Multilayer Social Networks

Multilayer networks, in particular, multilayer social networks, are an emerging and active research area in several disciplines, including social network analysis, computer science, and physics. They have traditionally been studied within these separate research communities, leading to the development of several independent models and methods to deal with the same set of problems.

This book unifies and consolidates existing knowledge in multilayer networks, making the relevant methods accessible to researchers and practitioners across an array of disciplines from data science to computer science, social network analysis, sociology, and physics. A range of practical and theoretical topics is covered, from data collection and analysis, modeling, and mining of multilayer social network systems to theoretical models behind the evolution of interconnected social networks and dynamic processes such as information spreading.

MARK E. DICKISON is a Data Science Manager at Capital One, where he attempts to put his knowledge of complex systems and technical skills at the forefront of solving business problems while still finding time to stay current with theory. He has been a postdoctoral fellow at Pennsylvania State University in its USP program, which supports the U.S. Defense Threat Reduction Agency, one of the first organizations to focus on multiple network models. His research interests fall within multidisciplinary network modeling, including network formation, and epidemiological and opinion spreading as well as data mining and machine learning.

MATTEO MAGNANI is Senior Lecturer in database systems and data mining at Uppsala University and has previously held positions at the Italian National Research Council (CNR), at the University of Bologna and at Aarhus University. His research interests lie in the general area of data science and engineering, including the modeling and mining of networks for the analysis of social systems.

LUCA ROSSI is Assistant Professor in the Communication and Culture research group of the IT University of Copenhagen. He has been a post-doctoral fellow at the University of Urbino Carlo Bo. His research explores the use of computational methods to study social phenomena and the use of social media data to describe social processes with a specific focus on activism and political participation.

Multilayer Social Networks

MARK E. DICKISON
Capital One, Virginia

MATTEO MAGNANI
Uppsala University, Sweden

LUCA ROSSI
IT University of Copenhagen, Denmark

CAMBRIDGE
UNIVERSITY PRESS

CAMBRIDGE
UNIVERSITY PRESS

One Liberty Plaza, 20th Floor, New York, NY 10006, USA

Cambridge University Press is part of the University of Cambridge.

It furthers the University's mission by disseminating knowledge in the pursuit of education, learning, and research at the highest international levels of excellence.

www.cambridge.org
Information on this title: www.cambridge.org/9781107438750

First published 2016

Printed in the United States of America by Sheridan Books, Inc.

A catalogue record for this publication is available from the British Library.

Library of Congress Cataloguing in Publication Data
Names: Dickison, Mark E., 1981– author. | Magnani, Matteo, author. | Rossi, Luca, 1979– author.
Title: Multilayer social networks / Mark E. Dickison (Capital One, Virginia), Matteo Magnani (Uppsala University, Sweden), Luca Rossi (IT University of Copenhagen, Denmark).
Description: Cambridge, United Kingdom ; New York, NY : Cambridge University Press, 2016. | Includes bibliographical references and index.
Identifiers: LCCN 2016013912 | ISBN 9781107079496 (hardback ; alk. paper) | ISBN 1107079497 (hardback ; alk. paper) | ISBN 9781107438750 (paperback ; alk. paper) | ISBN 1107438756 (paperback ; alk. paper)
Subjects: LCSH: Social networks–Mathematical models. | Social networks–Data processing. | Social sciences–Network analysis.
Classification: LCC HM741 .D53 2016 | DDC 302.30285–dc23 LC record available at https://lccn.loc.gov/2016013912

ISBN 978-1-107-07949-6 Hardback
ISBN 978-1-107-43875-0 Paperback

To my family and my fiancée. M. D.
To my family and lo scrondo. M. M.
To my family, Serena and $+2$. L. R.

Contents

List of Abbreviations

EA	edge assignment
ER	erdös-rènyi
ERGM	exponential random graph model
HIN	heterogeneous information network
NG	network growth
OSN	online social network
SNA	social network analysis

1

Moving Out of Flatland

Be patient, for the world is broad and wide.

– The Square

On May 1, 2011, Keith Urbahn, chief of staff of Donald Rumsfeld, wrote 77 characters announcing to the world that a turning point in contemporary history had been reached (Nahon and Hemsley, 2013):

So I'm told by a reputable person they have killed Osama Bin Laden. Hot damn.

These 77 characters started a chain reaction that led, within minutes, to the worldwide diffusion of the news and marked the beginning of the post-Osama era. First posted on Twitter, the news quickly reached millions of other Twitter users, then spread over tens of other online social networks, appeared in traditional media (e.g., television, radio), and became a common topic of discussion in the offline world, both in its original 77-character format and rephrased so that only its information content was preserved.

We can think of this event from many perspectives. We could focus on its historical value or observe how social media, like Twitter, are challenging the traditional relationship between politics and journalism. We could also use this tweet and the reactions to it to describe how information virality works in contemporary society and why the Internet has made it different from everything else we have seen in the history of humanity. For the concerns of this book, we can say that Mr. Urbahn provided yet another example of the multidimensional nature of our social experience.

1.1 Multiple Social Networks in Our Everyday Experience

Our social experience is inherently a multifaceted reality made of multiple interconnected networks defining our understanding of the world and our role

1

in it. These networks do not exist autonomously; they are defined by our social relations and connected into a larger system by our activities. This is exactly what Keith Urbahn did when he tweeted something that a reputable person had told him: he defined a bridge between two networks. More precisely, he moved a specific piece of information out of an offline and exclusive network into a worldwide online digital network, and in switching between them, he was surely aware of the consequences. Dealing with multiple social networks is part of our daily experience: we continuously and effortlessly juggle our networks; we bridge them to move valuable information from one network to another; or we keep them separate to protect our privacy, to preserve face, or to offer a specific representation of ourselves to our potential audiences (Hogan, 2010). However, the fact that we continuously deal with multiple social networks and that we do it with no effort does not mean that this is a trivial activity or that we can overlook it. Quite the opposite is true: our *networked society* – described by Rainie and Wellman (2012) as being characterized by multiple overlapping social and media networks – provides us with a number of examples why these networks should be more and more relevant.

Let us be clear that the coexistence of multiple social networks is not a discovery of this book nor the result of recent research efforts. For example, the fact that we are connected to other people through multiple types of relational ties, although representing only one possible view of the problem, was known long before the field of social network analysis (SNA) was developed and has always been acknowledged in the SNA literature as a foundational feature of the discipline. Quoting Wasserman and Faust (1994, p. 18),

> the range and type of ties can be quite extensive, [including] evaluation of one person by another[,] transfers of material resources[,] association or affiliation[, etc.].

However, when we move from the qualitative description of the discipline to its mathematical definitions, quantitative measures, and practical applications, traditional SNA has typically focused on one type of actor and tie at a time:

> Most social network applications focus on collections of actors that are all of the same type....With multirelational data, we suggest that [actor centrality and prestige] be calculated for *each* relation. (p. 17)

Although this sort of structural approach to social understanding is still a very powerful tool for unfolding the hidden structures behind our social activities, over recent years, it has become more and more evident how a monodimensional analysis is unable to account for a growing number of phenomena.

Looking only at a single type of relational tie within a single social network risks either defining a world where different kinds of relationships are ontologically equivalent or overlooking the invisible relationships emerging from the interactions among different types of ties. This apparently harmless simplification can alter the topology of the network, producing inaccurate or misleading results (Magnani and Rossi, 2011). For example, Mr. Urbahn would not be regarded as an important user on Twitter if we were to measure importance solely by counting his number of followers, but in the larger system, including both his Twitter and offline social relations, he played a key role as a bridge between two complementary networks, one providing trust and the other speed of diffusion. Without an expanded perspective, we would not be able to describe the whole range of problems and structures that can be found in a world of multiple social networks. We would not even be able to conceive of multidimensional ideas within a monodimensional space. This is exactly the situation described in Abbott's (1884) famous novella, where a square explains how our senses and conceptual tools define what we can comprehend:

> I admit the truth of your critic's facts, but I deny his conclusions. It is true that we have really in Flatland a Third unrecognized Dimension called "height," just as it is also true that you have really in Spaceland a Fourth unrecognized Dimension, called by no name at present, but which I will call "extra-height." But we can no more take cognizance of our "height" than you can of your "extra-height." Even I who have been in Spaceland, and have had the privilege of understanding for twenty-four hours the meaning of "height"; even I cannot now comprehend it, nor realize it by the sense of sight or by any process of reason; I can but apprehend it by faith. (p. 7)

The good news is that we are luckier than our square friend: a gestalt SNA is possible, because our social experience is indeed multidimensional. Similarly to the Spacelanders who were looking for thickness on the two-dimensional objects in Flatland, we have always had the perception that there has to be something more. We have been confined by the world we created ourselves, but we have always had the clear understanding that a single dimension is not enough, as clearly stated in foundational SNA sources. This perception has been different in different disciplines: physical sciences, accustomed to looking for unifying models, have sometimes regarded any dyadic phenomena as a network, making no distinction between friends interacting on Facebook and proteins interacting in a cell; social scientists have struggled with this for many years in trying to understand how different kinds of ties affect each other (Borgatti et al., 2009). Nevertheless, for a long time, these interactions have largely been studied within what we call a single-layer perspective.

(a)   (b)

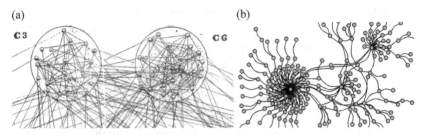

Figure 1.1. Visualizations of an offline and an online social networks: (a) a socio-metric diagram and (b) a Twitter reply network (2012). (Part (a) reproduced with permission of the American Society of Group Psychotherapy and Psychodrama from *Who Shall Survive?*, J. L. Moreno, M.D. Beacon House Inc. Beacon, N.Y., Second Edition, 1953).

For almost a century, one of the most effective SNA tools to measure our social interactions has been the *simple graph*, where *simple* is a mathematical term and does not imply that there is anything simple at all in our social lives. A simple graph is defined as a set of *nodes* (representing individuals or organizations, often called *actors* in the SNA tradition) with *edges* between them, also called *links* or *connections* (representing *relational ties*, e.g., friendship relationships) and with no edges connecting a node to itself. To provide some historical perspective, Figure 1.1 shows both one of the first known examples of a graph-based sociometric diagram, hand-drawn by Moreno (1934), and a more recent Twitter reply network drawn using one of the many currently available graph visualization tools[1] (Rossi and Magnani, 2012). Despite their mundane nature, it would be extremely complex (if not impossible) to accurately describe the aforementioned tweet about Bin Laden's death and its related events using a simple graph. How could we represent the differences between Mr. Urbahn's reputable source and his Twitter followers? Would it just be a matter of weights? And how could we represent the differences in network structure, localized social practices, and technological affordances that are necessary to fully explain what happened? These are all questions that cannot find a complete answer inside Flatland.

Moving out of Flatland does not mean that Flatland is wrong. It does not mean that we cannot explain anything within its boundaries: traditional SNA has repeatedly proved itself to have great explanatory power. To some extent, it is not even a matter of avoiding potential misleading results – even if that would be an indirect benefit. It is more a matter of introducing a new perspective, new ideas, and new dimensions that were not possible before. This is why this book should be perceived more as an extension of traditional SNA and network science into new directions than their as about their evolution.

---

[1] The igraph network analysis package, available at: http://www.igraph.org/.

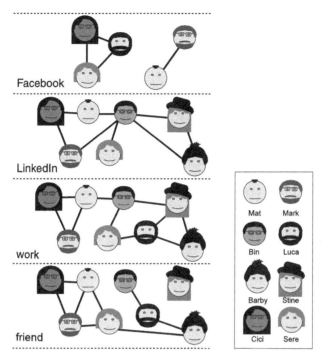

Figure 1.2. A multilayer social network with four layers and eight actors, used as a running example throughout the book.

1.2 An Introductory Example

A quick look at a simple example will help us provide a brief overview of the kinds of analyses enabled by what we are going to call the *multilayer social network model*. In Chapter 2, we precisely define what we mean by multilayer social network, but for now, we can think of it as a social network with nodes and/or edges organized into multiple *layers*, where each layer represents a different kind of node or edge, a different social context, a different community, a different online social network (OSN), and so on.

Consider the four layers in Figure 1.2, representing two offline relations (work collaborations and friendships) and two online, social media – based layers (LinkedIn and Facebook). These four layers are not independent, but they are connected through the common actors indicated in the right-hand side box. Each node in each of the four layers represents one of these actors or a social media account owned by one of them. These actors define bridges between the four layers, in the same way as Mr. Urbahn defined a bridge between the offline network of his reputable source and his Twitter followers.

Looking at the figure, we can observe some interesting patterns emerging from the dependencies between the four layers. For example, Cici, Mat, and Mark seem to form a cohesive group spanning multiple layers: they are all connected to each other (i.e., they form a *clique*) on the work and friend layers, and Cici is connected to both Mark and Mat also on LinkedIn. We can say that they form a strong group spanning several relational dimensions. However, Cici does not use Facebook to interact with Mark and Mat: different social networks can be strategically used in different ways, for example, to reach different audiences or to prevent some people from accessing information produced on a specific layer. If we count the total number of ties for each actor, we can see that both Sere and Cici have eight of them over the four layers. However, Cici is only connected to four actors (Mark, Mat, Luca, and Sere), whereas Sere is directly connected to almost everyone. In particular, she is directly connected with the same number of actors as Bin, despite that Bin has five connections just on the LinkedIn layer, more than anyone else – in contrast, Sere has at most three contacts on each single layer. At the same time, Sere can easily spread information to everyone in the four layers, assuming that this information is appropriate for all of them, for example, gossip might spread on Facebook more easily than on LinkedIn. Finally, we can look at the distance between Cici and Stine. Interestingly, without changing layers, they can reach each other only on the LinkedIn and work layers, through Mat and Bin. However, Cici can use her Facebook relationship with Luca to reach Stine in that context. The existence of multidimensional chains of social relationships (e.g., Cici is a Facebook friend with Luca, who works with Stine) is at the basis of many recent advances in this area, for example, identifying Luca's role in connecting people from different layers.

Although this multilayer network is too small to allow us to reach any significant conclusions on general network properties, this example shows how the joint analysis of multiple layers can provide knowledge that is not present in each layer when layers are considered independently of each other.

In addition, multilayer networks can significantly affect our understanding of a social system even when only single-layer data are available. A clear example are Facebook friendship connections, which may indicate friends, acquaintances, colleagues, family members, and so on. As a consequence, performing tasks like identifying communities becomes very complex because of the many overlapping social contexts, and if some data are missing only from one specific hidden layer, then some descriptive network measures can be either under- or overestimated, depending on the layer where the data are missing. In summary, advances in multilayer network analysis are also leading to a rethinking of how we analyze single-layer networks.

We now hope that the reader is looking forward to reading the rest of the book and getting more details about how to deal with these kinds of data. However, we first must raise one question. So far we have claimed that the topic of this book is very important, we have suggested that it may extend traditional SNA with a number of results not achievable otherwise, and we have mentioned how its importance has been acknowledged for a long time. So, why are we writing this book now? Why was it not written ten, twenty, or thirty years ago?

One possible answer to this question is related to the invisible nature of relational ties. Sociologists have known for a long time that invisible connections, often hard to describe, lie behind many social phenomena (Wellman and Berkowitz, 1988). SNA relies on making relational ties visible so that they can be studied as a social graph. However, recording these ties is complicated: until approximately a decade ago, network data collection was typically performed using questionnaires. Getting accurate information about relational ties, even a single type, would take great effort, and with scarce data, it is often difficult to develop popular models and analysis methods. Today, the explosion of OSNs and Web 2.0 has revealed the existing networks of relations bonding societies together and has highlighted their multidimensional nature (Rainie and Wellman, 2012). Although most of these relations have not been created by digital technologies, digital technologies have nevertheless made them visible, popularizing the concept of the network as a meaningful way to think about our social experiences. We all can see our networked world: links are everywhere, all around us, as Barabási (2002) pointed out in his popular book. So, it has become easier to reason about the relationships between all these links, especially when they belong to different social networks. In addition, the availability of large non–social network data sets, such as interconnected traffic networks (airplanes, trains, cars, etc.) and biological networks, has boosted the development of general measures and methods that have the potential to be applied also to a social context.

1.3 Scope and Other Learning Resources

The objective of this book is to provide an accessible presentation of recent research results on the analysis and mining of multilayer social networks. By *accessible*, we do not mean that we simplify the available material, but we try to provide a presentation that does not require a specific background to be appreciated or understood. Different disciplines, such as sociology, computer science, and physics, have contributed to this area, the first providing semantics and interpretative keys to new SNA measures, the second introducing new data mining algorithms, and the third formalizing general models and global dynamics of complex network systems. Interdisciplinary contributions have also been increasingly frequent in recent years. With this book, we want to take a step forward toward developing a homogeneous and interdisciplinary body of work on multilayer social networks. As such, although we try to be exhaustive whenever possible – something probably not completely achievable, given the vitality of the area – our main objective is to provide a consolidated presentation of the available material that makes sense from multiple points of view.

Some of the methods for multilayer social networks presented in this work can be applied to other kinds of (nonsocial) networks, making sure to take care to rethink their semantics so that they fit the different domains, and methods for generic multilayer networks can also be used to describe social networks. The reader interested in a more dense, general, and theoretical presentation of multilayer networks with less focus on data mining and social interpretations can refer to the excellent survey papers by Kivelä et al. (2014) and Boccaletti et al. (2014). Another valuable resource covering some of the literature on mining a specific kind of multilayer network called the *heterogeneous information network* has been published by Sun and Han (2012). For the reader more interested in concrete kinds of (nonsocial) networks and practical applications, a valuable collection of papers has been edited by D'Agostino and Scala (2014) that focuses on another specific kind of multilayer network called the *network of networks*. The confused reader who is getting lost with all these different names of related models may first check the next chapter of this book, where we provide more details about their differences and similarities. In addition, recent literature surveys have focused on the specific aspects of information diffusion (Salehi et al., 2015) and community detection (Bothorel et al., 2015) in multilayer networks. For more specific references, we refer the reader to the literature discussed in the different chapters.

As a final note, although we have tried to assemble an interdisciplinary group of authors, our presentation of the related material is biased toward our own backgrounds and certainly misses some important references of which we are not aware. This is a risk that must be run in an attempt to provide a uniform presentation of material developed in many different fields, and we apologize in advance for underrepresenting some disciplines or areas.

1.4 Outline of the Book

The book is divided into four parts. Part I ("Models and Measures") describes how to represent and compute quantitive descriptions of multilayer social networks. Part II ("Mining Multilayer Networks") explains how to discover hidden patterns such as communities or associations between edges on different layers. Part III ("Dynamical Processes") presents models of how multilayer social networks coevolve in time and how information, ideas, and behaviors diffuse in them. Finally, Part IV ("Conclusion") discusses our personal view on the future evolution of the discipline.

We have tried to keep each chapter as self-contained as possible. However, Section 2.1 introduces the models and terminology used in the book and may be useful to read first. Throughout the book, we refer to concepts defined in Chapter 3 ("Measuring Multilayer Social Networks"). Therefore, we have organized them so that they can be easily identified from the table of contents and checked without reading the full chapter, as needed. Although we will be happy if the reader decides to read the whole book, we will be even happier if he or she can save some time to use for something else, for example, reading some poetry or listening to some good music.

We conclude this introduction by providing additional details about the content of each chapter. Part I reviews alternative ways to represent and measure multilayer networks. In Chapter 2, we present the terminology and data model used in the book, in addition to various other data models for social networks allowing multiple types of nodes (also called heterogeneous, attributed, or multitype networks), multiple types of relational ties (also called multiplex or multidimensional networks), or explicitly representing the coexistence of separate, interdependent social networks. All these can be seen as specific cases of the general multilayer model used in this book. While going through all these different models, this chapter provides a historical account of the different approaches developed to study multilayer social networks in different disciplines. We also describe several application areas and provide pointers to the main existing data sets, some of which are used as working examples throughout the book. Chapter 3 presents the main measures for the quantitative description of multilayer social networks, complementing and extending traditional SNA metrics. In that chapter, we define and exemplify degree and neighborhood centrality, multidimensional distances, and derived measures such as betweenness, transitivity, relevance, and layer correlation. Other measures used to identify communities (modularity) and to predict the creation of new edges are treated in the corresponding chapters in Part II.

Part II focuses on identifying hidden patterns in multilayer social networks. We start focusing on the important aspects of data collection, preprocessing, and exploration. Chapter 4 discusses issues in data collection related to using sampling and to the presence of missing data and different approaches to transforming the collected data. Analyzing multiple layers is inherently more complex than dealing with a single layer, and too much information can generate noise and hide some important patterns that are present only in some of the layers or in their combinations. Therefore, it can be useful to simplify the data, from the extreme choice of creating a single *flattened* social graph to more sophisticated data transformations that remove or merge only some of the layers or portions of them. Then, after the data have been collected and prepared, a typical way to explore them is through visualization. Although only a few visualization methods have been specifically defined for multilayer networks, as reported in Chapter 5, they can be valuable in highlighting some basic patterns in the data, for example, the presence of well-separated communities or strong correlations or differences among relational ties in different layers. Chapters 6 and 7 focus on popular data mining tasks: identifying communities, predicting future relational ties, and computing layer correlations. Although community detection is one of the most widely studied network mining problems and has undoubtedly achieved many important results over the years, the complex conceptual and methodological problems associated with community detection methods rise to a new level when we consider multilayer networks. In Chapter 6, we provide wide coverage of existing approaches. Apart from community detection, other data mining problems have received less attention so far but are likely to become popular in the near future. In Chapter 7, we focus on predicting the appearance of new relational ties (a data mining problem known as *link prediction*) and discovering associations between ties in different layers.

Part III explores dynamical processes on multilayer social networks. Network formation models are among the most important tools in the field known as network science. A typical application of artificially generated networks is to provide *null* models that can be used to test new measures and make comparisons with real networks so that significant patterns can be highlighted in the real data. In addition, network growing models are useful for experimenting on the dynamics underlying the evolution of social relationships. In Chapter 8, we review some recent works modeling the coevolution of multiple layers representing interdependent social networks. Another important type of process happening in social networks is the diffusion of information, which can reach a very high speed when online social networks are used. However, information is not the only spreadable entity: diffusion processes in social networks can also involve opinions and behaviors. Traditionally, diffusion has been modeled with percolation or epidemic models, both of which have been shown to exhibit novel phenomena on multilayer networks, including new types of phase transitions and entirely new phases. In Chapter 9, we present material in these areas and explain how it can be applied to information and opinion diffusion.

The book does not have a classical conclusion chapter, because the field of multilayer networks is alive and continuously evolving. Instead, in Chapter 10, we describe what we see as the most promising future directions for research in this active and vibrant area.

1.5 Acknowledgments

We thank the several colleagues with whom we have discussed the topics of this book and those who have contributed to the advancement of this area. In particular, we thank Michele Coscia and Mostafa Salehi for providing several comments on an early version of the volume and Piotr Bródka for reading some selected parts of it. Personal thanks go to Fosca Giannotti and Dino Pedreschi for hosting one of the authors in their lab and giving him the opportunity to develop his research in this area. We also thank the Italian Ministry for Education, University, and Research for supporting this work through the FIRB funding scheme (RBFR107725) and Danilo Montesi and Giovanni Boccia Artieri for their involvement in the project. Last, but not least, we deeply thank Lauren Cowles from Cambridge University Press for approaching us and proposing that we write this book, and for all her subsequent support.

PART I

Models and Measures

2

Representing Multilayer Social Networks

As soon as you look at it with your eye on the edge of the table, you will find that it ceases to appear to you a figure, and that it becomes in appearance a straight line.

– The Square

Multilayer networks aim at providing a generalized way to deal with long-existing complex social phenomena that, over the years, have been observed using many different approaches. These phenomena have been described using the most diverse terminology belonging to different research areas, but they can be broadly grouped within three domains of problems: heterogeneity of relational ties, heterogeneity of actors, and interdependency between relations. After a short overview of these problems, which give ground for the development of multilayer social networks, in Section 2.1, we describe terminology and a mathematical model that constitute a foundation for all the measures and methods presented in the remainder of the book. Section 2.2 provides an overview of related models that have, in various ways, dealt with similar problems, and Section 2.3 describes a list of available data sets that the reader can explore and study using multilayer networks. All the terms introduced in this chapter, together with other basic terms in graph theory, SNA, and network science, are summarized in the glossary.

Modeling heterogeneity of social relations is an old problem that has often been addressed through qualitative approaches, not only within the borders of SNA. A classical example is the work by Gluckman (1955) that identifies the *multiplexity* of an African ethnic group's relations (the Lozi people) and defines it as the characteristic of being connected through multiple interdependent social ties. Multiplexity emerges, in Gluckman's work, as the key

15

element to understanding how individuals are part of more complex social structures. This approach has already moved beyond a simple structural analysis to describe the complex system of interdependent relations that Burt and Schott (1989) indicate as the substantive content of personal relationships. Within this perspective, multiplexity is not just an interesting but remote characteristic of social networks but rather the key element to understanding social structures and how individuals are connected. Heterogeneity of social relations maintains its centrality in the SNA field and has been indicated as the characteristic that defines the specific nature of SNA when compared to general network analysis (Borgatti et al., 2009). In fact, we find examples of multiplex networks in some of the earliest studies in SNA, as reported in Section 2.2.1.

References to heterogeneity of relations and to heterogeneity of actors underlie much of the sociological analysis of networks. According to Wasserman and Faust (1994), social networks contain at least three different dimensions: a structural dimension corresponding to the social graph, for example, actors and their relationships; a compositional dimension describing the actors, for example, their personal information; and an affiliation dimension indicating group memberships. These three dimensions, where affiliation defines – de facto – connections among different types of actors (e.g., members of the same family or organization), provide a minimal description needed to understand the full complexity of social structures. Sections 2.2.2 and 2.2.3 describe some models defined to handle these kinds of structures.

An alternative conceptual approach to dealing with the same set of problems is to think of multiple relationships as a set of connected levels, or layers, forming a single multidimensional social network. Figure 2.1 shows how this approach has been used by Padgett and McLean (2006) in their pivotal study about the rise of the Medici family during Italian Renaissance. In this example, layers are used to separate different contexts or edge types, but they can also be used to separate different types of actors.

Although heterogeneity of relations and heterogeneity of actors have been studied for many years within SNA, *layer correlation* (also called *layer interdependency* in more general terms), referring to the dynamics happening when different interdependent types of relations (often referred to as *networks of networks*) interact, has been mostly studied in the areas of physics and computer science. More details about approaches focusing on the aspect of interdependency are provided in Sections 2.2.4 and 2.2.5.

Despite the diverse origins and diverse fields of application, all the problems mentioned here show common aspects and can be modeled using the multilayer approach detailed in the next section.

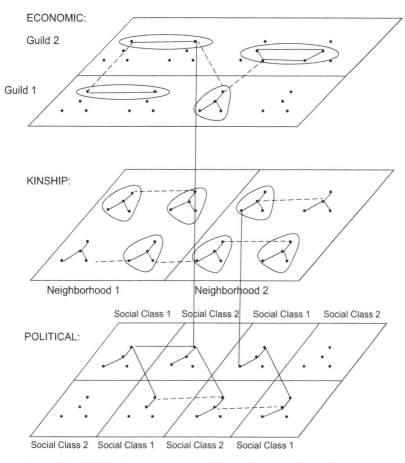

Figure 2.1. Multiple layers representing different kinds of relationships among families in Florence during the Renaissance. From Padgett and McLean (2006, p. 1469), used by permission of the University of Chicago Press.

2.1 Terminology and Model

Defining a uniform terminology for a topic that has independently evolved inside several disciplines, from social sciences to physics and computer science, can be regarded as a challenging (if not impossible) task. However, many concepts used in this area had already been developed in the field of SNA, and the existence of a common theoretical foundation for SNA and other disciplines dealing with networks, namely, graph theory, significantly simplifies this task.

Even when a *simple graph*, defined as a graph with single edges between nodes and no edges between a node and itself, has been used as a formal model of a social network, scholars in SNA have always stressed the distinction between a *node*, that is, an element of a mathematical model, and an *actor*, that is, the real-world concept represented by the node. As an example, Wasserman and Faust (1994) use the term *actor centrality* to indicate a set of measures characterizing the position/importance of a node in a social network.

Therefore, if we think of a social network not just as a simple graph but as a graph whose nodes are representations of real-world entities called actors, it is easy to see how this can be extended by defining additional social networks on top of the same set of actors. In this book, we call each of these social networks a *layer* and the whole structure a *multilayer network*. Different layers can also include different types of actors, for example, people and organizations. In this book, we refer to social networks with only one type of actor (e.g., user accounts on Facebook) and one type of edge among them (e.g., Facebook friendship) as *single-layer networks*.

As we will see in Section 2.2.4, different formal models have used the name "multilayer network" and have applied more or less similar concepts. In the remainder of the book, whenever we do not explicitly mention any specific formal model, we are indicating the general concept of a multilayer network, defined as follows.

Definition 2.1 (Multilayer network) Given a set of actors $\mathcal{A}$ and a set of layers $\mathcal{L}$, a multilayer network is defined as a quadruple $M = (\mathcal{A}, \mathcal{L}, V, E)$, where (V, E) is a graph and $V \subseteq \mathcal{A} \times \mathcal{L}$.

In principle, this definition can also be used to represent an infinite and continuous set of layers, for example, time layers, one for each possible instant in time. Temporal networks are not directly investigated in this book, where we mainly focus on finite, discrete, and unordered layers. However, many of the measures and methods presented in the next chapters can also be adapted to these networks.

Using multiple layers, we can represent different types of edges: those among nodes in the same layer, called *intralayer edges*, and those among nodes in different layers, called *interlayer edges*. Intralayer edges on different layers can also have different natures, for example, one layer may contain edges representing working relationships, one layer friendship relationships, and one layer can indicate which Twitter accounts follow each other. Figure 2.2 and Table 2.1 summarize the terminology defined in this section.

Interlayer edges are especially useful in representing the complex nuances of mediated communication. As an example, we can consider two layers

Table 2.1. *Terminology used in this book and synonyms used in the literature*

Term	Meaning
Actor	A person, an organization, or an entity that can have relationships with other actors.
Layer	The same actor can be present in different layers, where each layer represents a type of actors or a type of edge between actors.
Node	A specific actor on a specific layer. As an example, a node can represent a user account on an OSN. Multiple layers can be used to model different OSNs, and the same person (actor) can own accounts (nodes) on several OSNs (layers).
Edge	A relationship between two nodes, e.g., a *following* relationship between two nodes representing two Twitter accounts.
Multilayer network	A social network represented as a set of layers, where nodes in the different layers refer to a global set of actors and edges can also connect nodes in the same or different layers.
Single-layer network	A social network represented as a network with only one layer.

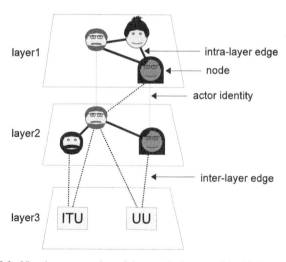

Figure 2.2. Visual representation of the terminology used in this book. We distinguish between nodes and actors, with the same actors (represented by the same icon) being potentially present in multiple layers. ITU and UU represent two organizations, for example, two universities.

representing, respectively, e-mail accounts inside an organization, say, Uppsala University, and private e-mail accounts owned by its employees, for example, Yahoo! mail or Gmail. Two employees of the university can communicate by exchanging e-mails using their university accounts (corresponding to directed intralayer edges on a university layer), or one can forward an e-mail from his university account to the private Gmail account of his colleague (corresponding to an interlayer edge from the university layer to a private e-mail layer). As a third alternative, one can receive an e-mail on her university account, copy the text into her Gmail web application, and send it using her private Gmail account to her colleague's private Gmail account. In this case, the presence of the same actor on the two layers (or, more precisely, the presence of nodes in the two layers representing accounts owned by the same actor) also allows information flows between layers without any e-mail exchanges across layers. Multilayer networks allow us to model this complex behavior that depends on layer-specific rules and actor's strategies, for example, e-mail messages exchanged among Swedish university accounts are legally considered public documents, which in theory can be accessed by anyone on request. Therefore switching layers from a university e-mail account to a private e-mail account might indicate the willingness (or rather the lack of willingness) of an actor to comply with an eventual request for information.

By representing these exchanges in a formal model, we enable the identification and numerical quantification of patterns induced by these external factors, and using the measures and methods presented in the next chapters, we can try to learn more about them. In summary, we can use our model as a proxy for understanding a reality that we would not be able to study without explicitly considering the different layers and their interactions.

2.2 Related Models

Multilayer social networks, being extremely abstract and flexible models, can represent a large variety of real-world scenarios. Many of these fall within the three domains of problems we briefly discussed during the introduction to this chapter: heterogeneity of relations, heterogeneity of actors, and layer correlation. These specific problems, or problems with similar characteristics, have been faced many times over the years and addressed through different approaches. It is thus important to recognize how these approaches are related and how they have contributed to the generalized concept of the multilayer social network.

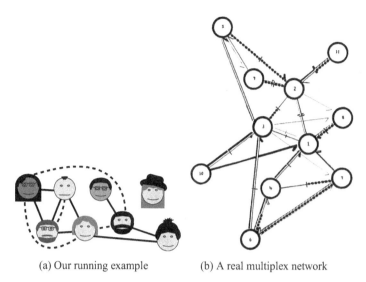

(a) Our running example   (b) A real multiplex network

Figure 2.3. Multiplex representation of two layers of the network introduced in Section 1.2 (Facebook and friend) and an example from the early SNA literature. (Reproduced with permission of the American Society of Group Psychotherapy and Psychodrama from *Who Shall Survive?*, J. L. Moreno, M.D. Beacon House Inc. Beacon, N.Y., Second Edition, 1953).

2.2.1 Multiplex Networks

In a multiplex network, a common set of actors is connected through multiple types of edges. Figure 2.3a shows a visual representation of part of the network we introduced in Section 1.2 when seen as a multiplex network, where two different types of edges (Facebook and friend) are indicated by continuous and dashed lines, respectively. This way of representing social networks has been in use for a long time. For example, among the papers mentioned by Freeman (1996) as the antecedents of SNA, we find a study by Bott (1928) measuring how a group of children talked, interfered, watched, imitated, and cooperated. These different kinds of relational ties are typically known as *multiplex ties* in the SNA literature. A visual representation as the one in Figure 2.3a appears in the book that is often considered the first text on SNA – see Figure 2.3b, taken from the book by Moreno (1934) – and the term *multiplex network* has been consistently used to refer to these networks across several decades (Verbrugge, 1979; Minor, 1983; Lazega and Pattison, 1999; Huang and Liu, 2010), although other terms, such as *multirelational network* (Cai et al., 2005a; Szell et al., 2010) and, more recently, *multidimensional network* (Contractor, 2009; Berlingerio et al., 2011c), have also been used.

	Cici	Mat	Mark	Sere	Bin	Luca	Stine	Baby
Cici	0	1	1	0	0	0	0	0
Mat	1	0	1	1	0	0	0	0
Mark	1	1	0	1	0	0	0	0
Sere	0	1	1	0	0	0	0	1
Bin	0	0	0	0	0	1	0	0
Luca	0	0	0	0	1	0	0	1
Stine	0	0	0	0	0	0	0	0
Baby	0	0	0	1	0	1	0	0

	Cici	Mat	Mark	Sere	Bin	Luca	Stine	Baby
Cici	0	0	0	1	0	1	0	0
Mat	0	0	1	0	0	0	0	0
Mark	0	1	0	0	0	0	0	0
Sere	1	0	0	0	0	1	0	0
Bin	0	0	0	0	0	0	0	0
Luca	1	0	0	1	0	0	0	0
Stine	0	0	0	0	0	0	0	0
Baby	0	0	0	0	0	0	0	0

Figure 2.4. Matrix representation of the (top) Facebook and (bottom) friend multiplex network in Figure 2.3.

A typical way of mathematically representing a multiplex network, already used by Bott (1928), is a set of *adjacency matrixes*, one for each type of edge, with one row/column for each actor and element (i, j) indicating if actors i and j are connected by an edge of the corresponding type. Figure 2.4 shows this representation for our Facebook and friend running example. However, multiplex networks are also often modeled as *edge-typed multigraphs*, that is, graphs allowing multiple edges between the same pair of nodes with an attribute on each edge indicating its type, for example, Facebook and friend in Figure 2.3a.

The idea of multiplex networks and more in general of multiplexity of social relations has important theoretical implications. Early works have observed how the presence of multiple relations between two actors is directly connected with the *strength* of the connection (Fisher, 1982). The strength of the connection has been used in many ways within SNA (Granovetter, 1978), and it has been generally considered as a good indicator of how intimate and durable relations can be (Wellman and Berkowitz, 1988). Multiplex relations between two actors are believed to be stronger because their redundancy can make them endure the rupture of a specific type of connection. For example, two people having both work and friendship connections can remain connected even if one of them changes job. This relationship between the multiplex nature of the network and the strength of the connections is highly intuitive, and it has been recently confirmed also for mixed online–offline connections (Hristova et al., 2014). Besides multiplexity intended as different types of ties reinforcing each other, other kinds of relations that can be distinguished in a directed multiplex network are *reciprocity*, where an actor i is connected to an actor j and j is also connected to i on the same relation type, and *exchange*, where the two connections happen on two different relation types (Lazega and Pattison, 1999; Skvoretz and Agneessens, 2007).

Connected with the use of multiplexity to evaluate the strength of the relationships is the use of multiplexity as a way to explain network evolution. As a simple example, it has been observed how the existence of a coworker relation can often be used to predict the possible emergence of a friendship-type connection (Monge and Contractor, 2003; Borgatti et al., 2009).

Both these ideas, largely supported by a growing amount of research over the years, are challenged by the contemporary sociotechnical scenario where different types of ties often appear decoupled or reflect more complex underlying social structures (Garton et al., 2006; Kane et al., 2012). During the last 20 years, the widespread adoption of Internet-based digital technologies has presented new opportunities and challenges. As Rainie and Wellman (2012, p. 13) suggested,

> The changing social environment is adding to people's capacity and willingness to exploit more "remote" relationships – in both the physical and emotional senses of the word.

Using again our running example, we should ask ourselves if we can really assume that the existence of a multiplex connection on the Facebook and work layers will predict a connection on the friend layer. Although being coworkers offers undoubtedly more opportunities to become friends, Facebook connections are used for a variety of goals not directly connected with friendship (Raacke and Bonds-Raacke, 2008). We discuss these aspects further in Chapter 3 (how to measure relationships between layers), Chapter 7 (how to predict the creation of new edges), and Chapter 8 (how different kinds of ties coevolve).

2.2.2 Multimode and Multilevel Networks

Whereas multiplex networks emphasize different types of relations within a set of nodes, a different way of extending single-layer networks is to consider multiple types of actors inside the same network. This extension has been used

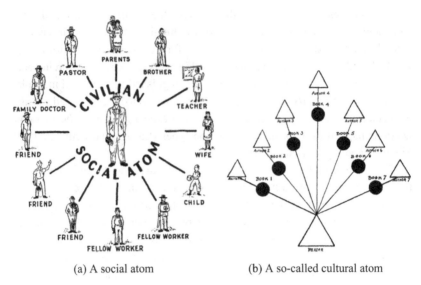

(a) A social atom   (b) A so-called cultural atom

Figure 2.5. Multiple types of actors in the early SNA literature. (Reproduced with permission of the American Society of Group Psychotherapy and Psychodrama from *Who Shall Survive?*, J. L. Moreno, M.D. Beacon House Inc. Beacon, N.Y., Second Edition, 1953).

in SNA since its origins, as shown in Figure 2.5 (Moreno, 1934), where basic components of a network (called *atoms*) are composed of different types of individuals (*social atom*) and individuals and resources, specifically books (*cultural atom*).

The most common application of this approach aims at modeling cases with two types of actors, for example, authors writing papers or users posting messages. A network where two types of actors can be identified is a *two-mode* (also called *bipartite*, or in some cases *affiliation*) network, where there are two types of nodes and edges connect pairs of nodes of different types (Iacobucci and Wasserman, 1990). This kind of network has been studied for a long time in anthropology (Davis et al., 1941) and can be used to model different types of scenarios, for example, authors and conferences/journals as well as members of various boards or offices. Two-mode networks have been typically handled by transforming them into simple graphs through a *projection* operation (see Section 4.2.1).

An early multilayer model based on these ideas was introduced as an extension of two-mode networks, where instead of allowing only edges between nodes from the two different sets, relationships are also allowed to exist within the sets (Iacobucci and Wasserman, 1990; Wasserman and Iacobucci, 1991).

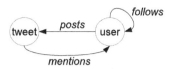

Figure 2.6. A HIN schema for a Twitter network defining two types of actors and three types of edges.

This can be seen as an early example of a *multilevel network*, which is today a popular network model. Different levels in a multilevel network have often been used to represent different aggregations of the actors: if we consider a two-mode affiliation network, we can see it as a level containing individuals and a level containing organizations to which these individuals belong – see, for example, the studies by Lazega et al. (2008), Zappa and Robins (2016), and Zappa and Lomi (2015). Recently, the terms *multilevel* and *multilayer* network have both extended the range of systems to which they are applied, leading to some level of convergence of the two concepts – at least when social systems are concerned.

2.2.3 Heterogeneous Information Networks

In the field of computer science, several data mining algorithms have been developed for a graph-based model allowing different types of nodes and edges, called a heterogeneous information network (HIN) (Cai et al., 2005b; Sun and Han, 2012).

A peculiar feature of HINs is the so-called *network schema*, that is, a set of constraints summarizing the structure of the network. As an example, using HINs to model a Twitter data set, we can constrain edges of type *follows* to be between two actors of type *user*, edges of type *posts* to be between an actor of type *user* and an actor of type *tweet*, and edges of type *mentions* going from tweets to users. This schema, represented in Figure 2.6, can be used to formulate patterns. For example, the pattern $user_1 \rightarrow user_2 \rightarrow tweet$ indicates a user following another user who posted a tweet. These patterns can be used to express information extraction queries, for example, *retrieve all the followers of users who posted a specific tweet*, and also for predicting events, such as the creation of new relationships – this last aspect is described in Chapter 7.

Networks with multiple types of nodes, where types are sometimes represented as *colors*, have also been called *multitype networks* in the literature (Vasquez, 2006; Allard et al., 2009; Brummitt et al., 2012). Different colors can be associated to different node properties, for example, lower or higher probabilities of establishing ties with other nodes (Söderberg, 2003).

2.2.4 Multilayer(ed) Models

The term *multilayer network* has been recently used to indicate different models (Kazienko et al., 2010; Magnani and Rossi, 2011; Kivelä et al., 2014), all related to the definition used in this book but also presenting specific features. The common aspects of all these models are as follows:

1. the fact that actors are organized into different layers and
2. the fact that nodes in different layers can correspond to the same actor.

Therefore, we would no longer say, for example, that Mark is connected to Luca (as in a single-layer social network), but we would say that Mark on layer A is connected to Luca on layer A and that there is one Luca on layer A who is represented by a different node than is Luca on layer B.

One early model that was called *multilayer* but is slightly different from the definition used in this book is the ML model, where one node in one layer can correspond to multiple nodes in another, potentially leading to *many-to-many relationships* across layers instead of simple node identity (Magnani and Rossi, 2011). This was specifically defined to study OSNs, where the same actor can open multiple accounts on some social media, for example, Luca can have two Twitter accounts, one used to work and one to hang out with friends. This work, together with the work by Kazienko et al. (2010), was one of the first proposals explicitly representing the same actor as a set of multiple nodes. However, though being able to model a more complex scenario than other proposals, and providing a more realistic description of the data available from OSNs, to the best of our knowledge the feature of having multiple instances of the same actor on the same layer has not been further developed so far, mainly because of the difficulty in getting real data with these characteristics.

In the work by Kivelä et al. (2014), layers are not considered as indivisible units but are defined as a combination of different *aspects*. For example, given a set of researchers, we can record interactions among them happening at two different conferences, for example, VLDB and WWW, at two different times, for example, 2015 and 2016. These two aspects (conferences and times) define four layers (VLDB-2015, WWW-2015, VLDB-2016, and WWW-2016). In addition, not being specific for social networks, this work does not use the term *actor* but just refers to nodes being present on multiple layers.

2.2.5 Networks of Networks

Another type of system that can be described using a multilayer model is known as a *network of networks*. Networks of networks are often used to represent interactions between nonsocial networks and are therefore significantly different – on a semantic level – from the models we have described so far. Networks of networks usually contain different types of nodes, such as a power grid and a control network, where one node in a network can be related to multiple nodes in the other. As for HINs, they are not particularly important because of the mathematical definition of the model itself, which is not significantly different from many other models, but rather because of the phenomena that have been studied using them and the set of methods developed on top of them. Although HINs are valuable because of their data mining algorithms, and other features, such as the network schema, networks of networks have been used to study cascading effects, that is, how events in one network affect nodes in other networks, potentially leading to chains of reactions (Buldyrev et al., 2010; Kenett et al., 2014). Several examples of networks of networks, mostly nonsocial, are discussed in the book by D'Agostino and Scala (2014).

Networks of networks can be represented as multilayer networks, with a layer representing each network, and have also been used to study social systems where different groups of actors are separated into different layers. Examples of these systems, which have also been called *interconnected networks* (Dickison et al., 2012), are individuals living in different cities, where each city is represented by a layer, or people using different e-mail providers, where each e-mail provider is represented by a layer. In these cases, the types of interactions modeled by inter- and intralayer edges are of the same kind, for example, texting another person living in the same city (intralayer) or in a different city (interlayer). A feature of these examples is that nodes in different layers mostly correspond to different actors, especially if there is not much overlapping between groups. Therefore interconnected networks can be significantly different from multiplex models where the same actors are present on all the layers.

2.2.6 Temporal Networks

Longitudinal studies, that is, studying the evolution of some variables through repeated observations at different times, constitute an important investigation tool in the social sciences and medical research. Although running a longitudinal study often requires many resources – more than what is needed to collect a snapshot of the data corresponding to a single specific time – it can answer questions that cannot be addressed by looking at a single snapshot. This kind of study has been a common tool in the domain of SNA, and data collected from longitudinal network surveys are very related to multilayer models: we can think of different layers as representing different snapshots of the same evolving social network in time.

As different points in time can be considered as different layers, in theory a social network observed at different times can be analyzed using multilayer methods. At the same time, this book is not about temporal aspects, which we leave to others (Holme and Saramäki, 2012), and we think that specific approaches and interpretations should be developed that take the temporal semantics under consideration: we cannot treat two accounts on different OSNs in the same way as a single account at two different times. In addition, time is a kind of continuous attribute, making it quite distinct from discrete layers – even if some methods for temporal networks are defined on discretized versions of the data. Therefore we will not specifically treat this kind of networks, although many measures defined in the book can in theory also be used in this context.

In some cases temporal aspects have been combined with other kinds of layers, as in the Tailor Shop data set (Kapferer, 1972) and in the work by Barigozzi et al. (2010), where trade networks are studied with regard to different product categories and times.

2.2.7 Exponential Random Graph Models

Exponential random graph models (ERGMs) follow a significantly different approach to representing social networks. For all the models discussed so far, the choice of the aspects of the social network represented in the model is fixed – nodes, edges, sometimes types or other node/edge attributes. Then, on top of this representation of the data, we can formulate analytical questions. With ERGMs, these two aspects (how to represent the data and which knowledge to extract from it) follow the opposite order: we first define a set of questions, then we build a model tailored on these questions. In the following we provide an intuitive explanation of ERGMs through an example.

To use an ERGM, we first need to define some questions we want to ask regarding the empirical data we want to study, and these questions can be formalized in terms of *network configurations*, that is, basic patterns that can appear multiple times in a graph. As an example, assume that we are interested in the four configurations in Figure 2.7. The first represents an actor, the second an edge, the third a 2-star, and the fourth a triangle. Including a triangle as one of the configurations we want to study implies that we are interested in knowing if there are any social dynamics determining the creation of edges among people with common neighbors.

Second, we need to understand the concept of the *random graph*. A random graph model can be used to generate graphs with specific features. The most famous type of random graph is the erdös-rènyi (ER) random graph model $G(n, p)$, which works as follows: we create n nodes, and for each pair of nodes,

Figure 2.7. Four configurations that we may use to define an ERGM.

we add an edge between them with probability p. Figure 2.8a shows an example of a graph generated using a $G(34, .139)$ model. This is only one of the specific graphs that can be generated by this model: if we run the generator multiple times, we may end up with different graph structures; therefore a random graph model does not define a specific graph but a set of possible graphs that can be generated by it. As an example, the graph in Figure 2.8b can also be generated by our $G(34, .139)$ model.

However, running the generator a large number of times, we would see that graphs like the one in Figure 2.8a will appear more frequently than graphs like the one in Figure 2.8b. In summary, a random graph can be defined as a probability distribution over a set of graphs: Figure 2.8a and Figure 2.8b can be both generated by the $G(34, .139)$ model, the first with a higher probability than the second.

Using the configurations we have chosen to study these graphs, we can make this statement more clear by looking at the number of times they appear in each of the two graphs and comparing these statistics with the expected number of configurations defined by the model. If we look at all the graphs that we can generate using a $G(34, .139)$ model, we would have on average 34 nodes, around 78 edges, around 347 2-stars, and around 16 triangles. If we look at the graph in Figure 2.8a, we can find 34 nodes, 78 edges, 334 2-stars, and 14 triangles. These network statistics are very close to the average values associated to the $G(34, .139)$ model, so we can say that the $G(34, .139)$ model is likely to be the model used to generate this graph. If we look at the graph in Figure 2.8b, we still have 34 nodes, but only 47 edges, 116 2-stars, and 6 triangles. Therefore we can say that the $G(34, .139)$ model is not as likely to be the one used to generate this graph.

We can now get to the main idea behind ERGMs: given a random graph model with some parameters and a specific social network representing empirical data, we can fit the model to the graph; that is, we can estimate the values of the parameters that would most likely generate that specific graph. In our example, using a $G(n, p)$ random graph model, we could try to estimate n and p for each of the two graphs in Figures 2.8a and Figure 2.8b. However, ER random graphs are not powerful enough to represent networks with more complex dependencies between edges. For example, checking the network statistics of the graph in Figure 2.8c (34, 78, 528, 45), we can see how the number of

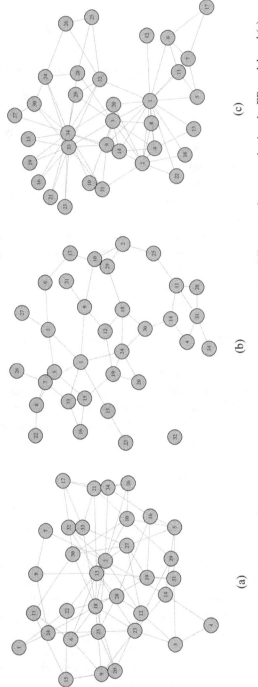

(a)

(b)

(c)

Figure 2.8. Different kinds of graphs: (a) a graph generated using the ER model; (b) a different graph generated using the ER model; and (c) the Zachary Karate network (Zachary, 1977).

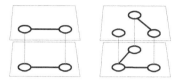

Figure 2.9. Two possible configurations to study in a multilayer social network.

triangles is significantly higher than the average expected for $G(34, .139)$ models, despite the number of nodes and edges being exactly the same: ER random graphs are not likely to generate graphs like this, independently of how we set their parameters.

To conclude this intuitive presentation of ERGMs, we can think of a specific ERGM as analogous to an ER random graph model, where instead of having n and p as parameters, we use the network statistics defined by the configurations we choose. As a consequence, when we fit an ERGM defined on some configurations to a specific graph, we get as a result an estimate of how much the social dynamics associated to each of these configurations are expected to have contributed to the generation of this graph. For example, defining an ERGM on the four configurations in Figure 2.7 and fitting it to the graph in Figure 2.8c, we would see that the triangle configuration is significant in determining the structure of that specific graph.

The application of ERGMs to multilayer networks follows the same idea: if multilayer configurations are specified, then the model will tell us about the importance or unexpectedness of each of them. For example, we can define an ERGM based on the multilayer configurations in Figure 2.9, to study if some empirical data contain an unexpectedly large number of edges between the same actors on multiple layers and of triangles that are closed thanks to the contribution of edges in two different layers. As said, analysts can choose other configurations (and thus define other ERGMs) to study other aspects of the multilayer network.

For an introductory text on ERGMs, the reader can consult the book edited by Lusher et al. (2012), which contains both a basic presentation of the main concepts needed to use ERGM software packages and details on the underlying theory, whereas Wang et al. (2013) discuss how to apply ERGMs to multilevel networks. In the SNA literature, ERGMs have been one of the models of choice to study both multiplex (Lazega and Pattison, 1999) and multilevel networks (Zappa and Lomi, 2015).

Two features to be considered when choosing a model and that are worth mentioning with regard to ERGMs are simplicity and efficiency. Given two models able to represent the same data, using a more complex or less intuitive model (as may be the case for ERGMs) might lead to misinterpretations of the results. In addition, although, to the best of our knowledge, the scalability of specific software and algorithms has not been studied in detail within this specific context, it is known that ERGM models can deal with single-layer networks up to the order of 1000 nodes (Goodreau, 2007). When multilayer configurations are used, these limits can be significantly reduced, making the analysis impractical, except for very small networks.

2.3 Data Sets

Multilayer social networks appear in a number of different contexts, where data are characterized by different sizes (from a handful of nodes to several millions), different natures (e.g., online, offline, hybrid), and different layer semantics (contact, communication, time, context, etc.). The objective of this section is both to present a set of examples where multilayer networks can be used as a tool to study social systems and to indicate a list of available data sets that can be used for training or research purposes. Table 2.2 summarizes all the mentioned data sets.

Many multirelational networks, that is, actors connected by multiple types of ties, have been collected during SNA studies and are still largely used as reference networks to experiment on new measures and methods. These networks are often characterized by a small size, because they were often collected through offline questionnaires or interviews, so although they cannot be used to test the scalability of algorithms, they can be very useful in qualitatively checking the behavior and results of new methods. Some of these can be downloaded from the UCI repository:[1] Florentine Families, Sampson's Monastery, Bank Wiring, and Tailor Shop. Another interesting multirelational network about criminal relationships is described by Bright et al. (2015).

More recently, with the advent of online social media, additional data have become available. A way to collect multilayer networks from OSNs consists in retrieving information about the accounts of the same set of users on different platforms. This has been often done extracting data from *social media aggregators*. These meta-services can be ad hoc websites or stand-alone applications and allow people to manage in a unified way their multiple online identities, for example, to receive all updates from their OSNs as a single stream. Aggregators used in the literature include Friendfeed (Celli et al., 2010; Magnani and Rossi, 2011), Foursquare (Rossetti et al., 2012), and general systems like Google+ and

---

[1] Available at http://vlado.fmf.uni-lj.si/pub/networks/data/UciNet/UciData.htm.

Table 2.2. *Multilayer social network data*

Name	Description
Florentine Families	These data, collected by John Padgett from historical documents, describe relations among 16 politically prominent families in the city of Florence around the year 1430: business ties (specifically, recorded financial ties such as loans, credits, and joint partnerships) and marriage alliances. Two factions appear in the data, with families strongly related to the Medici or to the Strozzi family, making the data useful for testing community detection methods.
Sampson's Monastery	A group of eight monks was asked to specify their top three choices on four pairs of positive/negative relations: esteem and disesteem, liking and disliking, positive influence and negative influence, praise and blame. The limit of the top three preferences imposed in the survey can bias the results of measures based on degree, as the out-degree of each actor is 3 by construction of the data.
Bank Wiring	These data, first presented by Roethlisberger and Dickson (1939), describe 14 employees of the Hawthorne Plant (Western Electric) working in the bank wiring room. The employees had different roles (two inspectors, three solderers, and nine wiremen or assemblers), making the data useful for testing role/position detection methods. The available layers describe participation in horseplay, participation in arguments about open windows, friendship, antagonistic (negative) behavior, helping others with work, and the number of times workers traded job assignments.
Tailor Shop	Collected by Kapferer (1972), these data represent work and friendship interactions among 39 workers in a tailor shop. Two versions of the social network are available, recorded at two different times.
Terrorist	A data set made available by Roberts and Everton (2011) and mainly extracted from data collected by the International Crisis Group, with relationships among 78 Indonesian terrorists (mutual trust, common operations, exchanged communications, and business relationships).
Criminal	This data set has been analyzed by Bright et al. (2015), who focused on eight types of edges related to the exchange of a particular resource (e.g., drugs, money) in a criminal network with 128 actors.

(*cont.*)

Table 2.2. *(cont.)*

Name	Description
AUCS	These data, described by Rossi and Magnani (2015), were collected at a university research department and include five online and offline layers. The population of the study consists of 61 employees (out of the total number of 142) who decided to join the survey, including professors, postdoctoral researchers, PhD students, and administrative staff.
Facencounter	This hybrid online/offline data set is described by Gaito et al. (2012), where a two-layer network storing, respectively, Facebook friendship and offline encounters has been collected on a set of 35 students. These data have been used to compute structural differences and information transfer across layers.
French School	A data set collected by Mastrandrea et al. (2015) about more than 300 high school students recording face-to-face contacts (measured using both wearable sensors and contact diaries), self-reported friendships, and online social links.
FYT	This data set has been obtained starting from Friendfeed, a social media aggregator (Magnani and Rossi, 2011). In this system, while users can directly post messages and comment on other messages, much like in Facebook and other similar OSNs, they can also register their accounts on other systems. The original data acquisition consists of 322, 967 users who registered at least one service outside Friendfeed, with a total number of 1, 587, 273 services. From these, two multilayer networks were retrieved, one with users who registered exactly one Twitter account and whose Twitter account was associated to exactly one Friendfeed account (155, 804 users) and one smaller data set with an additional YouTube layer.
Foursquare	Another service that has been used to build multilayer networks, this is a location-based social network. A data set collected starting from this service has been described by Rossetti et al. (2012), including 7500 actors.
Twitter-XF	This data set contains Twitter replies and retweets produced by a small set of users (5137) interacting online during the final episode of a popular TV show (*XFactor Italy*). Rossi and Magnani (2012) have used these data to analyze the effect of online conversations on the connections in the contact networks, that is, how users started following each other after having interacted on topics of common interest.

Table 2.2. *(cont.)*

Name	Description
Friendfeed	This large data set, described by Celli et al. (2010), contains public interactions among users of the Friendfeed OSN collected over one month. Commenting and liking constitute two layers, which can also be overlaid with the users' contact network to create a hybrid contact and communication multilayer social network.
MMORPG	A large data set about interactions in a massively multiplayer online role-playing game, studied by Szell et al. (2010).
DBLP[a]	This data set can be obtained from the DBLP repository and has been used in a large number of studies, especially in computer science and using HINs. Undirected edges among researchers indicate coauthorship, while no information on citations is present. Different layers correspond to different conferences and years where the corresponding papers were presented.
AMiner[b]	This is a large collection of citation networks including information about authors, papers, conferences, publication years, and citations among papers.

[a] http://dblp.uni-trier.de.
[b] https://aminer.org/billboard/AMinerNetwork.

Facebook, even if extracting data from the latter is not easy because of its strict privacy settings.

Although social media aggregators may represent a viable solution to the problem of mapping users across multiple OSNs, access to these aggregated data is not easy, and even when anonymized, they can pose serious ethical and privacy concerns. Nevertheless, these data sets have some peculiar features distinguishing them from the previous cases and making them potentially valuable for research. First, they explicitly expose multiple online identities of the same individuals: different accounts on different social media may be considered as different entities, even if owned by the same actor, because they can be used to present different aspects of the person and can be used strategically to reach different audiences. Nodes corresponding to the same actor on different layers do not directly represent the actor but only user accounts, which makes these nodes clearly distinct from each other. We can say that these data clearly fit a multilayer model, whereas multirelational networks can often be described just using an edge-typed multigraph where no distinction is made between an actor and the same actor operating on different types of relationships. In addition, although this aspect has not been explored in the literature so far, there can be many-to-many relationships between nodes in different layers, that is, a single node can correspond to multiple nodes in another layer, and vice versa. Statistics about this phenomenon are presented by Magnani and Rossi (2011).

Although multilayer social networks from multiple online social media are hard to collect due to the complex problem of mapping users across different services, multilayer networks can be used to study other kinds of online data. Social media platforms (from Facebook to Twitter and YouTube) often offer the opportunity to communicate outside of the topological network defined by users' connections. Twitter hashtag-based conversations, as well as Facebook groups or YouTube comments on a video, represent examples of how, within these services, users can communicate independently from the structure defined by their specific connections, for example, friendship on Facebook and following on Twitter. In these cases the topological network (e.g., friendship) can be modeled as a layer of a multilayer network, and any other communicative action (e.g., commenting on the same public page) can be represented by additional layers. Some studies of these kinds of multilayer networks have shown interesting coevolution patterns of the two layers (Magnani et al., 2013), for example, the fact that contacts created after commenting on the same global discussion tend to be more stable.

A different type of digital data source that has been used to reconstruct social interactions are massively multiplayer online role-playing games, where it is possible to log all the players' activities and to reconstruct multiple layers that can include chatting, fighting, exchange of goods, co-location, and so on. (Szell et al., 2010). These types of data are typically owned by the companies selling the game and cannot be accessed without specific agreements.

Besides offline multilayer social networks, often collected with traditional methods, and online multilayer social networks, often relying on social media data, there are also hybrid networks trying to combine the two approaches. Among these, in this book, we often use the AUCS data set to exemplify the presented concepts. In this data set about the relationships among employees of a university department, five structural variables have been recorded, namely, current working relationships, repeated leisure activities, regularly eating lunch together, coauthorship of a publication, and friendship on Facebook. These variables cover different types of relations between the actors based on their interactions. All relations are dichotomous, which means that they are either present or absent, without weights. Measurements of the first three variables (offline data) were collected using a questionnaire that had been distributed among the employees. On top of this, the respondents were asked to provide their user information for some major OSNs. Seventy-seven percent of the respondents who filled in the questionnaire stated that they had a Facebook account and provided their usernames and lists of friends. Information about the coauthorship relation was obtained from an online bibliography database without the need to directly ask the actors. A coauthorship of at least one publication by a pair of actors resulted in an edge in that layer. The bibliography database gets new publication data with a delay of several months, and therefore the work network is quite distinct from it. Moreover, the work network includes other types of interactions than cooperation on papers (e.g., cooperation on administrative work). Other hybrid networks are studied by Gaito et al. (2012) and Mastrandrea et al. (2015).

Finally, another typical source of multilayer social networks are online bibliographic databases, from which it is possible to obtain coauthorship relations and citations among researchers publishing in different contexts (e.g., conferences or research areas) and at different times. Typical examples are the DBLP and arXiv online digital archives.

3

Measuring Multilayer Social Networks

The greatest length or breadth of a full grown inhabitant of Flatland
may be estimated at about eleven of your inches. Twelve inches may be
regarded as a maximum.

– The Square

In this chapter we present a set of measures that can be used to compute quantitative descriptions of multilayer networks. Some of these measures have counterparts in classical SNA, whereas others focus on the different layers or on their interplay and do not have specific equivalents among traditional measures.

We organize the chapter in to two main sections. Actor measures are used to describe the characteristics of actors with respect to their connections on the different layers. Some are extended versions of existing SNA measures, for example, degree, betweenness, and clustering coefficient, whereas others are specific to multilayer networks and can be used to quantify the *relevance* of one or more layers for an actor. Layer measures, alternatively, focus on the relationships between layers, for example, their similarity.

Along with the description of the measures, we also show their application to our running example, represented in Figure 1.2. In addition, we apply a selection of these measures to a real multilayer network to better illustrate their goals and consequences. The real multilayer network we are going to use for our analysis is the AUCS network, described in Section 2.3 and containing five types of relationships among the employees of a university department: Facebook friendship, having lunch together, being coauthors of published research papers, collaborating at work, and spending leisure time together.

The aim of this chapter is not only to introduce metrics to describe multilayer social networks in the same way we used to describe single-layer networks but

38

also to stress how and why multilayer networks present a unique set of features and problems requiring specific approaches to be addressed.

3.1 Four Main Approaches

When we study multilayer networks, the additional complexity introduced by relations existing between the layers can be handled in different ways, depending on the interpretation of the network data and on the goals of the analysis. On a general level, and with the due level of abstraction, we can identify four different approaches.

The first approach consists in merging the layers to obtain a single-layer network. This process, often called *flattening* and further detailed in Section 4.2.1, can be performed in different ways. One simple way is to create a new graph with one node for every actor and an edge between two nodes if the corresponding actors are connected in any of the layers. To preserve more information, we can also add a weight to each edge in the flattened network, representing the number of layers on which the actors are connected. Once we have obtained a flattened network, traditional SNA measures can be computed, as reported in the first row of Table 3.1, where the five layers composing the AUCS network have been flattened into a single layer and then summarized. The reader not familiar with some of these measures can find their definitions in the glossary at the end of the book.

The second approach, already used in traditional SNA, consists in applying existing measures to each layer separately and then comparing these results. This approach is complementary to the first one, where we try to preserve information that might be contained in some of the layers but gets hidden by the flattening process.

As Table 3.1 shows, the various layers of the AUCS network have very different sizes, for example, almost every actor belongs to the lunch or the work layer, whereas fewer than half of them are part of the coauthor layer. Different layers also show remarkably different characteristics in terms of graph density, clustering coefficient, centralization, and network diameter when observed one at a time. Every single layer has its own specific characteristics representing specific social dynamics. For example, the high density of the flattened network seems to be determined by the Facebook connections, acting as a sort of social glue filling holes in the rest of the connective structure. However, this analysis is still limited: without information on actual social interactions happening on top of these connections, we cannot know if Facebook ties are practically relevant or just social place-holders, and without information on the correlations

Table 3.1. *Descriptive measures for the flattened AUCS network and for its five layers: number of actors, density, clustering coefficient, degree centralization, average path length, diameter*

Network	n	Dens	CC	DCentr	Avg length	Dia
Flattened	61	0.34	0.48	0.48	2.06	4
Coauthor	25	0.07	0.43	0.14	1.50	3
Work	60	0.11	0.34	0.35	2.39	4
Lunch	60	0.11	0.57	0.15	3.19	7
Leisure	47	0.08	0.34	0.22	3.12	8
Facebook	32	0.25	0.48	0.23	1.96	4

between the different layers, we cannot be sure that the high density is not determined by a combination of the other layers. As another example, we can also appreciate the remarkably high clustering coefficient of the lunch layer compared to the other layers. This is not difficult to understand: people go to the canteen in more or less stable groups.

In practice, this approach can be useful for producing an initial overview of the data, before applying truly multilayer measures.

Differing from these two conservative approaches, the third and fourth classes of measures represent multilayer networks with ad hoc conceptual models and are the main focus of this chapter. The third approach considers multiple layers at the same time, but without treating them as being ontologically different. Measures based on this approach explicitly consider the difference between interlayer and intralayer edges and also make numerical distinctions between different layers, for example, through weights, but at the end they typically produce single numerical values merging the contributions of the different types of edges. A typical way of doing this, used by De Domenico et al. (2015a), is to run extended *random walks*, that is, processes describing an item – often called a walker – randomly flowing through the available relational ties and also able to switch layers. For example, in Figure 3.1a, we can see a random walker starting from Mark on the LinkedIn layer. Each step in the process is indicated by thick arrows and sequential numbers (1 to 4): first, a neighbor of Mark, Bin in this example, is chosen at random, and the walk proceeds on the same layer (Mark → Bin). Then a neighbor of Bin is chosen, and the walk continues (Bin → Sere). Because this approach is based on a multilayer network model, there is also the possibility for a walker to move cross-layer, as in our example, where Sere propagates the item to Luca after switching to another layer (Facebook). In addition, at each time stamp, it is common to allow the walker to restart, either from the same node or from a randomly chosen node (a process

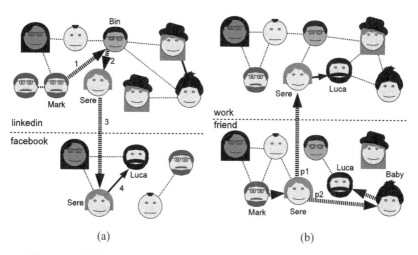

Figure 3.1. (a) A random walk made of four steps crossing network boundaries thanks to the same actors (in this case, Serena) being active on multiple layers. (b) Two alternative paths p1 and p2 from Mark to Luca.

called *teleportation*), to avoid effects like the walker getting trapped inside a portion of the network with no outgoing edges. This process can be executed multiple times, and as the choice of each propagation step happens at random, different paths can be traversed at each time.

During recent years, approaches based on random walkers have generated a considerable amount of interest among researchers. They are useful to study both structural and dynamical processes, have the ability to calculate the centrality of actors without knowledge of the full topology of the network (Newman, 2005), and can be used to approximate measures that would otherwise take a long time to be computed exactly.

Several traditional measures can be extended to multilayer networks using this approach. For example, we can run multiple extended random walks and count how many times Bin is traversed when moving from one actor to another. This provides an idea of how central Bin is with respect to information exchanged between other actors. This class of approaches considers multiplicity as an unavoidable characteristic of networks requiring a new set of tools to be handled properly. In this case the focus is not only on obtaining additional information from the adoption of a multilayer network perspective but also on avoiding possible distortions due to a flattening process and underestimations of the correlations between the layers.

However, extended random walks introduce an underlying assumption that edges on different layers are of a comparable nature. It is of course possible to specify parameters stating that it is more probable to stay inside Facebook than staying on LinkedIn, but when measures must be computed, paths traversing different layers are treated indistinguishably. As an example, while counting how many times Bin has been traversed by a walk, it would not make any difference if the walk happened on Facebook, on LinkedIn, or on a combination of the two layers. This might limit our ability to deal with the intrinsic multiplexity of social networks where actors are connected by qualitatively different ties and the quality of the tie defines the possibilities of the connection.

Within this perspective, and on a more abstract level, multilayer networks could be described as a set of behavioral contexts (Barrett et al., 2012). Different edge types, network structure, and social relations are not separate entities and should not be observed separately, but at the same time, we may believe that traversing two actors on the Facebook layer is not equivalent to traversing two actors on the coworker layer and that the difference cannot be expressed by a number, for example, an edge weight. These considerations lead us to our fourth approach, where edges involving different layers are analyzed together but not mixed with each other.

As an example, within this approach, the two paths in Figure 3.1b,

P1 $Mark_{friend} \rightarrow Serena_{friend} \rightarrow Serena_{work} \rightarrow Luca_{work}$

P2 $Mark_{friend} \rightarrow Serena_{friend} \rightarrow Barby_{friend} \rightarrow Luca_{friend}$

are considered incomparable: within this approach, it does not make sense to say, for example, that one of the two is shorter than the other, as they use conceptually different kinds of ties. Therefore, within this perspective, it is necessary to introduce measures that describe this additional information without summarizing it into a single value but maintaining, as much as possible, the distinction between the different kinds of relational ties. This idea constitutes the background for the fourth set of measures, where the emphasis is on the qualitative distinction existing between the various layers as well as on the structural properties of the multilayer network. Several authors, such as Berlingerio et al. (2011c), Magnani and Rossi (2013b), and Solé-Ribalta et al. (2014), have tried to adopt this complementary approach, defining measures based on a multilayer network model but, at the same time, keeping the different layers semantically distinct.

3.2 Actor Measures

In this section we focus on four main classes of measures to describe actors in a multilayer social network. The first three sets of measures are direct extensions of their single-layer counterparts: measures characterizing a single actor based on its local edges, measures based on the relationship (in particular, the distance) between pairs of actors, and measures based on groups of three actors. Although this classification is not strict, as, for example, we can define measures sharing aspects from both the first and the second class, it emphasizes the three main components of a social network: single actors, *dyads* (pairs of actors), and *triads* (groups of three actors). In addition, we can define measures characterizing the relevance of a specific layer (or set of layers) within the context of the actor's connectivity. These measures have no counterpart for single-layer networks.

3.2.1 Degree and Neighborhood Centrality

Centrality is not a single measure but rather a family of measures aimed at identifying the most important actors in a social network (Wasserman and Faust, 1994). The family of centrality measures is probably the most widely applied set of SNA tools in practical contexts. At the same time, centrality is a defining concept of this field: SNA focuses on the relations between units instead of trying to sort units into categories defined by their inner attributes (Wellman and Berkowitz, 1988; Wasserman and Faust, 1994). Within this perspective, centrality is an intrinsically relational concept, because to be central, an actor needs to have relations: there is no such thing as centrality without relations.

Nevertheless, the concept of importance is vague and needs to be better defined. An actor might be important for many reasons: he might be important because he is connected to a large number of different nodes or because he is connected to other important nodes. An actor can also be considered important because her absence would result in a loosely connected social network made of many isolated components. Centrality is also often described in terms of the power that an actor could receive from it, for example, an actor strategically located within a network will have a high control over the information flowing through the network. These examples should show how centrality can be interpreted in different ways from different perspectives. Whereas sociologists and social scientists might think of that in terms of power or amount of social capital, computer scientists might think of that in terms of reachability. Both interpretations make perfect sense within a specific context, and this is why centrality should be considered a contextual concept. Its interpretation, and more specifically the type of centrality that we should use to identify the most important actors, is first and foremost dependent on the nature of the network itself.

In traditional SNA, centrality measures were first presented as a unique coherent framework by Freeman (1979). In his framework, degree, closeness, and betweenness centrality are introduced together as measures based on three different conceptual foundations. In the context of this book, although the general conceptual framework introduced by Freeman still stands, we need to take into consideration the complexity introduced by the different layers of a multilayer network.

Degree-Based Measures

A way to compute the degree of an actor consists in flattening the network and computing her degree (i.e., the number of edges adjacent to her) on the resulting network. For example, we can generate a weighted network, where edge weights reflect the number of layers where those actors were connected, and we can remove the edge whose weight is below a given threshold before computing the degree (Bródka et al., 2011a, 2012).

As we discussed in the introduction to this chapter, this approach does not recognize the different nature of different layers; an alternative is to perform a qualitative analysis where each layer is treated as a distinct entity. Within this perspective, connections existing on two different layers are qualitatively different and should not be reduced to a single value: as an example, using this approach, we would not arbitrarily sum up connections between coworkers with Facebook friendships.

To cope with this complexity, Berlingerio et al. (2011c) extended the traditional concept of degree into a multilayer network perspective that takes into consideration the possibility for an actor a to exist throughout a set of layers L out of all the possible layers $\mathcal{L}$. Here the degree of an actor on a set of layers is simply the number of his relational ties on all these layers.[1]

Definition 3.1 (Degree centrality) Let $a \in \mathcal{A}$ be an actor, $L \subseteq \mathcal{L}$ a set of layers, and $G = (\mathcal{A}, \mathcal{L}, V, E)$ a multilayer network. The degree centrality of a on L is defined as

$$\text{degree}(a, L) = |\{\{(a, l), (a', l')\} \in E \text{ s.t. } l, l' \in L\}|$$

This function can be computed on any set of layers, and we only give a basic version of this definition here, which can be adapted not to consider inter-layer edges (setting $l_1 = l_2 \in L$), to calculate incoming and outgoing degrees in directed networks or adding weights to each edge. The definition can also be

---

[1] All definitions presented in this chapter have been adapted or extended to fit a multilayer network model; therefore they can present differences with respect to the definitions in the original papers.

Table 3.2. *Layer-specific degree centrality for users Luca and Cici*

User	Facebook	Friend	LinkedIn	Work	Flattened
Luca	2	2	(*NA*) 0	3	7
Cici	2	2	2	2	8

extended to distinguish between the case where a is not present in any of the layers in L (e.g., returning N/A) and the case where a is present in some of the layers in L but has no connections.

We can then consider two extreme cases: when $L = \mathcal{L}$, we have the degree of the actor within the whole multilayer network (as in the first approach based on flattening), whereas when the set of layers contains only one layer, we have a classical degree for the actor in that layer (as in the second approach). If we consider our running example, Luca and Cici's degrees are summarized in Table 3.2. In between, we have a number of options. In particular, it is also possible to compute an actor's degree on multiple layers. For example, we might want to compare online and offline relationships, in which case we would compute degree(Luca, {Facebook, LinkedIn}) = 2 and degree(Luca, {Friend, Work}) = 5.

Figure 3.2 shows how the various layers of the AUCS multilayer network have different distributions of degree: whereas coauthor, work, and leisure have very skewed distributions, this is not so evident for Facebook data, and lunch clearly shows a more bell-shaped distribution.

Degree centrality is still a very simple measure, even in its extended version. The importance of this function mainly lies in the measures that can be defined on top of it. An initial exploration of the specific possibilities of a multilayer analysis consists in investigating how actors structure their presence through different layers: is Cici evenly present on every layer of the multilayer network? And what about Luca's presence? *Degree deviation* measures their different behaviors.

Definition 3.2 (Degree deviation) Let $a \in \mathcal{A}$ be an actor, $L \subseteq \mathcal{L}$ a set of layers, and $G = (\mathcal{A}, \mathcal{L}, V, E)$ a multilayer network. Degree deviation is defined as the standard deviation of a's degree over the layers in L, that is,

$$\sqrt{\frac{\sum_{l \in L} \left(\text{degree}(a, \{l\}) - \frac{\text{degree}(a,L)}{|L|} \right)^2}{|L|}}$$

Whereas Cici has the same degree on every network, corresponding to 0 deviation, Luca shows a more unstable presence. His average degree on the

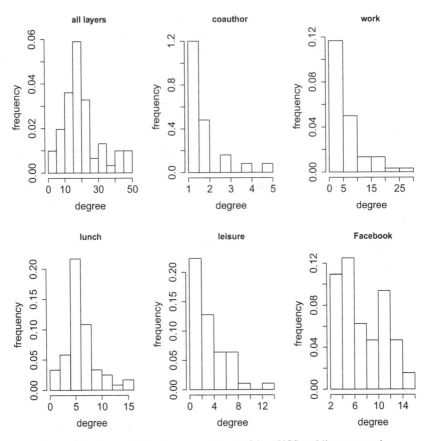

Figure 3.2. Degree distribution on each layer of the AUCS multilayer network.

four layers is $\frac{2+2+0+3}{4} = 1.75$, and his degree deviation with respect to all the four layers corresponds to $\sqrt{\frac{(2-1.75)^2+(2-1.75)^2+(0-1.75)^2+(3-1.75)^2}{4}} = 1.09$.

Degree deviation is an indicator of the actors' presence in the multilayer network but not a way to identify meaningful correlations between different layers. In Figure 3.3 we show the distribution of the degree deviation over the 61 actors in the AUCS network. Most actors have a low degree deviation, indicating that they are either active or inactive in a comparable way on the different layers. A few individuals show a clear selectivity, with a large presence on only some of the layers.

Neighborhood-Based Measures

Whereas in a single-layer social network, the degree centrality of an actor corresponds to the number of adjacent actors, this is no longer true in a multilayer

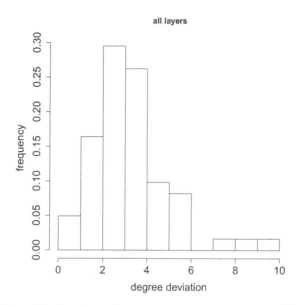

Figure 3.3. Distribution of degree deviation for the actors in AUCS.

network where actors can be connected to different individuals, depending on the layer. The difference between actors and potential number of adjacent edges is the key concept behind the definition of *neighborhood centrality*. Following Berlingerio et al. (2011c), the neighbors of an actor a are those distinct actors that are connected to a on a specific layer or set of layers.

Definition 3.3 (Neighbors) Let $a \in \mathcal{A}$ be an actor, $L \subseteq \mathcal{L}$ a set of layers, and $G = (\mathcal{A}, \mathcal{L}, V, E)$ a multilayer network. The neighbors of a on layers L are defined as follows:

$$\text{neighbors}(a, L) = \{a' \in \mathcal{A} \mid \{(a, l), (a', l')\} \in E \text{ and } l, l' \in L\}$$

The corresponding measure, called *neighborhood centrality*, simply counts the number of neighbors of an actor on one or more layers.

Definition 3.4 (Neighborhood centrality) Let $a \in \mathcal{A}$ be an actor, $L \subseteq \mathcal{L}$ a set of layers, and $G = (\mathcal{A}, \mathcal{L}, V, E)$ a multilayer network. The neighborhood of a on layers L is defined as follows:

$$\text{neighborhood}(a, L) = |\text{neighbors}(a, L)|$$

Just as the concept of degree can be extended for directed and weighted networks and can be modified by not considering interlayer edges, we can do the same for the concept of neighborhood.

When computed on a single layer, degree and neighborhood centrality coincide. However, the comparison between these two measures becomes interesting when we consider multiple layers. For example, the ratio between neighborhood and degree tells us something about how a single actor is connected through the different layers. When actors are connected to the same neighbors on multiple layers, we have high values of *connective redundancy*.

Definition 3.5 (Connective redundancy) Let $a \in \mathcal{A}$ be an actor, $L \subseteq \mathcal{L}$ a set of layers, and $G = (\mathcal{A}, \mathcal{L}, V, E)$ a multilayer network. Connective redundancy is defined as

$$\text{connective redundancy}(a, L) = 1 - \frac{\text{neighborhood}(a, L)}{\text{degree}(a, L)}$$

When connective redundancy is computed on the set of all layers and equals 0, every edge on every layer is necessary for an actor to keep her total connectivity. Applying this concept to our running example, we see how Luca's neighborhood is 5 with a degree of 7 and a redundancy of .29. Comparing these data with Cici's values (neighborhood 4, degree 8, and redundancy .5), we can clearly detect how Cici's network has a higher level of multiplexity. A visual inspection of our running example shows how Cici is connected to Mark and Mat on the LinkedIn, work, and friend layers, which increases her connective redundancy.

Another way to explore the role of specific layers for specific actors is using the concept of *exclusive neighborhood*. This considers the actors that are connected exclusively on a specific layer or set of layers.

Definition 3.6 (Exclusive neighborhood) Let $a \in \mathcal{A}$ be an actor, $L \subseteq \mathcal{L}$ a set of layers, and $G = (\mathcal{A}, \mathcal{L}, V, E)$ a multilayer network. Exclusive neighborhood is defined as

$$\text{xneighborhood}(a, L) = |\text{neighbors}(a, L) \setminus \text{neighbors}(a, \mathcal{L} \setminus L)|$$

where $\setminus$ indicates the set difference operation.

In our running example, Luca has one exclusive neighbor on every layer where he is present (Facebook, friend, and work); therefore removing or losing information about one of these layers will remove one social tie that does not exist anywhere else.

Although in the examples described so far, we have often compared single layers within multilayer networks, we would like to stress again that one of the most powerful opportunities of these measures is the option of computing them on a specific set of layers that might be perceived as homogeneous for any reason. Let us say, for example, that we want to group together online relations on Facebook and LinkedIn to compare them with the offline layers friend and work. All the measures defined so far can also be used in this scenario.

Random Walk–Based Extensions of Degree Centrality

Several network analysis approaches based on random walks have been proposed for single-layer networks (Newman, 2010), and they can be fruitfully extended to apply to multilayer networks. If, on one hand, random walk–based methods lack the ability to deal with qualitative differences existing between different layers, on the other hand, they offer a powerful tool to define multiple measures on top of a single basic concept. The most relevant feature of extended random walks is their ability to deal with interlayer connectivity, treating the possibility for an actor to switch between two different layers as an additional connection traversing the node. Although this is theoretically possible also with other approaches, dealing with interlayer connectivity between qualitatively different layers does not seem to be a trivial problem. Within this approach, a measure related to degree centrality in multilayer networks is *occupation centrality*, as defined by De Domenico et al. (2015a).

Definition 3.7 (Occupation centrality) The occupation centrality of an actor $a \in \mathcal{A}$ in a multilayer network $G = (\mathcal{A}, \mathcal{L}, V, E)$ is the probability that a random walker on G is found on any node corresponding to a.

In this case, a walker in node (a, l) might jump to one of its neighbors (a', l) within the same layer l with uniform probability or might switch to its counterpart (a, l') on a different layer l'. The interlayer connection is treated as an edge that can be chosen randomly among all edges traversing the node. This formulation can be easily extended for weighted networks assuming a layer-switching probability proportional to the strength of the connection. In the specific case when interlayer edges have the same strength for all nodes, occupation centrality is strongly correlated with degree centrality. Related definitions based on random walks, also known as (extended) PageRank centralities after the name of the algorithm initially used by the Google search engine to rank web pages, are described by Halu et al. (2013) and can be used to rank layers in addition to actors (Ng et al., 2011).

The practice of random walk sampling carries with it the inherent danger of errors arising in the measurement of the network: in particular, with the high degree of triadic closure in social networks (Heider, 1946), random walkers may be trapped for a long time in local subgraphs (Leskovec et al., 2008). A variety of modifications to the standard random walk process exists to address this problem for single-layer networks (Avrachenkov et al., 2010; Ribeiro and Towsley, 2010), and similar methods should be considered important in

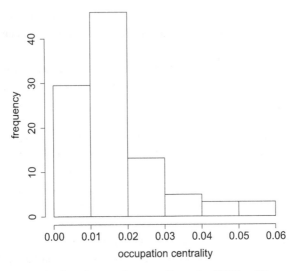

Figure 3.4. Distribution of occupation centrality on the AUCS multilayer network, with teleportation probability .2, and for each layer a probability of .4 to remain in the same layer and a uniform probability to move to any of the other layers.

multilayer networks as well. As a final note, while it may seem that Definition 3.7 depends on the starting node of the random walker, given enough time and a connected network with finite variance (guaranteed by the finite size of real networks), the starting point no longer has an effect on the probability distribution of the location of the walker. Figure 3.4 shows the occupation centrality distribution for the AUCS multilayer network.

3.2.2 Distance-Based Measures

Whereas the original definition of degree centrality is conceptually based on direct connections among actors, the two other main centrality measures introduced by Freeman are conceptually based on *shortest paths*, that is, shortest sequences of edges leading from one actor to another. The number of edges in a shortest path is called *geodesic distance*, or just *distance*.

The distance between two actors is one of the most complex and interesting concepts we need to extend to define new measures on multilayer networks. A first consideration is that the shortest path might not be the best option for evaluating the separation between the two actors. Under the availability of multiple layers, instead of using a shortest path, actors could prefer to switch layers and reach their destination through a longer, but maybe more reliable, path. To understand this, let us assume that in our running example, Sere has work-related problems with Bin. She might address this through the shortest path on the work layer (where she is directly connected with him), or she might prefer to talk to her friend Mat and ask him to talk to Bin as a friend, trying to solve the problem stepping outside of the formal context of working relationships. In this example, as in many others, shortest paths (where *short* refers to the total number of traversed edges) are not necessarily the preferred way to navigate the network from one user to another and could therefore produce a wrong estimation of the actors' actual distances and positions.

This is not a feature only of multilayer networks. Despite the fact that the most commonly used centrality metrics, closeness and betweenness, rely on the assumption that shortest paths should be the preferred way to compute the distance between two actors in a network, there are many other measures based on alternative ways to evaluate the distance between two actors. Among these, the extension of betweenness centrality based on random walks, proposed by Newman (2005), is probably the most notable.

Within multilayer networks, not only can we say that nonshortest paths can also contribute to the computation of distances between actors but the very concept of shortest path becomes difficult to define because it would require the comparison of ontologically different layers, like offline and Facebook friendships. In addition, multilayer paths can include changes of layer, which we may want to consider while computing the length of the path.

Paths and Path Lengths

As for other measures, path lengths can be computed by flattening the network and computing single-layer distances over it, as proposed by Bródka et al. (2011b). This said, we now focus on a more general concept of *multilayer distance* that makes a substantial, ontological difference between edges on different layers (Magnani and Rossi, 2013b). As an example, in Figure 3.5(a,b), we can see two possible paths from Cici to Luca. If we want to describe their length, we can be tempted to say that both involve four steps and that their distance is thus four. However, if we look at them more carefully, we can see that the first consists of two steps on the work layer, a layer switch from work to friend, and one step on the friend layer, whereas the second has two friend steps, a layer switch from friend to work, and one work step. Therefore we can more accurately represent the length of a path using a matrix counting these steps layer by layer.

Definition 3.8 (Multilayer path length) The multilayer length of a p on layers $\mathcal{L} = \{l_1, \ldots, l_m\}$ is a matrix L where L_{l_i, l_j} indicates the number of edges traversed from a node in layer l_i to a node in layer l_j.

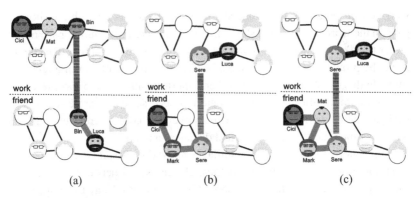

(a)   (b)   (c)

Figure 3.5. Three alternative paths from Cici to Luca; (a) and (b) have the same number of steps but different lengths on different layers, whereas (c) is longer than (b).

Following this definition, the lengths of the two paths in Figure 3.5(a,b) can be represented respectively as

$$\begin{pmatrix} 2 & 1 \\ 0 & 1 \end{pmatrix} \quad \begin{pmatrix} 1 & 0 \\ 1 & 2 \end{pmatrix} \tag{3.1}$$

where the first row/column of each matrix represents the work layer and the second row/column represents the friend layer.

From this matrix, we can obtain different representations of the lengths, depending on the level of detail we want to keep. For example, we can omit interlayer switching costs, only keeping the diagonal of the length matrix. In this case, our two distances can be expressed using the following vectors:

$$\begin{pmatrix} 2 & 1 \end{pmatrix} \quad \begin{pmatrix} 1 & 2 \end{pmatrix} \tag{3.2}$$

As an extreme solution, we can sum all values into a single number, reducing our multilayer concept to a traditional length – in our example, both paths would appear having the same length.

The relevant aspect of a multilayer distance is that even if it keeps a difference between edges of different kinds, it still allows us to identify shortest paths containing different edge types. In Figure 3.5, while paths (a) and (b) are incomparable, path (b) is shorter than path (c), because it involves a shorter path on the friend layer and the same number of steps on the work layer.

Definition 3.9 (Shorter-than relation) Let R and S be two multilayer path lengths. R is shorter than S iff $\forall i, j \, R_{ij} \leq S_{ij} \wedge \exists ij \, R_{ij} < S_{ij}$.

Table 3.3. *Multilayer shortest path distance between Serena and Cici*

Dist#	LinkedIn	Work	Facebook	Friend
1	3			
2	2	1		
3	1	2		
4		3		
5			1	
6	1			1
7		1		1
8				2

A clear difference between a distance on a single-layer social network and a generalized distance on a multilayer network is that, in the first case, we only have one number, whereas in the second case, we may need to consider multiple incomparable shortest distances, each represented by a matrix or by an array. Table 3.3 shows the multilayer distance between Serena and Cici on our running example, using the vectorial simplification of the matrix – that is, its diagonal, only representing intralayer steps. From this, we know that to connect Sere with Cici, we need to traverse three edges on the LinkedIn layer, or two on LinkedIn and one on work, or we can use a direct connection on Facebook, and so on.

This definition has some attractive properties: it considers all paths that can be shortest under some monotone evaluation function (e.g., a function assigning a weight to each dimension), does not consider paths that cannot be the shortest given any evaluation function, and reduces to a traditional length in the single-layer case. In other words, multilayer shortest paths maintain on a general level the idea that a shorter path is on average better than a longer path, but the distance between two actors is expressed as a set of incomparable shortest paths that can traverse multiple layers. This concept is easily extensible to allow weighted edges by replacing the number of steps with the sum of weights along the path.

By defining distance as a set of distances, we assume that the concept of shortest path can be misleading in many real-world scenarios if we do not take the qualitative aspect of the existing relations into account. As we can easily understand from our everyday experience, the way in which we communicate using our interpersonal social networks is highly dependent on the content that we need to communicate and on the intended audience of that content. Whereas we can easily postpone a meeting just by sending an e-mail, we might prefer a different medium if we have to discuss personal issues, even if this requires involving more actors on the way. Within this perspective, every actor has a clear set of expectations when it comes to evaluating his own network to decide which layer should be used to communicate a specific message. It is no longer a matter of who is close and who is far.

In the following, we describe some basic distance-based measures, some defined as outcomes of random walks and others using the aforementioned generalized concept of distance.

Closeness Centrality in Multilayer Networks

Closeness is traditionally defined as the inverse of far-ness, where far-ness is the sum of the distances (lengths of a shortest path) between a node and every other node in the network (Sabidussi, 1966). Therefore closeness centrality relies heavily on the idea that the minimum number of steps between two actors is a reliable measure of efficiency in actors' communication within the network (Hakimi, 1965; Wasserman and Faust, 1994). A way to challenge this assumption and to include short-but-not-shortest paths into this centrality measure when dealing with multilayer networks has been defined by De Domenico et al. (2015a) with the concept of *random walk closeness*.

Definition 3.10 (Random walk closeness) The closeness of an actor a is defined as the inverse of the average number of steps that a random walker, starting from any other actor in the multilayer network, requires to hit a for the first time.

In contrast with degree and betweenness centralities, the discriminatory power of closeness centrality decreases when the size of the social network increases (Newman, 2010). Even in very large social networks, it is typical to find a limited number of actors with very large values of degree and betweenness centrality. Instead, the closeness centralities of different actors become small and very similar.

Betweenness Centralities in Multilayer Networks

A powerful aspect of random walks is that the same idea can be easily extended to redefine multiple measures, including *random walk betweenness centrality* (De Domenico et al., 2015a).

Definition 3.11 (Random walk betweenness centrality) Given an actor $a \in \mathcal{A}$, random walk betweenness centrality is defined as the number of random walks between any pair of nodes that pass through any node corresponding to a, averaging the value over all possible starting layers.

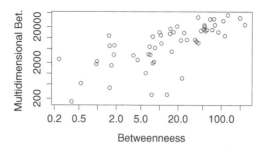

Figure 3.6. AUCS data show a high correlation between the traditional between-ness centrality on the flattened network and the multilayer betweenness centrality. The *x* and *y* axes are log scale; correlation coefficient = .72.

We can see how this definition is very conservative with respect to the single-layer case: the only differences are that multiple nodes contribute to a common actor and that values are averaged over the layers. Although a multidimensional distance does not lead to a straightforward extension of closeness centrality – as, on the opposite, do approaches based on random walks – it can be used to extend betweenness centrality. Traditionally, the potential influence of actors with high betweenness centrality derives from being on multiple shortest paths. A large part of the research that has been done on the idea of betweenness centrality has been on how to combine the shortest paths with other existing nonshortest paths or on removing shortest paths for extremely long geodesic distances (Stephenson and Zelen, 1989; Borgatti and Everett, 2006). However, the original and still the most used definition of betweenness on single-layer networks counts the number of shortest paths passing through a given node. The same definition can thus be used to characterize betweenness in a multidimensional network by replacing the concept of shortest path with a concept of multilayer distance (Magnani and Rossi, 2013b).

The general interpretation of multilayer betweenness centrality is similar to the traditional interpretation for betweenness centrality, but with the ability to detect the interplay existing between different layers; therefore nodes that will be traversed by the largest number of multilayer distances will have a higher multilayer betweenness centrality. Even though we generally expect to find a high correlation between these two measures, we may find some significant differences when we compare the two rankings.

Figure 3.6 provides an example of the difference between the two between-ness measures by showing how the correlation in the AUCS network is undoubtedly positive (.72) but less strong than the one we can observe compar-ing degree and neighborhood. If we compare the top six actors ranked accord-ing to the two definitions of betweenness (Tables 3.4 and 3.5), we can see that

Table 3.4. *Top six actors ranked according to their betweenness*

	Actor	Betweenness	M_Betweenneess
1	U4	235.34	23 324.00
2	U123	196.90	35 911.00
3	U91	125.89	43 008.00
4	U67	112.95	11 351.00
5	U79	106.25	29 733.00
6	U71	88.62	14 413.00

only three actors are present in both rankings (U91, U123, U79) and none of them has the same position. Actor U1 is a remarkable example of this behavior: although it has the second highest value of multilayer betweenness centrality, it only ranks 18th with respect to traditional betweenness centrality.

Other Distance-Based Measures

Some additional measures based on distances have been defined in the literature or can be defined extending existing concepts but have not been studied experimentally yet, at least in the context of social networks. An interesting measure based on shortest paths is *interdependence*, defined by Morris and Barthelemy (2012) as the proportion of shortest paths traversing multiple layers over the number of all shortest paths. This concept is of interest because it is a truly multilayer measure; however, as said, its explanatory power is still unexplored.

Another possible usage of multilayer paths could consist in computing the maximum number of edge-independent (i.e., not sharing any edge) shortest paths between each pair of actors. This measure, together with the path lengths, might indicate how robust the relationship between these individuals is, as their

Table 3.5. *Top six actors ranked according to their multilayer betweenness*

	Actor	Betweenness	M_Betweenneess
1	U91	125.89	43008.00
2	U1	41.87	37409.00
3	U123	196.90	35911.00
4	U130	75.57	33627.00
5	U32	65.41	33074.00
6	U79	106.25	29733.00

distance would increase only removing at least one edge from each of these paths. As said, to the best of our knowledge, these concepts still deserve experimental evaluation.

3.2.3 Measures of Relevance

One of the most intriguing aspects of multilayer network analysis is its ability to understand the relation between an actor and a specific layer as well as between different layers within the same multilayer network. We can easily agree on the fact that even if we participate in several social contexts at the same time, not all of them are always equally important for us; we do not rely on them in an equal way, and we have different expectations for the other actors involved. In other words, even if in our daily lives we traverse many different social contexts, and even if so far we have claimed that it is safe to represent these contexts as an interconnected network of different layers, we must admit that there are layers that might be more relevant than others. This diversity of social contexts is a habit that we seldom question. For example, we find it perfectly normal to assume that Sere will expect a higher level of emotional support from Barby and Mark than from Bin and Luca because they belong to her network of friends. This kind of unquestioned assumption is often behind the identification of what is supposedly the proper network data to collect to explore specific phenomena. If we had to choose between a given set of layers, we would find it perfectly normal to use friendship relationships instead of the LinkedIn layer to study the aforementioned emotional support. If we do want to consider multiple layers at the same time, we must be able to explore how single layers relate to the whole network structure and to what extent a single layer is an important part of an actor's social network.

The metrics discussed in this section deal with this problem. A full understanding of the meaning that every layer has for every actor is beyond the possibilities of a quantitative analysis; nevertheless, a first attempt has been made by Berlingerio et al. (2011c) with the concept of *relevance*.

Definition 3.12 (Relevance) Let $a \in \mathcal{A}$ be an actor, $L \subseteq \mathcal{L}$ a set of layers, and $G = (\mathcal{A}, \mathcal{L}, V, E)$ a multilayer network. Relevance is defined as follows:

$$relevance(a, L) = \frac{neighborhood(a, L)}{neighborhood(a, \mathcal{L})}$$

Relevance computes the ratio between the neighbors of an actor connected by edges belonging to a specific set of layers and the total number of her neighbors. The set L might also contain only a single layer, of which we might want

Table 3.6. *Relevance for the actors in our running example*

	User	Facebook	Friend	LinkedIn	Work
1	Cici	0.50	0.50	0.50	0.50
2	Mat	0.25	0.75	0.50	0.75
3	Mark	0.25	0.75	0.50	0.50
4	Bin		0.17	0.83	0.50
5	Serena	0.33	0.50	0.17	0.33
6	Barby		0.50	0.50	0.50
7	Stine			0.67	1.00
8	Luca	0.40	0.40		0.60

to study the specific role within the multilayer network. Using again our running example, we notice that the work layer has a high relevance for Stine (relevance = 1), because it contains all the three neighbors that she has on the whole multilayer network. The same work layer has a lower relevance for Sere (relevance = .33), who has only two neighbors on it out of six total neighbors. Within this perspective, every actor has a specific signature, represented by her presence on the different layers, contributing in different ways to the actor's total neighborhood.

While we can assume that a layer with a high relevance is meaningful for an actor, this still does not provide a full characterization of the role of that layer. As an example, this measure does not capture the fact that, for an actor, a layer could be the only way to directly reach a subset of its neighbors. In other words, we might be interested in knowing how much the general connectivity of an actor would be affected by removing a single layer. To capture this aspect, we can use a variant of relevance (see Tables 3.6 and 3.7).

Table 3.7. *Exclusive relevance for the actors in our running example*

	User	Facebook	Friend	LinkedIn	Work
1	Cici	0.50	0.00	0.00	0.00
2	Mat	0.00	0.25	0.00	0.00
3	Mark	0.00	0.25	0.25	0.00
4	Bin		0.17	0.33	0.00
5	Serena	0.17	0.50	0.00	0.00
6	Barby		0.25	0.25	0.00
7	Stine			0.00	0.33
8	Luca	0.20	0.20		0.20

Definition 3.13 (Exclusive layer relevance) Let $a \in \mathcal{A}$ be an actor, $L \subseteq \mathcal{L}$ a set of layers, and $G = (\mathcal{A}, \mathcal{L}, V, E)$ a multilayer network. Exclusive relevance is defined as follows:

$$\text{xrelevance}(a, L) = \frac{\text{xneighborhood}(a, L)}{\text{neighborhood}(a, \mathcal{L})}$$

that is, the fraction of neighbors directly connected with actor a through edges belonging only to layers in L.

In our example, Sere's friend layer has a high level of exclusive relevance (.5) because three out of six actors in her neighborhood are present only there.

In this section we have presented the concepts of relevance and exclusive relevance as defined in the literature. However, computing layer relevance based on how selecting or removing layers affects neighborhood is only one specific way of doing it. These two concepts can be extended to any other kinds of measures: we can choose any measure m, for example, closeness or betweenness, and see how it changes by selecting or removing a specific set of layers. We can also extend this idea to a whole multilayer network, to check how whole-network measures like the number of connected components are affected.

3.2.4 Transitivity and Clustering Coefficient

Group measures are among the most used tools in SNA. Starting from triads, that is, groups of three actors (Simmel, 1902a,b; Krackhardt, 1999), and continuing to larger sizes, SNA has always tried to use the network structure to detect groups of related actors, the roles of the actors inside the groups, and the influence of the groups on the actors' actions.

Transitivity and *clustering coefficient* measure the largely acknowledged tendency of social network actors to form triangles following the old popular saying "a friend of my friend is my friend." Extending local cohesion measures to multilayer networks means investigating how the various layers are involved in the creation of the cohesive structure between a single actor and his neighbors. Some recent studies have extended these concepts. Among them, it is interesting to point out the work done by Barrett et al. (2012), because they offer an interesting perspective on how multilayer networks in general could be used to observe and understand not only social phenomena but also cognitive processes. Besides this contribution, the general approach on multilayer network triadic measures has been dealing with the scenario illustrated in Figure 3.7 (Bródka et al., 2012; Battiston et al., 2014; Cozzo et al., 2015). In addition to triangles existing on a single layer, multilayer structures allow triangles

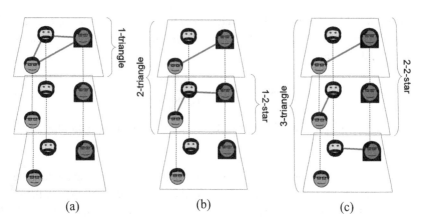

Figure 3.7. In a three-layer network, a triangle can be closed by (a) edges belonging to a single layer, (b) edges belonging to two different layers, or (c) edges lying all on different layers.

distributed on multiple layers. We can then identify two additional possibilities: triangles that are closed by an edge belonging to one layer and two edges belonging to a second layer (2-triangle) and triangles that can be closed only through edges lying on three different layers (3-triangle). Similarly, a 1-2-star centered on actor i, for instance, $j - i - k$, is a triad in which both edge $j - i$ and edge $i - k$ are on the same layer, whereas a 2-2-star is a triad whose two links belong to two different layers of the system.

Given these definitions, Battiston et al. (2014) extend clustering coefficient to the multilayer context. $C_{i,1}$ is defined, for each actor i, as the ratio between the number of 2-triangles with a vertex in i and the number of 1-2-stars centered in i. This clustering coefficient in terms of a multilayer adjacency matrix A where $A_{ij}^{[\alpha]}$ indicates if actors i and j are connected on layer α is expressed as

$$C_{i,1} = \frac{\sum_\alpha \sum_{\alpha' \neq \alpha} \sum_{j \neq i, m \neq i} (A_{ij}^{[\alpha]} A_{jm}^{[\alpha']} A_{mi}^{[\alpha]})}{(|\mathcal{L}| - 1) \sum_\alpha \sum_{j \neq i, m \neq i} (A_{ij}^{[\alpha]} A_{mi}^{[\alpha]})}$$

$$= \frac{\sum_\alpha \sum_{\alpha' \neq \alpha} \sum_{j \neq i, m \neq i} (A_{ij}^{[\alpha]} A_{jm}^{[\alpha']} A_{mi}^{[\alpha]})}{(|\mathcal{L}| - 1) \sum_\alpha k_i^{[\alpha]} (k_i^{[\alpha]} - 1)} \qquad (3.3)$$

Because each 1-2-star can theoretically be closed as a 2-triangle on each of the $|\mathcal{L}|$ layers of the multilayer network, excluding the layer to which its edges belong, to have a normalized coefficient, it is necessary to divide the term by $|\mathcal{L}| - 1$.

A second clustering coefficient for multilayer networks is the ratio between the number of 3-triangles with node i as a vertex and the number of 2-2-stars centered in i. In terms of adjacency matrixes, this can be expressed as

$$C_{i,2} = \frac{\sum_\alpha \sum_{\alpha' \neq \alpha} \sum_{\alpha'' \neq \alpha, \alpha'} \sum_{j \neq i, m \neq i} (A_{ij}^{[\alpha]} A_{jm}^{[\alpha'']} A_{mi}^{[\alpha']})}{(|\mathcal{L}| - 2) \sum_\alpha \sum_{\alpha' \neq \alpha} \sum_{j \neq i, m \neq i} (A_{ij}^{[\alpha]} A_{mi}^{[\alpha']})} \qquad (3.4)$$

where a normalization coefficient $|\mathcal{L}| - 2$ has been added.

Whereas $C_{i,1}$ is a suitable definition for multilayer networks with $M \geq 2$, $C_{i,2}$ can only be defined for systems composed of at least three layers. Averaging over all the nodes of the system, it is easy to obtain the network clustering coefficients C_1 and C_2.

Closely related to the clustering coefficient, transitivity has been introduced as an alternative way to measure the probability for two neighbors to be both connected with a third one (Newman et al., 2002; Girvan and Newman, 2002; Schank and Wagner, 2005). Within a single-layer network, transitivity measures the ratio between the relative number of triangles in the network and the total number of connected triples. Although the two measures represent the same phenomenon, they have found popularity in different research fields. Given the definitions provided earlier, we can derive two measures for transitivity: T_1, as the ratio between the number of 2-triangles and $(|\mathcal{L}| - 1)$ times the number of 1-2-stars in the multilayer network, and T_2, as the ratio between the number of 3-triangles and $(|\mathcal{L}| - 2)$ times the number of 2-2-stars in the system.

Additional measures for larger groups of actors are presented in Chapter 6, in the context of community detection.

3.3 Layer Measures

When an actor can be present on multiple layers, some basic questions emerge. What is the role of a layer (or a set of layers) with respect to its actors? What is the relationship between different layers (or sets of layers)? The first question finds an answer in the measures of relevance defined in Section 3.2.3. For the second, we need to discuss measures of layer similarity.

The relationships between layers can be studied from two different perspectives: on one side, we can describe the differences between different layers as a sign of different behaviors of the actors, strategically selecting what kinds of connections they want to establish on every layer (we define this as an *actor-centered perspective*); on the other side, we can describe these

Table 3.8. *Interlayer correlation in our running example*

	Facebook	Friend	LinkedIn	Work
Facebook	1.00	0.09	0.00	0.17
Friend	0.09	1.00	0.14	0.29
LinkedIn	0.00	0.14	1.00	0.50
Work	0.17	0.29	0.50	1.00

differences in terms of interlayer influences (we define this as a *layer-centered perspective*). Although the second approach is probably the most coherent with a structural network approach, we think it might be interesting for researchers to be aware of this possible double interpretation enabled by the more complex structure of multilayer network models. The easiest way to investigate this is by applying existing methods to compute correlation and similarities to multilayer networks, targeting the presence of edges among the same actors on different layers. This is the approach followed by Berlingerio et al. (2011c) when they developed the idea of *layer correlation* as a multilayer network version of the classical Jaccard correlation coefficient able to cope with more than two layers at the same time.

From Table 3.8, we can see how, in our working example, the LinkedIn layer shows a high level of correlation with the work layer, whereas the Facebook layer shows a low level of correlation with the friend layer. If these were real-world data, the first result would be expected, while the second would definitely be surprising. These values can be tested for significance using the QAP procedure as described by Krackhardt (1988). Table 3.9 applies the same idea to the AUCS multilayer network, making interpretation of the results easier. In this case, it is interesting to observe the generally low level of correlation between every pair of layers, suggesting a limited influence of any layer over the others. The strongest level of correlation is visible between lunch and work and between lunch and leisure, suggesting an easily predictable social dynamic that sees coworkers having lunch together and, sometimes, hanging out together. Although the low correlation level between coauthor and every other layer is somehow expected, it is interesting to see how Facebook does not show any specific correlation with any layer.

Interlayer correlation can provide many interesting insights into the ongoing social dynamics within multilayer networks. As for every correlation, it would be wrong to assume any causal relation between the two observed layers, but it is still important to be able to detect levels of similarity within multilayer network structures. Other ways to compute the number or frequency of edge

Table 3.9. *AUCS layer correlation*

	Coauthor	Facebook	Leisure	Lunch	Work
Coauthor	1.00	0.06	0.10	0.06	0.09
Facebook	0.06	1.00	0.16	0.18	0.19
Leisure	0.10	0.16	1.00	0.28	0.21
Lunch	0.06	0.18	0.28	1.00	0.34
Work	0.09	0.19	0.21	0.34	1.00

overlapping across layers can also be used, and it is important to check if these measures are influenced by the size of the layers. More details on size-aware computation of layer dependencies are given in Section 7.2, where we discuss the automated identification of highly correlated sets of layers.

An actor-centered approach has been followed by De Domenico et al. (2015a) in trying to quantify the similarity between the degree of nodes across various layers. In this case, it is possible to use the Pearson coefficient, often used to estimate the amount of linear degree–degree correlation and to assess the assortative – disassortative mixing patterns in single-layer networks (Newman, 2002). Assortativity measures the preference of a network's nodes to have connections with other nodes that are similar in some way. Often, as in this case, similarity is computed with regard to the degree of the node. Instead of quantifying the level of assortativity between various nodes in the same layer, we can easily extend the idea to quantify the amount of assortative – disassortative mixing of a single actor over different layers of a multilayer network.

When we extend the actor's assortative or disassortative behavior to the whole network, we obtain the *interlayer assortativity coefficient*. This coefficient is defined in the range between -1 (fully disassortative mixing) and $+1$ (fully assortative mixing). Two layers show assortative (resp. disassortative) interlayer correlations if they are positively (resp. negatively) correlated. Table 3.10 shows Interlayer assortativity coefficient for the running example.

Table 3.10. *Interlayer assortativity coefficient, running example*

	Facebook	Friend	LinkedIn	Work
Facebook	1.00	0.42	-0.65	-0.29
Friend	0.42	1.00	-0.38	-0.50
LinkedIn	-0.65	-0.38	1.00	0.19
Work	-0.29	-0.50	0.19	1.00

Table 3.11. *Interlayer assortativity, AUCS*

	Coauthor	Facebook	Leisure	Lunch	Work
Coauthor	1.00	0.03	0.01	−0.01	0.13
Facebook	0.03	1.00	0.17	0.28	0.42
Leisure	0.01	0.17	1.00	0.32	−0.05
Lunch	−0.01	0.28	0.32	1.00	0.29
Work	0.13	0.42	−0.05	0.29	1.00

Observing the interlayer assortativity coefficient in the AUCS multilayer network gives us an interesting perspective on actors' interlayer behavior. Reading Table 3.11 we can see how users who are popular on one layer are often popular also on other layers. At a general level of analysis, we do not see any case of negative correlation (or disassortative behavior), but we see how the general assortativity of the various layers shows different levels of correlation. The extremely low level of assortativity between leisure and work suggests how actors who are extremely popular from a professional point of view might not be that popular when it comes to drinking a beer together. In fact, in a university department, as is the original context of our data, it is reasonable to expect that some of the actors on the top of the hierarchical structure will have multiple collaborations (therefore they will be extremely well connected on the work layer), whereas at the same time, for the same hierarchical structures or for other plausible reasons (age, role, etc.), they will not be extremely popular on the leisure layer, which is based on completely different social norms. This simple example shows how the interlayer assortativity coefficient can be used to detect quite complex social dynamics that can be fully explored and understood only within a multilayer network perspective.

PART II

Mining Multilayer Networks

4

Data Collection and Preprocessing

It is a Law of Nature with us that a male child shall have one more side than his father, so that each generation shall rise (as a rule) one step in the scale of development and nobility.

– The Square

The first step in the analysis of an empirical multilayer network is to obtain and prepare the data. Although this may sound obvious, it is easy to underestimate the impact of the data collection and preprocessing phase in a data mining process, or the proportion of time spent on these activities and the subsequent interpretation of the results if compared with the time needed to execute the selected data mining algorithms. In fact, this is often the most time-consuming and crucial part of the process and has a great impact on the results of the analysis.

Even if it has become common for researchers in different areas to collect large amounts of digital data, with more or less reasonable assumptions of completeness (Morstatter et al., 2013), we must consider that, in most cases, not all the desired data are available or that the data can be too large to be processed with the available computational resources. In this case, sampling can be necessary, leading to an incomplete data set. However, these are only some of the reasons why our data can be inaccurate or incomplete. In Section 4.1, we discuss several sources of missing or inaccurate data in multilayer social networks.

Then, after the data have been collected, they may not be ready to be analyzed. In a typical data mining process, a main part of data preprocessing consists in choosing the right features to represent the data, for example, descriptive variables like age or income, also called attributes. This may involve the selection of some specific values from raw data; the transformation of some of them, for example, expressing numerical attribute values in the range [0, 1]; or the combination of some attributes to generate new features. If we consider a multilayer social network, we can see each layer as a feature describing the actors in the model, very much like age or income, but focusing on the actors' relationships instead of their personal characteristics. In a similar way as we need to remove or transform features when we analyze nonnetwork data, before analyzing a multilayer network, we may want to keep only some relevant layers among the ones that were initially collected or to combine multiple layers into a new one providing a different view over the data. We call this process *network simplification*, and we discuss alternative methods to perform it in Section 4.2.

4.1 Issues in Data Collection

Before collecting multilayer social network data, we need to define what data to collect and which data to exclude from our study, this implying that some potentially available data will be missing by design. For example, some available data may simply not be relevant to a particular question: if we want to study a group of people using a specific Twitter hashtag during a given time frame, any user who does not use that hashtag is not relevant. The potential consequences of excluding data by design are discussed in Section 4.1.1. However, excluding data by design is not the only potential source of missing data: even after deciding to focus on specific data, it may still be difficult or impossible to collect them. This can be due to the size of the data or to the cost to collect them, in which case sampling strategies can be necessary, as discussed in Section 4.1.2. Another problem concerns the unavailability of some information, for example, some user profiles on an OSN can be private, and individuals providing information about their connections through a survey may omit some information. This problem is touched upon in Section 4.1.3. Finally, a peculiar and complex problem in multilayer data collection is the identification of correspondences between nodes in different layers, for example, user accounts on different OSNs owned by the same actor. This problem is discussed in Section 4.1.4.

4.1.1 Data Missing by Design

Boundary specification and fixed choice are two types of design choices made to collect single-layer social networks, and both may lead to data incompleteness. These choices are sometimes unavoidable because of limited resources and may affect the results of the computation of actor and network measures. In this section, we explain them in the context of multilayer networks.

Boundary specification (Laumann et al., 1989) is the choice of which actors and relations should be included in the data, for example, the choice to study only the users commenting on a given Facebook group and only their interactions happening inside this group. Even if this may look like a conscious and harmless choice, setting a boundary may have a significant impact on the results of the study. What if two actors are disconnected inside the boundaries we are observing but have a common neighbor who is not part of our study? This would still determine a relationship between these two actors that is not captured by our data and would not be reflected by measures computed inside the boundaries we have specified.

The boundary specification problem is well known in the traditional SNA literature, and we refer to the work by Kossinets (2006) for a more extensive discussion of how it may affect single-layer network measures. Here we focus on the fact that multilayer networks add a new dimension to this problem: what if two of the actors we are studying, for example, Stine and Bin, who do not appear to be connected as friends, are in fact members of the same karate club, and this gives them the opportunity to meet twice a week – even if they do not consider themselves as friends? In practice, within multilayer networks, we can have two kinds of boundaries: *horizontal*, as in single-layer networks, where the boundary regards the actors included in a given layer, and *vertical*, where the boundary concerns the choice of which layers (or types of edges) to consider (Sharma et al., 2014, 2015). This problem has been studied by Kossinets (2006) using a bipartite network model with an actor layer and an affiliation layer and by Sharma et al. (2015) for a more general multilayer network model.

The vertical boundary specification problem should be carefully considered before collecting multilayer social network data and also when the data are prepared for the analysis and some layers may be removed because they are considered not relevant or redundant: a layer may contain several relational ties that are not present in other layers, leading to inaccurate actor and network measures. Without clear theoretical guidance, the selection of a specific set of relations will define what kinds of research questions can actually be addressed (Robins, 2015). A possible way to address the problem of which layers to select is to perform an extensive data collection campaign, retrieving as many layers as possible, and reduce the number of layers at a later time. This reduction is usually done by merging one or more layers (or parts of them), and we provide a general overview of empirical methods to do so in Section 4.2. Otherwise, if possible, we can base this process on theoretical arguments. For example, if we are studying a university department, we might decide to merge the connections between coworkers and those between coauthors, because the latter often imply the existence of the former. Also in this case, the operation does not have to be completely manual, but measures of layer correlation/similarity can be used to guide the process, as described in Section 4.2.2.

Another way to define the boundaries of our network is often based on selection strategies that are not based on including/excluding full layers or all actors inside an organization. For example, we can decide to focus only on users above a specific threshold of degree or who have posted at least a minimum number of messages to a discussion board. This has also been called *node censoring* and can also be based on edges instead of nodes, for example, considering only edges between actors of different gender.

In the context of multilayer networks, the strategy used for censoring may be different in various layers: someone might have 100 friends but just 2 coworkers; therefore we may decide to remove only the node from the coworker layer, or we may remove the actor (i.e., both nodes) because it does not pass the threshold on one layer, or we may keep both nodes because the threshold is passed on at least one, and so on. We call a selection strategy that takes into account the various layers *multidimensional actor censoring*.

A specific type of problem related to edge censoring is known as the *fixed-choice effect* (Holland and Leinhard, 1973) and occurs when we ask actors to mention only a fixed number of connections. An example in the context of multilayer networks can be found in the Sampson's Monastery data set referenced in Table 2.2, where monks were asked to specify their top three choices on four pairs of positive/negative relations.

4.1.2 Sampling

Sampling strategies allow to make inferences about the whole network starting from a set of observations performed on a small set of data. For this to be possible, the whole population should be known and have a well-defined boundary. However, this is rarely the case when studying online social networks.

The specific problems concerning network sampling have been investigated for many years (Granovetter, 1976), and the different approaches that have been adopted have focused on different sampling units: nodes, edges, walks, and various types of subgraph configurations (Frank, 2011). A full description of single-layer network sampling is beyond the goal of this book, but the reader interested in this topic can consult the work of Frank (1979, 2005).

When we focus on multilayer social networks, it is important to question the validity of the data with respect to the data sampling strategy. In some cases, the boundary is well defined and the layers are collected in the same way, as it happens when we study a small group of individuals, such as the students in a class or the employees in a company division, and we ask them about their different relationships. This can still result in missing data problems, as explained in Section 4.1.3. However, the main problems related to sampling processes occur where one of the layers is given priority over the others.

In particular, care should be taken when actors are sampled from a specific layer, and the corresponding nodes from other layers are then retrieved. For example, we can collect a network of users from an OSN, for example, by snow-ball sampling, and then get the neighbors of these users on other OSNs using sophisticated actor-matching techniques (see Section 4.1.4) or *social media aggregators*, that is, services where people register multiple OSN accounts. However, snowball sampling would guarantee the collection of a connected component only on the initial layer, but not on the others, providing a poten-tially distorted view of the real structure of those layers. Unfortunately, existing works using these kinds of data have not acknowledged and studied this prob-lem, probably because of the difficulty of getting real online multilayer data.

Multilayer networks have also been used by Gjoka et al. (2011) to address some of the limitations that specific sampling techniques (e.g., random walk strategies) may encounter in single-layer networks, for example, when the indi-vidual layers are disconnected or highly clustered.

4.1.3 Other Sources of Missing Data

So far we have discussed cases where the study is designed not to include all the data (Burt, 1987) or where we are at least aware that some data will not be collected, often because of limited resources but also to restrict the focus of the research. However, in some cases, data that were intended or expected to be obtained may still not be retrieved. Several sources of missing data besides the aforementioned boundary specification and node/edge censoring problems have been studied in multiple occasions in the context of single-layer networks (Roethlisberger and Dickson, 1939; Travers and Milgram, 1967; Bearman et al., 2004). According to Kossinets (2006), other main sources of missing data in single-layer social network analysis are due to *respondent inaccuracy* (Bernard et al., 1984; Marsden, 1990) and *missing responses* in network surveys (Rum-sey, 1993). The former concerns actors providing information about their con-nections that may be perceived in a subjective way: actor A may believe that actor B is a friend, but not vice versa, or actor A may forget having had a recent interaction with actor B, and so on. The latter refers to actors omitting some information, which in some cases can also be seen as a respondent inaccuracy.

When we have to articulate our data collection through many different types of relations, respondent inaccuracy and missing responses are more likely to occur. However, the most important issue to consider is that, when we deal with multilayer networks, data might be missing from different layers for different reasons and in different ways. For example, people might refuse to respond to some questions regarding their sentimental relationships but provide all the requested information when asked about their work ties. This can have different effects, depending on the way in which the network is studied. As an example, if we consider two layers with data missing from only one of them, this will either have no effect on shortest path lengths between nodes or it will increase them. Therefore, when path lengths are concerned, we would know that what we are measuring can be overestimated because of missing data. On the contrary, if one of the two layers has a high clustering coefficient while the second has a low one, depending on which layer is affected, the overall clustering coefficient can either increase or decrease. As a consequence, whereas for single-layer networks and for many network analysis measures, we have a basic understanding of the effects of missing data, effects in a multilayer context can become more unpredictable, requiring even more care (Sharma et al., 2014, 2015).

4.1.4 The Identity Resolution Problem

Multilayer network models also face a specific type of missing data that does not affect single-layer networks: the same actor can be present in two layers, but the information that allows us to map two nodes to the same actor might not be available. A classical example would be a multilayer network study trying to observe how users publicly share information on Facebook and Twitter. Although collecting the two layers can be relatively easy, being able to map which node on the Twitter layer corresponds to which node on the Facebook layer can be the most challenging data to collect, typically resulting in uncertain mappings (Magnani and Montesi, 2010). We call this the *identity resolution problem*.

Given the practical relevance of the problem, several methods have been developed to reconcile user accounts from different OSNs. These approaches are typically based on the comparison of a large number of features, to identify similarities between the accounts' metadata and their usage patterns. An obvious source of information to match users are profile names (You et al., 2011; Zafarani and Liu, 2013), which can be compared not only character by character but also using a number of features like the appearance of specific words and characters; the impact of the type of keyword in the definition of random user names; language and cultural references; and patterns to transform user names from one OSN to another, for example, the addition of a number to the end of the profile name. However, profile names are insufficient alone to reach high accuracy, and several other features can be used, including friends lists (Labitzke et al., 2011; Bennacer et al., 2014), social tags (Iofciu et al., 2011), temporal patterns of activity (Atig et al., 2014; Johansson et al., 2015), writing style (Bhargava et al., 2013; Johansson et al., 2013; Atig et al., 2014), and even distortions introduced by the mobile phone camera used to take pictures posted on the OSN (Bertini et al., 2015). Several works have indicated how combinations of different features can enhance the accuracy of the matching task (Vosecky et al., 2009; Raad et al., 2010; Malhotra et al., 2012; You et al., 2013; Jain et al., 2013; Johansson et al., 2013).

However, despite the excellent results obtained under controlled experimental tests, often using limited data sets, our general belief is that real identification of common identities is still a very complicated task. A recent work supporting this belief has been published by Goga et al. (2015), testing different approaches on large networks and obtaining significantly worse results than those mentioned in the aforementioned papers. In addition, specific factors can make this task more complex, from users who do not want to be identified and purposely modify their behavior to multilayer networks where the same actor uses different layers to expose different personalities and reach different audiences, which often also corresponds to different behaviors.

4.2 Network Simplification

One way to address the vertical boundary specification problem is to collect as many layers as possible and reduce them to a smaller and more focused number at a later time. A basic way to reduce the number of layers is to (partially) remove some of them or to merge some into a single layer. Ultimately, we can reduce any multilayer network to a single-layer network and analyze it using traditional methods, and even though the general message of this book is that, in doing so, we risk losing relevant information, this can still be considered a way to perform a first exploration of the data. This approach is called *flattening* or *projection*, depending on whether the merged layers contain the same actors, for example, multiplex networks, or actors of different types, for example, affiliation networks. We cover these preprocessing methods in Section 4.2.1.

If we do not want to reduce the network to a single layer, manually choosing which layers to remove may be difficult, especially when several layers have been collected or their semantics are unclear. Therefore, in Section 4.2.2, we discuss how to automatically choose a set of layers so that the lost information is minimized. We refer to this approach as *global simplification*, because layers are removed or preserved in their entirety.

At the same time, layers are complex objects, sometimes corresponding to a whole OSN. Therefore, instead of removing a full layer, we may want to remove only some parts of it that are considered unimportant for the analysis we are performing. In Section 4.2.3, we discuss an approach that simplifies specific portions of a layer, depending on the local neighborhood of its nodes – we call this *local simplification*.

4.2.1 Flattening and Projection

A basic approach to dealing with multilayer networks is to reconstruct a (weighted) single-layer social network so that existing methods, such as community detection, can be directly applied. Two such general approaches can be used, depending on the nature of the nodes. If nodes on the different layers correspond to a common set of actors, we normally talk of flattening, that is, the process of merging all nodes corresponding to the same actor into a single node. When we have multiple types of nodes, a common operation consists in projecting the network only on one type of node, discarding the others.

Flattening

A basic flattening process consists in creating a layer with one node for each actor and an edge between two nodes if an edge among two nodes corresponding to those actors exists somewhere in the multilayer network.

Definition 4.1 (Basic flattening) A basic (unweighted) flattening of a multi-layer network $G = (\mathcal{A}, \mathcal{L}, V, E)$ is a graph (V_f, E_f), where $V_f = \{a \mid (a, l) \in V\}$ and $E_M = \{(a_i, a_j) \mid \{(a_i, l_q), (a_j, l_r)\} \in E\}$.

A simple variation of basic flattening consists in adding a weight to each edge in the flattened network proportional to the number or edges between the actors corresponding to those nodes. A more general approach consists in assigning a weight $\theta_{q,r}$ to each pair of layers (l_q, l_r), so that the resulting single-layer network can be expressed as a linear combination of the original multilayer network.

Definition 4.2 (Weighted flattening) Let $G = (\mathcal{A}, \mathcal{L}, V, E)$ be a multilayer network. Given a $|\mathcal{L}| \times |\mathcal{L}|$ matrix θ, where $\theta_{q,r}$ indicates the weight to be assigned to edges from layer l_q to layer l_r, a weighted flattening of G is a weighted graph (V_f, E_f, ω), where (V_f, E_f) is a basic flattening of G and $\omega(a_i, a_j) = \sum_{\{(a_i, l_q), (a_j, l_r)\} \in E} \theta_{q,r}$.

This definition generalizes the simple weighted flattening strategy described in the previous paragraph, which can be expressed by setting $\theta_{q,r} = 1 \; \forall q, r$,

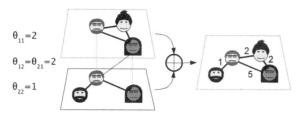

Figure 4.1. Weighted flattening of two layers, with varying weights depending on the starting and ending layers of edges in the original multilayer network.

and can also be used to remove some of the layers by setting their weights to 0. In addition, it can be used as a preprocessing operation to compute metrics where the impact of the different layers is known in advance. Other nonlinear combinations can also be specified: for example, if we know for each layer the probability that information will be propagated through its edges, we can combine these values to obtain the probability that information is flowing from one actor to the other and compute distances on a flattened network weighted according to these probabilities.

Figure 4.1 shows an example of weighted flattening with

$$\theta = \begin{pmatrix} 1 & 2 \\ 2 & 2 \end{pmatrix} \tag{4.1}$$

where the first row/column corresponds to the top layer in the figure and the second to the bottom one.

Projection

Network projection is a traditional approach used to simplify two-mode networks, which can be modeled as multilayer networks where each node type (say, A or B) is represented by a layer. In a similar way, we can extend the idea of a two-mode network to take into account a multiplicity of relations, as is done in multipartite graphs (Hoffman and Rodger, 1992).

The most straightforward approach to network projection consists in removing type B nodes and adding an edge between any pair of type A nodes originally connected to the same type B node (Seierstad and Opsahl, 2011). As an example, the coauthor layer of the AUCS network had originally been collected as a two-mode network, and an edge between two researchers (type A nodes) was established whenever they had authored a common publication (type B node).

This approach suffers from some well-known problems (Padrón et al., 2011): on one side, it removes information about nodes that are connected

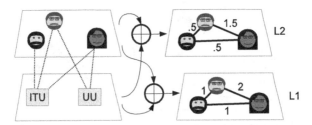

Figure 4.2. Two ways of performing a projection from a two-mode network to a single-layer network.

to more than one type B node, and on the other side, it often generates large cliques, especially in the presence of very popular type B nodes.[1] Attempts to overcome these limits have been introduced by Padrón et al. (2011) in the form of a weighted projection. In this approach, type A nodes get connected by a weighted edge with weight w defined as $w(i, j) = \sum_p 1$, where p indicates the type B nodes connected to both i and j. This is the case for layer L1 in Figure 4.2: Luca, Cici, and Mark would form an unweighted clique under a simple projection, but Mark and Cici are both connected to two type B nodes, ITU and UU. Therefore the weight of the edge between them is twice the weight between Cici and Luca, who only share one type B node (ITU).

Newman (2001b) pointed out how, in specific contexts, if we share something (like a collaboration on an article) with a limited number of actors, this will be more valuable than sharing it with a lot of other actors. This is closely related to the concepts of network relevance and exclusive network relevance presented in Section 3.2.3. Therefore Newman (2001b) proposed a different weight assignment: $w(i, j) = \sum_p \frac{1}{N_p - 1}$, where N_p is the number of nodes of type A connected through the pth type B node. This is the case for layer L2 in Figure 4.2: Luca and Cici are connected to a single type B node (ITU), with $N_p = 3$, resulting in a weight of $\frac{1}{3-1} = .5$ among them. Mark and Cici are connected to two type B nodes, ITU and UU, the first with $N_p = 3$ and the second with $N_p = 2$, resulting in a weight of $\frac{1}{3-1} + \frac{1}{2-1} = 1.5$ among them. Interestingly, this creates a projected network where the total strength of the edges adjacent to a node (i.e., the sum of their weights) equals the number of edges adjacent to the node in the original two-mode network; however, these weights are now redistributed according to the exclusivity of the collaborations (Opsahl, 2013).

---

[1] As an example of the impact of this phenomenon, the reader may consider that an article recently published in *Physical Review Letters* counted 5154 authors.

4.2.2 Global Simplification

The problem addressed by global simplification as defined by De Domenico et al. (2014) is to what extent it is possible to automatically aggregate layers with a small loss of information. A global simplification process requires two measures: one computing layer similarity and one indicating the quality of a merging. Then, the process articulates on four main steps: (1) for every pair of layers, their similarity (or distance) is computed; (2) then, one performs hierarchical clustering of the layers and produces a dendrogram whose leaves represent the initial layers and internal nodes denote layer merging; (3) at each level of the dendrogram, layers with the smallest dissimilarity are merged into a single layer, and the quality of the new layer is quantified by the quality function; and (4) the maximal value of the quality function corresponds to the best simplification of the multilayer structure. In practice, the quality function defines a compromise between simplicity and information loss: the more layers that are merged, the higher the simplicity is, positively affecting the quality function. However, the more layers that are merged, the higher the information loss is, negatively affecting the quality function. The reader familiar with clustering will recognize a very typical agglomerative hierarchical clustering method, and for a specific choice of functions, the work by De Domenico et al. (2015b) can be consulted, where Von Neumann entropy and the Jensen-Shannon distance are used to test this approach on different data sets.

Although the evaluation of the obtained hierarchical clustering on real-world multilayer networks is still under development, initial results on biological and socioeconomical networks are promising. Moreover, the results obtained on several synthetic multilayer networks show a reasonable behavior of the method where layers with high edge overlap and similar structure, for example, characterized by highly overlapping communities, tend to be aggregated earlier.

4.2.3 Local Simplification

Local simplification is a different and complementary approach to preprocessing a multilayer network and reducing the noise generated by too many layers. This approach is defined starting from the idea that, in a social network, what is relevant should be understood within a relational – dyadic – perspective and that what is relevant can be different in different parts of the same layer.

If we consider the AUCS network, and we define a layer to be locally relevant if it is the only layer allowing a specific actor to be connected to a large portion of his neighbors, then we can expect that for some of the actors belonging to the AUCS department, the lunch layer will be very relevant, for example, because lunch breaks are the only times when they can meet each other, whereas for a different group of researchers, the facebook layer can be more relevant, for example, because they do not work in the same building and they have no other way of staying in touch. A direct consequence of this idea is that multilayer network simplification can define the relevance of the various layers not using their informational value from a global, layer-by-layer perspective, but evaluating relevance from a local perspective: a layer can be relevant only for some of its actors, whereas it might be just a source of noise for other actors. This means that the final simplified multilayer network will preserve the multilayer structure but only keep some relevant portions of each layer.

So far, we have used a rather unspecific concept of relevance. What does *relevant* mean? The idea underlying this concept, introduced by Rossi and Magnani (2015), is that relevance can be expressed using a variety of different measures, depending on the kinds of patterns we want to emerge. Having a way to quantify what *relevant* means, we can thus remove users (and their connections) from layers that are not relevant for them and create a new multilayer network providing a combination of local views from its actors' perspective. In practice, we no longer ask ourselves if two layers should or should not be merged, and we do not try to measure whether two layers are globally similar, but we ask these questions locally acknowledging that the answer can change when we focus on different portions of a layer.

In summary, a local simplification process works as follows: given a measure $r(a, l)$ indicating how much a layer l is relevant for actor a, and a threshold θ, for each layer l and for each pair of actors a_1, a_2, we keep an edge between them on this layer if and only if (1) an edge exists, (2) $r(a_1, l) \geq \theta$, and (3) $r(a_2, l) \geq \theta$. This indicates that the dyadic relation between a_1 and a_2 is considered an important one by both actors and should thus be preserved.

In Section 5.5, we show practical applications of this simplification approach to identifying and visualizing structures hidden within the AUCS multilayer network.

5

Visualizing Multilayer Networks

As early as the eleventh century of our era, triangular houses were
universally forbidden by Law.

– The Square

Visualization has two main goals: it can be used as an exploratory tool to gain
a basic understanding of the network structure and of some network properties, for example, the presence of communities, or it can be used to present the
results of a preexisting analysis in an easily accessible way. In both cases, good
visualizations can play an important role in a SNA process. However, although
today it is relatively easy to produce beautiful network diagrams using one of
the many SNA software packages, producing insightful diagrams can be more
challenging, especially when the network is large. We can emphasize many
aspects while visualizing a social network, and some of them may create visual
noise and hide other properties. Not surprisingly, when multilayer social networks are involved, these aspects are even more important. Therefore, in this
chapter, we present different visualization approaches and exemplify them on
our running example to highlight the kind of information that they can extract
from a real multilayer network.

5.1 Four Main Approaches

There are two main aspects where visual representation of social networks can
play a major role: the visualization of network structure, that is, the spatial
disposition of its nodes and edges, and a visual representation of its numerical
properties, corresponding to the various metrics that exist in SNA or to those
described in Chapter 3. These two kinds of goals can also be merged into a

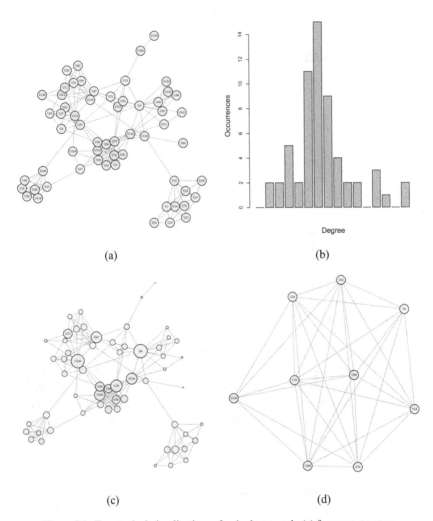

(a)   (b)

(c)   (d)

Figure 5.1. Four typical visualizations of a single network: (a) focus on structure, (b) focus on metrics, (c) augmented visualization, and (d) simplified visualization (6-core of the network).

single visualization, either by augmenting a graph with information about the metrics or using the metrics to remove irrelevant information from the graph. We have illustrated these four approaches in Figure 5.1, as described in the following.

Among the visualizations focusing on the network structure, graphs and their application to social networks, known as sociograms (Moreno, 1934), have seen, so far, the most widespread adoption (von Landesberger et al., 2011).

This adoption has been so large and diffuse that outside of academic discourse, SNA and sociograms are sometimes perceived as synonyms. An example of this is the sociogram of the lunch layer in the AUCS network, shown in Figure 5.1a. Sociograms put a lot of emphasis on layout, because positional differences are the most accurately perceived graphical attribute (Cleveland and McGill, 1984) and also because some network properties, such as modular structure and node centrality, may emerge out of a good layout. In the case represented in Figure 5.1a, we can easily see the existence of several subgroups and how specific actors act as bridges between them.

While probably the most appealing, the visualization of the network structure is not the only way to make sense of a network: sometimes it might be more convenient to rely on more traditional data visualization techniques. This might be the case when the network structure does not fit any standard layout or when the network is too large. In these cases, we can still describe a network using numbers, either single values or distributions, and use traditional visualizations not specifically developed for graphs. A simple example in this context is the study of the degree distribution of a network, which is often illustrated using a log-log plot (for long-tail distributions) or simple histograms like the one about our lunch layer shown in Figure 5.1b. In this case, though there is an obvious connection between the degree distribution within a network and its structure, the focus of the visualization is not on the structure itself but rather on the specific metric we are visualizing.

The two aforementioned options – structure and measures – can also be merged, and sociograms can be enriched with information about metrics. In Figure 5.1c, the same lunch sociogram is again visualized, but now the size of the nodes represents the node's degree. In practice, network measures can be used to augment a sociogram. In this way, it is possible to communicate information about the network structure (e.g., the presence of clusters) and information regarding single nodes (e.g., degree centrality) at the same time.

The opposite way of combining the two basic visualization strategies is to use network metrics to filter or simplify the network. The underlying idea is that network edges may carry overabundant information, and visualizing everything may lead to noise hiding relevant knowledge. Figure 5.1d shows a visualization that focuses on the nodes in the *k-core* of the network. A *k*-core is obtained by removing nodes connected to fewer than *k* other nodes and repeating this until no more nodes can be removed: removing a node may result in other nodes exiting the core and being removed. Although this kind of simplification may not be deemed necessary for this small social network, it can provide an otherwise impossible visual understanding for large networks.

5.2 Visualizing Multilayer Network Metrics

A first problem that we should address when we want to visualize multiple relations is how to represent the same metric on different layers. Histograms showing the distribution of some metrics, like degree centrality in Figure 5.1b, can certainly be used for multiple networks by computing the chosen measure separately on each layer. The next step is then to find a way to combine the various diagrams to be able to visualize how the specific measure changes through the various layers. To do so, it is useful to combine the layer-specific diagrams into a single diagram that emphasizes the relationships between the different layers. There are two main strategies to achieve this goal: one way of doing so is to explicitly represent each actor and show how its values change for a given measure over the different layers using a parallel coordinates visualization, and a second way is to directly plot a measure of layer similarity using a block matrix visualization for layer correlation.

5.2.1 Parallel Coordinates

As we have seen in Chapter 3, the same actor can behave differently on different layers, for example, a user might be highly connected on Facebook and have almost no followers on Twitter. These differences of behavior provide some information about that user and about the correlation between the two social networks. Information here arises not only from the measurement of a specific measure on a specific layer but also from how the values measured on different layers relate to each other.

Parallel coordinates are typical tools for visualizing multidimensional data (Moustafa, 2011). Figures 5.2a and 5.2b use two variations of parallel coordinates plots to visualize, respectively, relevance and neighborhood.

Figure 5.2a shows the value of relevance as defined in Section 3.2.3 for every user on every layer of the AUCS multilayer network. The darkest shade of gray represents maximum relevance (1, i.e., all the actor's neighbors in the multilayer network are present on that specific layer) and the lightest represents minimum relevance (0, i.e., none of the actor's neighbors in the multilayer network is present on that specific layer).

Figure 5.2b shows the number of neighbors for every user on every layer of the multilayer network. The value of neighborhood is defined as the number of nodes directly connected with one node in a specific layer, and the shape of each line in the parallel coordinates plot represents a specific profile of how a single user is connected through the various layers. At the same time, by observing all the different lines together, we obtain information about how the

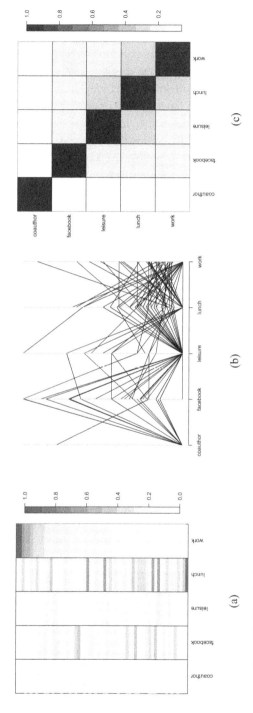

Figure 5.2. Visualization of different measures emphasizing the relationships between the different layers. (a) The value of relevance for each actor on each layer of the AUCS data set. (b) Number of neighbors for each actor on each layer. (c) Jaccard correlation coefficients for each pair of layers.

83

various layers relate: several parallel or almost parallel lines indicate a correlation among the different layers. Traditional limitations of this visualization still apply to this context: the order of the parallel axes is arbitrary, but some specific orders can emphasize correlations that would otherwise be lost, and a common scale is required. The latter is a minor concern because the visualization is supposed, in this specific context, to show the same metric using the same scale on every single layer. Regarding the first, a visualization algorithm could try to put highly correlated layers close to each other, but finding the best sequence is an intractable problem for networks with many layers.

5.2.2 Block Matrix

Multilayer network analysis also introduces the possibility to investigate the correlation between pairs of layers. A block matrix visualization can be used to visualize this kind of information. Figure 5.2c shows the values of Jaccard correlation for the various pairs of layers of the AUCS network. Although, in this case, we do not show any information about the single actor on the various layers, we get a better understanding of the global similarities existing within the multilayer network. In the case of the AUCS data, we can see how the work and lunch layers appear to have a relatively high level of correlation, as do the leisure and lunch levels.

In all the diagrams discussed in this section, each layer has been compared with the others. Although, in this case, interpretation is straightforward, it is still interesting to notice how, following a similar approach, it is possible to analyze existing correlations not only between pairs of layers but also between any pair of sets of layers. In our running example, we might be interested in comparing relevance or degree between the work-related layers (work and LinkedIn) and the friendship-related layers (friend and Facebook). This can be done by first aggregating these pairs of layers, generating a two-layer network, and then proceeding as in the previous examples. However, it is necessary to explicitly specify which layers we want to aggregate, which requires either some knowledge of the different layers that might not be available during the preliminary data exploration or the application of a network simplification process as described in Section 4.2.

5.2.3 Edge Co-Occurrence Graph

Another way to visualize the relationships between different layers is to use the representations in Figure 5.3. Figure 5.3a shows the percentage of edges

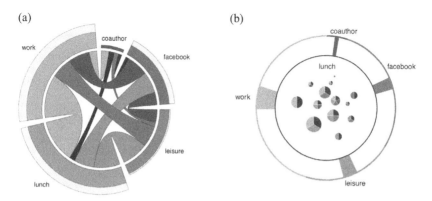

Figure 5.3. Edge co-occurrences across layers: (a) global view; (b) local view.

co-occurring in each pair of layers; therefore it conveys similar information as Figure 5.2c, while also providing an intuition about the size of the
layers.

A similar approach allows us to move the focus of the visualization to a
specific layer. For example, Figure 5.3b shows a local view of the same data
centered on the lunch layer. In this case, in addition to edge co-occurrences
between the lunch layer and the other layers, we can see a distribution of multiplex patterns, indicated inside the circle. The idea behind these pies is that, in
addition to visualizing pairwise relationships, we can also show the frequency
of more complex multiplex patterns involving more than two layers. In the figure, each pie represents a pattern indicating some typical connections, that is,
pies having similar distributions have been merged, and the size of each pie
represents the number of pies merged, giving an indication of the frequency of
patterns with approximately that shape. More details about these approaches
are described by Redondo et al. (2015).[1]

5.3 Visualizing Multilayer Network Structures

When we move from a single to a multilayer network perspective, the additional complexity in the added relations makes the computation and even the
definition of an appropriate layout more challenging. In Figure 5.4, we can see
again the lunch layer of the AUCS network (Figure 5.4a) and the whole network
with the four additional kinds of relations (Figure 5.4b).

---

[1] We thank Arnaud and Dino for generating these figures.

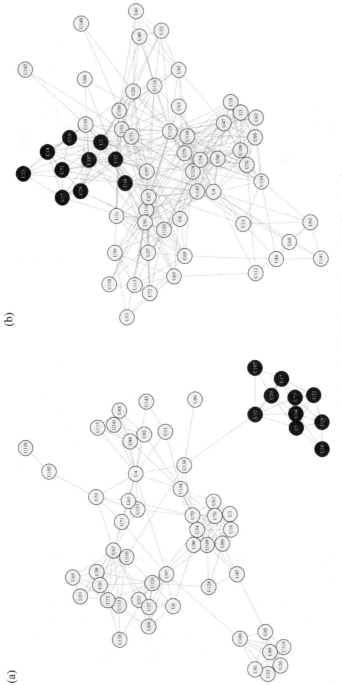

Figure 5.4. One and five layers of complexity: (a) a single layer, lunch; (b) the full flattened AUCS network.

Comparing the two visualizations, we can see how the clear structure of the lunch network becomes more blurred and confused if we take connections from all the layers into consideration. As an example, we have highlighted a clearly visible cluster on the left-hand side layer (black nodes). The same nodes are also black-marked in the flattened graph on the right, and we can see that the cluster has been partially attracted toward the center of the figure and that some of its nodes are now more connected to other nodes outside the cluster.

In addition, although the graph in Figure 5.4b shows some specific structural features, for example, some denser locations, information about the different layers is completely lost. Within this perspective, the traditional way to preserve layer-related information by assigning different colors to different layers, adopted by most of the works and software on multiplex networks and multigraph visualization, might not be extremely effective. It may work well when the number of layers is small, but it certainly becomes difficult to distinguish different colors or traits in a large multilayer network, or even in a small network where actors are connected to different individuals in the different layers.

5.3.1 Layer Slicing

A possible solution to this problem is obtained through the idea of layer slicing. Two alternative visualizations are shown in Figures 5.5 and 5.6. Both methods slice the network into its composing layers. To simplify a comparison between the layers, in Figure 5.5, the nodes have been placed using the same layout in each slice.[2] A very similar approach can be used, as it is done by the software MuxViz (De Domenico et al., 2014), to obtain an interactive 3-dimensional visualization of a multilayer network – also called a 2.5-dimensional representation, because it is made of 2-dimensional planes. Such a visualization of the AUCS network is shown in Figure 5.7. The possibility to interactively explore a multilayer structure is extremely interesting and fascinating; however, if different layers contain different connections, their internal structure can become invisible if it is not highlighted by a layer-specific layout. This is evident, for example, in comparing the lunch layer in Figure 5.4 with the same layer visualized in Figure 5.5 (fourth slice). If we use a specific layout for every layer, as in Figure 5.6, we can better appreciate the structure of each layer, but we lose the possibility of detecting structures developing over multiple layers.

---

[2] In this specific case, we have computed the common layout on the flattened graph, but any layer can be used to this aim.

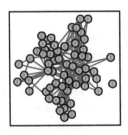

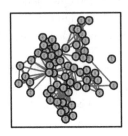

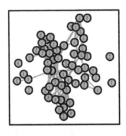

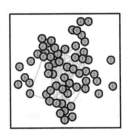

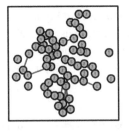

Figure 5.5. Sliced visualization, same layout.

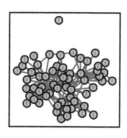

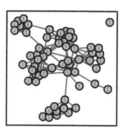

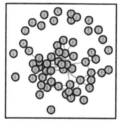

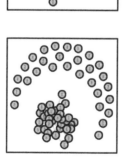

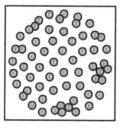

Figure 5.6. Sliced visualization, independent layouts.

89

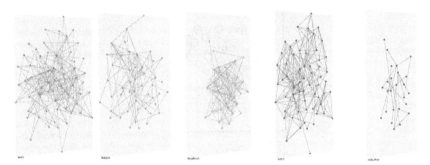

Figure 5.7. Sliced three-dimensional visualization of the AUCS network.

5.4 Augmented Networks: Structure + Measures

Similarly to the process for single-layer networks, multilayer metrics can be used to increase the information contained within the graphical visualizations introduced in the previous section. The next step in our exploration of visualization strategies is thus to use some metrics to produce augmented versions of the multilayer sociograms.

Figure 5.8 shows again the AUCS network where every actor contains information about its degree (size of the circle representing the actor) and its neighborhood in the various layers (pie chart). Here we are combining the layout structure defined on the flattened network with metrics computed both on the flattened network (degree) and on the multilayer network (neighborhood). Although this may look like an interesting visualization, it is hard to claim that it provides a clear understanding of the underlying network structure, of node patterns on the various layers, or even of the degree distribution within the whole network.

An alternative approach following an idea by Longabaugh (2012), which we call a *ranked sociogram*, abandons the traditional sociogram visualization – where edges go from one node to the other – and replaces it with ranking-based positioning of nodes and edges where the ranking is based on a specific metric. In ranked sociograms, actors are represented as horizontal lines and plotted according to a chosen metric on a classical x-y plot (Figure 5.9 ranks them according to their aggregated degree). Every node has a length on the x axis that is defined by a set of edges connecting the vertical position of node a to the vertical position of node b. All the edges expand only on the y axis and show the distance between the nodes according to the chosen ranking. Every edge is also represented using a different color, according to its corresponding layer.

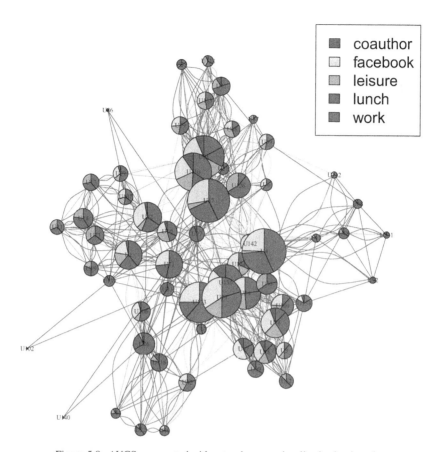

Figure 5.8. AUCS *augmented* with actor degrees, visualized using igraph.

This produces a clear perception of how many connections every actor has on each layer and how far the connected nodes are in terms of the chosen measure both on the flattened network and on the multilayer network.

In Figure 5.9, the user with the highest degree (U4) is mainly connected through the work layer, the lunch layer, and the Facebook layer (as it would be easier to see using colors to distinguish edges on the different layers instead of shades of gray), whereas this individual has no connections on the leisure or coauthor layer. It is also interesting to notice how U4 is connected with users with very different degrees (as indicated by the lengths of the edges), whereas this is not happening on the Facebook layer, corresponding to the second set of edges starting from U4 in the figure and spanning a shorter range of contacts. Another interesting element that can be noticed studying Figure 5.9 is that between the top five users, only two (U91 and U79) show a relevant

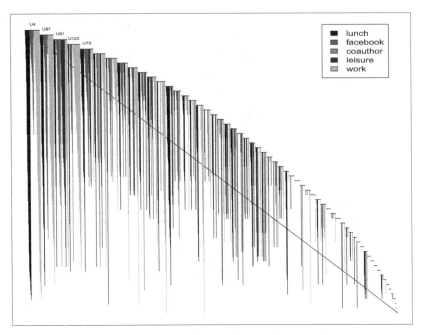

Figure 5.9. Ranked sociogram of our working example.

presence on the leisure layer, while this type of edge appears to be absent for the other users.

Although this kind of visualization does not provide the same immediate understanding that we have learned to experience from traditional sociograms, it provides a still largely unexplored way to investigate networks and relationships between nodes. At the same time, it allows us to combine various measures – both single layer and multilayer – and it can provide a quick overview on many network properties. Among other clues, ranked sociograms with nodes ranked according to their degrees give us insight into the layers' assortativity or disassortativity.

5.5 Simplified Network Visualization

An opposite way to visualize a network is to use analytical measures to simplify it instead of augmenting already complicated sociograms with even more information. Going back to Figure 5.8, we can see that all the layers are entirely included in the picture. Acknowledging this aspect, we can try to produce sociograms based on the local simplification technique introduced in Section 4.2.3. Locally simplified sociograms maintain the classical look of sociograms, as well as their intuitive nature, but redefine the meaning of edges connecting the nodes. Using this approach together with the multilayer measures defined in Chapter 3 makes it possible to visually isolate relevant network structures hidden inside the multilayer network.

Figure 5.10a shows the local merging sociogram defined according to the relevance measure with a threshold of .6, represented as a multigraph. Defining a locally simplified sociogram based on this value means showing an edge between two nodes of the multilayer network only when a specific layer is more relevant than .6 for both actors. This kind of visualization considers the relevance value for the dyad and not for the single actor, therefore edges are represented only if they belong to a layer that is relevant for both actors of the dyad; this is why this has been called local simplification (Rossi and Magnani, 2015).

Looking at Figure 5.10a, we can see that edges considered relevant by both their end points are not uniformly distributed in the network, but tend to aggregate into cohesive structures corresponding to groups of actors using the network in different ways. From this figure, it should be clear how this method preserves only specific (and local) portions of each layer.

Figure 5.10b shows another simplified network based on exclusive relevance. While in a multilayer network, nodes and connections are often replicated through several layers, exclusive relevance measures those connections that are available only on a single layer. From an actor-level perspective, we can assume that within a multilayer network, a layer that shows a high level of exclusive relevance is used by the node in a different way from the other layers. Actors might have many different reasons to maintain different connections in different layers and not to bridge different layers that they want to maintain separated. As in the previous example, only the edges belonging to a layer with an exclusive relevance higher than a given threshold (.3 in our example) for both the actors of the dyad are visualized. These edges are therefore those connecting actors that are both using that specific layer in a peculiar way (where they have connections that are not replicated in any other layer).

If we look at Figure 5.10b and we examine the small clique in the lower right corner composed of users U141, U68, U48, and U92, we notice that these users share their exclusive connections on the lunch network. If we were to check their connections on the other layers, we would notice that they are all connected on the work layer with U4, who is also connected to the four nodes on the lunch layer. However, the lunch layer does not have a high value of exclusive relevance for U4. A possible interpretation is that U4 is a central hub on the work layer and she has lunch with many collaborators. Nevertheless, these collaborators get together only during lunch, therefore their interactions

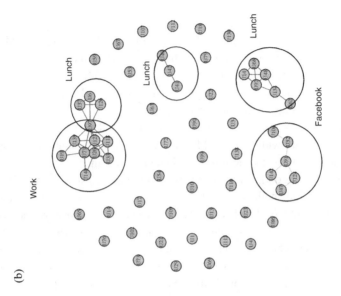

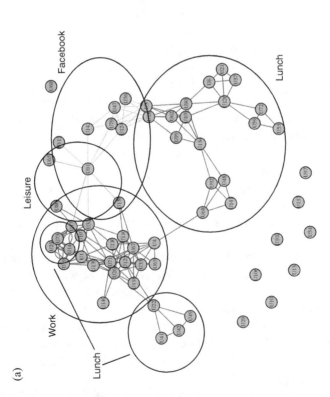

Figure 5.10. Local merging: (a) relevance $\geq$ .6; (b) exclusive relevance $\geq$ .3.

94

with other coworkers of U4 can only happen on the lunch layer. This explains why this clique emerges from the simplified network visualization as a relevant structure to be highlighted.

The idea of network simplification for visualization is also adopted in the work by Renoust et al. (2015), where instead of performing a preprocessing task to remove irrelevant data, some simpler networks are extracted from the multilayer network. In particular, the network is split into a so-called *substrate network*, corresponding to the flattened network, and a so-called *catalyst network*, representing relationships between the different layers (in a similar way as network schemas for HINs) and allowing interacting network manipulation to focus on subsets of the data, for example, specific sets of actors or layers.

6

Community Detection

The Configuration of the Circles, to which all other objects are
subordinated.

– The Square

SNA is at least as much about connections within groups of individuals highly
connected to each other as it is about connections between two actors. As
Kadushin (2012) has suggested, as soon as we move beyond a dyadic perspective, we can see how the role played within larger social contexts by groups of
actors, their sense of belonging, and the social support those groups can provide
are among the main focuses of SNA.

The apparently simple fact that social networks contain subregions that are
densely connected has consequences both at an actor level and at a network
level. Tightly connected subregions have an impact at an actor level when we
observe how actors with common attributes are often connected together, and
they have a direct impact on network dynamics when we observe how they
influence phenomena like the speed of information propagation. Communities,
with their intermediate nature connecting individual actors' social experience
with larger network dynamics, play a central role within any sociological theory that tries to understand how human societies evolved from small *mechanic*
groups, that is, from homogeneous individuals connected because of their similarities, toward more complex *organic* societies, characterized by an interdependent set of complementary groups or individuals, still maintaining a necessary level of internal support and solidarity (Tonnies, 1957).

The study of these intermediate structures between the individual and the
societal level has a long tradition. *Community* is a frequently used term to indicate these structures, despite the fact that this term carries connotations of sociological aspects that are not always observable within the structural perspective of SNA (Bernard, 2012). SNA scholars have often used the term *cohesive*

subgroup to refer to a related concept stressing its structural perspective, and at the same time, computer scientists have often referred to the same idea with the term *cluster*. Within this chapter, we try to provide a common framework for the community detection task on multilayer networks, without changing, when possible, the original terms connected with the concepts we are describing.

As we have seen, the concept of community is generally linked to the goal of identifying close, strong, and meaningful connections from the larger group of everyday connections that we experience. Freeman (1992) defines groups as relatively small, informal, and formed by close personal ties. These considerations lead one to expect greater homogeneity among members of the same group. Collins (1988) connects these elements, noting that

> there are two factors operating here, which we can see from network analysis: how many ties an individual has to the group and how closed the entire group is to outsiders. Isolated and tightly connected groups make up a clique; within such highly cohesive groups, individuals tend to have very homogeneous beliefs. (p. 417)

It is interesting to point out how this resonates with what we have said about how multiplex network models have tried for a long time to use multiplexity as a way to evaluate intimacy of relations (see Section 2.2.1): intimate friends will be connected through multiple types of edges, and at the same time the more tightly a group of individuals is connected, the less it will be affected by the values existing in the rest of the network or, we could say, the more clearly defined that community will be.

Wasserman and Faust (1994) identify three ideas behind the identification of cohesive subgroups: reachability, adjacency, and nodal degree. Although the difference between these ideas is based on how we define cohesiveness, four general properties of cohesive subgroups have influenced most of the social network formalizations of the concept:

- the mutuality of ties;
- the closeness or reachability of subgroup members;
- the frequency of ties among members;
- the relative frequency of ties among subgroup members compared to non-members.

It is important to stress how these properties can be observed in a different way within multilayer models and how they can be described using some of the measures introduced in Chapter 3.

Besides the new models of representation made available by multilayer approaches, there are other contextual reasons why community detection offers a new range of research challenges. While a relevant part of traditional SNA has been based on data collected from preidentified sociospatial contexts, like companies, clubs, and monasteries (Reitz, 1988; Zachary, 1977), the goal of community detection becomes more and more important when, as it happens today, large-scale social network data are digitally available online (Jin et al., 2001; Newman, 2004). This represents a challenging task not only because of the larger scale of online data but also because of intrinsic characteristics of online behaviors, such as the tendency of multiple online communities or subgroups to overlap and collapse within a single digital platform.

According to Leskovec et al. (2009), some of the characteristics we observe in OSNs, such as the presence of a large core with no apparent community structure – also known as *fur ball networks* (Tsatsaronis et al., 2011; Alamsyah and Rahardjo, 2014) – arise from several overlapping communities where high density corresponds to individuals belonging to multiple clusters, as in Figure 6.1: in OSNs the tendency to belong to several groups at the same time becomes visible and reaches unprecedented levels. Although this phenomenon has been defined as *context collapse* and studied extensively within the field of Internet studies from the point of view of privacy and identity disclosure (boyd, 2008; Vitak et al., 2012; Marwick and boyd, 2011), we are mainly interested here in how to deal with it from a network analysis perspective. As a matter of fact, an approach able to deal with multiple social groups maintaining their specific social value might play a very relevant role in understanding many of contemporary online social dynamics. So far the SNA approaches that have faced this problem have often struggled between two possible strategies: if we consider every group as if it were an independent network and thus we consider every network separately, then community structures may be easy to identify, but we would lose the additional value of a multilayer network structure, and it would be impossible to detect communities emerging from interlayer interactions. Quite the opposite: if we merge all the groups and relations into a flattened structure forming a single network, we typically find ourselves back at the *fur ball* scenario sketched in Figure 6.1. Although this might seem a necessary compromise to be made between the amount of data and the interpretability of them, a new set of community detection techniques based on multilayer networks can provide substantial advances.

Beyond these general considerations, we can say that, overall, there are three main approaches to community detection in multilayer networks. A first approach is based on applying existing algorithms to simplified data that have been first reduced to a single-layer network, or at least to a less entangled network, as described in Section 4.2.1. The second approach considers one layer at a time, and after single-layer communities have been identified, they are merged

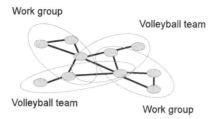

Figure 6.1. In large networks, a dense core surrounded by smaller extensions (whiskers) can be the result of several overlapping clusters, where peripheral nodes are the ones belonging to one or few clusters, whereas central ones belong to many.

into larger structures spanning multiple layers. The third class contains extensions of the most common single-layer network methods to a multilayer model, including modularity optimization, random walks, spectral clustering, and label propagation. Despite the availability of multilayer approaches, there might be practical reasons for researchers to use flattened network methods. Additionally, the superiority of one approach over the other has not been proved yet through systematic comparisons.

Sections 6.1, 6.2, and 6.3 present a set of methods representative of these three classes. Then, Section 6.5 covers the main measures used to evaluate the result of a community detection algorithm. The reader interested in a detailed coverage of community detection for single-layer networks can consult the excellent survey papers by Coscia et al. (2011) and Fortunato (2010).

6.1 Methods Based on Simplification

Network simplification methods can provide good answers to the difficult task of finding cohesive subgroups in real social networks when some reasonably well-separated groups exist. This is strictly related to the way in which community detection algorithms have been defined: some try to maximize modularity, favoring well-separated clusters; some use random walk approaches, where the probability that a walker crosses two clusters depends on the number of edges between them; some exploit measures like betweenness, which is high when few other edges connect distinct portions of the network (Fortunato, 2010). However, when we deal with real data, the presence of overlapping layers or of layers with poor relational value but characterized by a high density can easily undermine these techniques. One way to deal with this problem is to perform an initial simplification of the network aimed at presenting what can be considered as a meaningful set of social relations.

6.1.1 Flattening

A way to simplify a multilayer network is to use one of the flattening approaches defined in Section 4.2.1, as proposed, for example, by Berlingerio et al. (2011a). Figure 6.2 illustrates this through a simple example. The analysis of the combination of the three layers (A + B + C), that is, the flattened network, does not reveal any interesting patterns, as there are too many edges in the top-right network and no clear groups emerge. Similarly, a simple weighted flattening process would not show any clear structure, and the observation of each single layer does not provide any valuable information either. However, by performing a flattening that removes layer A and combines layers B and C, some more evident structures appear: two clusters, denoted by gray and white nodes, respectively. Figures 6.3 and 6.4 show different selections of layers from the AUCS network, to provide an intuition of how different combinations of layers can sometimes reveal more evident community structures.

This combination of layers can be chosen manually whenever we have some specific qualitative knowledge of the network indicating which combination might be relevant. However, this qualitative knowledge of the network is not always available, and when we are working within domains where this is missing, we must rely on different approaches to find a good selection of layers. In the work by Berlingerio et al. (2011a), all the layers are used, and after communities have been identified on the flattened network, they are ranked based on the number of edges that were originally replicated on multiple layers – a measure called *redundancy*.

Rocklin and Pinar (2013) proposed an interesting generalization of this problem by reframing it as the problem of finding one or more appropriate combinations of weights for the layers given a predefined community structure. An inverse problem with respect to the one studied by Rocklin and Pinar (2013) would be to find which weights correspond to the best community structure. Within this perspective, various combinations of weights within a flattening process should be tried until we can observe the emergence of visible structures. Although this approach is undoubtedly interesting, it runs the risk of producing visible structures through combinations that have little or no connection with the underlying social relations.

A completely different perspective was introduced by Bonchi et al. (2012): in contrast to other flattening approaches, which assign individuals connected on multiple networks to the same group because they are connected by strong edges in the flattened network, considers a set of individuals as a good cluster if their relationships are as specific and homogeneous as possible, that is,

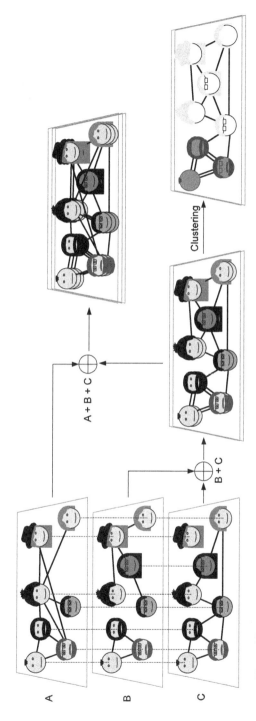

Figure 6.2. Multiple layers are combined to obtain a single network, then traditional community detection algorithms can be used. However, communities may appear when a specific subset of the layers is used (B + C) and disappear or become less dense when less or more layers are used (like A, or A + B + C).

101

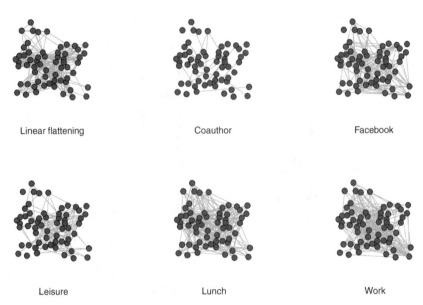

Linear flattening   Coauthor   Facebook

Leisure   Lunch   Work

Figure 6.3. Flattening applied to the AUCS network, showing some community structure. The five layers are also shown individually.

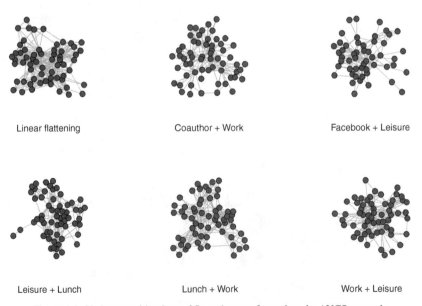

Linear flattening   Coauthor + Work   Facebook + Leisure

Leisure + Lunch   Lunch + Work   Work + Leisure

Figure 6.4. Various combinations of flattenings performed on the AUCS network. Different combinations of layers show different group configurations.

they almost all appear on one and only one layer. This approach challenges the assumption, widely accepted in SNA, that the presence of multiple connections should be considered an indicator of the strength of the relation. Although this method was not designed for social networks, and thus may not prove to be a superior choice over previous models, it is still interesting in that it considers exclusiveness as a measure of tie strength.

6.1.2 Local Simplification

Local simplification, similarly to other flattening approaches, tries to achieve the same goal of producing more compact and essential network structures without losing relevant information. Despite this common goal, the methods applied and the underlying assumptions are radically different. If flattening starts essentially from single layers merged together or selecting specific combinations to highlight underlying structures, local simplification draws the required information from the multilayer network. This means that the information used to simplify the network is not available on a single layer, nor is it available anywhere outside of the relations existing between the various layers within the multilayer structure.

As described in Section 4.2.3, local simplification adopts some of the assumptions made for global simplification and brings them one step further by considering dyadic information between pairs of nodes.

Figure 6.5 shows the AUCS network when we apply a local simplification based on layer relevance. In this case, only the actors that are connected on a layer that has relevance higher than a given threshold (.6 in this case) for both of them are included. A few elements make this approach rather specific. On one hand, it is based on the assumption that different actors might consider different layers locally relevant, and this might be different in different parts of the same layer. On the other hand, it is worth noticing that what defines inclusion in the same structure is not the existence of an edge between two actors (which is more and more probable, as long as the total number of layers increases) but the existence of a connection between nodes having a similar relevance for both actors. This idea connects quite directly with the idea of mutuality embedded in our understanding of subgroups and communities.

Although local simplification undoubtedly introduces innovative ideas to deal with the complexity of multilayer network structures, this method has been introduced only recently, and it will take some time before we can truly compare its results with the approaches based on flattening or with those dealing with the full interconnected structure of the multilayer network.

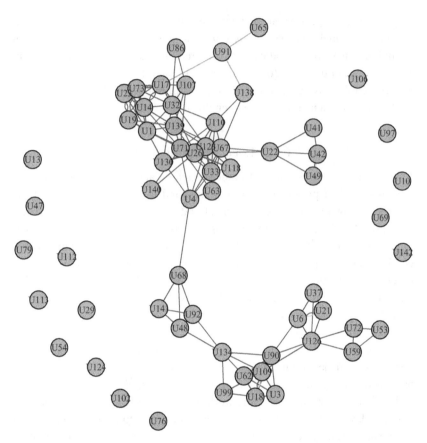

Figure 6.5. Local simplification used as a way to detect underlying multilayer structures. Only actors that are connected on a layer that has relevance higher than a given threshold for both of them are visualized.

6.2 Combination of Single-Layer Communities

This class of approaches is based on the idea of detecting communities on single layers, using existing methods, and then aggregating them into larger structures spanning multiple layers. As some of these approaches are based on the identification of cliques, we begin with a short digression on this important structure and on how it can be extended to multilayer networks.

Cliques are one of the basic concepts in graph and network theory and are characterized by a wonderfully simple definition that captures much of our intuitive understanding of communities and cohesive subgroups.

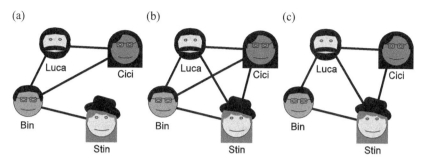

Figure 6.6. Various examples of cliques and noncliques: (a) a 3-clique, (b) a 4-clique, and (c) a .5-quasi-clique.

Definition 6.1 (Clique) A clique is a set of nodes connected to all other nodes in the clique.

Figure 6.6a shows an example of a 3-clique (Bin, Luca, and Cici). However, although any three nodes in Figure 6.6b also make a clique, we will not call that a maximal one, because we could add the fourth node and still have a clique.

Definition 6.2 (Maximal clique) A maximal clique is a clique that is not contained in a larger clique.

A (maximal) clique clearly corresponds to a set of very well connected nodes, which should thus belong to the same cohesive subgroup. There are two concepts here that are important. The first is that we cannot have a cohesive subgroup (nor a group) of two actors: cohesive subgroups start beyond the dyadic nature of the couple. The second is that, although a number of actors fully mutually connected belong to the same clique, a single actor can be part of several cliques at the same time.

However, while the concept is rather intuitive, large cliques are extremely difficult to find in real data, because one single missing edge is sufficient to break the clique, and in social networks, edges can be missing for many reasons (from unreported data to two individuals who do not get along well together). Alternatively, when dealing with large, extremely dense networks, such as those common online, we may find the opposite problem: cliques are numerous but largely overlapping and provide no substantial understanding of the network. While in the latter case, the study of how cliques overlap is a way to dig into the underlying network structure, in the first case, it is wiser to look for more relaxed structures called quasi-cliques.

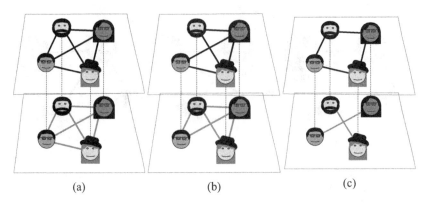

Figure 6.7. Multilayer cliques: (a) a multilayer clique, (b) a quasi-clique with $\lambda = 1$ and $\gamma = .5$, and (c) a quasi-clique with $\lambda = 1/2$ and $\gamma = 1$.

Definition 6.3 (Quasi-clique) A quasi-clique is a set of nodes where each node is connected to at least a fraction γ of the other nodes in the quasi-clique.

Although alternative definitions are possible, for example, using a strict > or considering the percentage over all nodes in the quasi-clique – the underlying concept remains the same. Algorithms to discover quasi-cliques typically take γ as a parameter. In Figure 6.6b, we have illustrated a .5-quasi-clique, and in Figure 6.6c, we have four nodes that do not constitute a .5-quasi-clique, because Bin and Cici are connected to only one-third of the other nodes.

The concept of a clique can be extended to multiple layers just by propagating its definition to each of the layers.

Definition 6.4 (Multilayer clique) Given a set of layers L, a multilayer clique is a set of actors connected to all other actors in the clique on each of these layers.

This concept can be relaxed according to different dimensions in the multilayer case. We can be less strict on the number of actors connected to each other, as in the single-layer case, but also on the number of layers.

Definition 6.5 (Multilayer quasi-clique) Given a set of layers L, a multilayer quasi-clique is a set of actors where each actor is connected to at least a fraction γ of the other actors in the quasi-clique on at least a fraction λ of the layers composing the multilayer network.

Figure 6.7 illustrates these alternative concepts. When $\lambda = 1$ and $\gamma = 1$, this definition corresponds to the preceding one. When $\lambda \in [\frac{2}{|L|}, 1]$, we can also talk of multiplex cliques, with $\lambda = 1$ indicating the maximum degree of multiplexity, because we require each pair of actors in the clique to be connected with multiple edge types. When $\lambda = \frac{1}{|L|}$, cliques may emerge from the contribution of different layers where no clique structure would be otherwise observable. Although multilayer cliques are quite easy to define and visualize, their distribution in real social networks, their role in various social processes, and their actual interpretation require more research.

Research in this area has mainly targeted the concept of multiplex quasi-cliques. Consistently with the flattening approach to detect clusters in multilayer networks, this implies that clique identification methods have been based on the underlying assumption that the redundancy of connections between two nodes should generally be understood as an indicator of the strength of the relationship (Provan and Sebastian, 1998). Following this assumption, Pei et al. (2005) have introduced algorithms to discover quasi-cliques in all layers that compose a multilayer network, and Wang et al. (2006) and Zeng and Wang (2006) have studied algorithms to identify quasi-cliques in at least a given percentage of layers. A slightly different approach has been developed by Boden et al. (2012). Also, this method looks for sets of nodes that make a clique in each single layer. Then, combinations of the layers containing these cliques are checked to see if these basic clusters aggregate into larger meaningful structures. A major problem with this approach is that by basing multilayer cliques solely on single layers, there is the risk of missing layers that play a relevant role in connecting clusters into larger meaningful structures but that do not show any clusters themselves (thus they would not be selected initially). A second issue with this approach is that different combinations may lead to very similar overlapping communities, with only one or a few nodes distinguishing them. Therefore it is important to remove duplicate or nearly duplicate results from the output by providing a threshold for the number or percentage of different nodes or edges.

Starting from different premises, the ABACUS algorithm proposed by Berlingerio et al. (2013) also applies a similar definition: first, clusters are identified in each layer, then those actors belonging to the same cluster in at least a given percentage of layers are also included into a global cluster in the result. In this approach, the clusters on single layers can be computed with any clustering algorithm, so it is not based on cliques, but it is also based on the idea of aggregating single-layer clusters.

It is worth noticing that these methods have been developed for generic multilayer networks without focusing on the application domain of multilayer social networks. In this specific domain, while we may agree that a clique spanning all the layers represents a strong global cluster, we should consider a wider range of meaningful hypotheses. It could be relevant to identify cliques or quasi-cliques that are densely connected on a few specific layers (e.g., we might find a group of students who go to the same school and play on the same basketball team). We could also identify cliques or quasi-cliques that are detectable only when taking multiple layers into consideration. Even more conceptually challenging, we could use multilayer information to see how groups that appear densely connected on one layer are, in fact, kept separate on different layers – this can easily happen in online social networks where traditional groups and relational contexts collapse within the same digital network (boyd, 2008).

How can we use the additional information stored within the multilayer structure to interpret these more nuanced configurations? This is, to a large extent, an open problem.

6.3 Multilayer Modularity Optimization

Modularity is a measure of how well actors can be separated into dense and independent components (Newman, 2004). One could say that modularity is a measure of how well subgroups are separated with the network. Figure 6.8 shows four possible combinations when the actors of a network are assigned

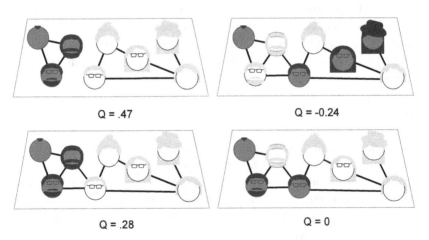

Figure 6.8. In each of these four examples, actors are assigned to either a gray or a white group; the corresponding modularity is indicated under each example. The top-left network contains two isolated groups, and one is a clique (maximum internal connectivity, minimum external connectivity), leading to the highest modularity.

to two groups, for the case of a single social network. The modularity value below every single option shows how good that specific combination is, that is, how well it corresponds to the underlying social ties. Thus modularity is not a measure that refers to the connectivity of a single actor, nor to the network's general structure; rather, it refers to a specific way of grouping the actors and evaluates the quality of that specific grouping. In Figure 6.8, it is clearly visible how assigning highly interconnected actors to the same group and separating groups of actors with only a few connections between them corresponds to a higher value of modularity (top-left assignment). In this respect, modularity follows the same idea behind clique and subgroup identification that we have explored so far: actors that belong to the same group have a high level of internal connectivity, or at least higher than what they have with the rest of the network.

Although this measure suffers from some resolution problems (discussed by Fortunato and Barthélemy (2007) and Lancichinetti et al. (2011)), in particular, the fact that groups of different sizes can be favored or penalized depending on the number of nodes in the network, it has become a very popular choice to explore and characterize network structures. The formal definition of modularity is:

$$Q = \frac{1}{2m} \sum_{ij} \left(a_{ij} - \frac{k_i k_j}{2m} \right) \delta(\gamma_i, \gamma_j) \tag{6.1}$$

where $\delta(\gamma_i, \gamma_j) = 1$ when actors i and j belong to the same cluster, and 0 otherwise. Therefore the sum is computed only for those pairs of actors assigned to the same group. For each of these pairs, if there is a tie between those actors, this improves the quality of the assignment: a_{ij} equals 1 when i and j are directly connected, 0 otherwise. As we are dividing everything by m (the number of edges in the network), assigning two connected actors to different groups negatively affects modularity, because that edge is not considered in the numerator (as $\delta(\gamma_i, \gamma_j) = 0$) but it is counted in the denominator. Finally, the formula considers the fact that two actors with high degree would be more likely to end up in the same group by chance, just because they have a lot of ties, therefore their contribution is reduced ($-\frac{k_i k_j}{2m}$, where k_i and k_j are the degrees of actors i and j).

An extension of modularity for multilayer networks was proposed by Mucha et al. (2010). In Figure 6.9, it can be seen that even if we assign each node to one single group, thanks to the multiple layers, actors can belong to different groups at the same time. For example, Barby and Stine are connected on two layers (chat and e-mail), and Stine is assigned to two different clusters in layers chat (black community) and [e-mail, friendship] (white community).

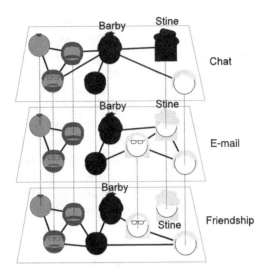

Figure 6.9. When multiple layers exist, the same actor can belong to different groups on different layers. Here we show three groups (white, black, and gray).

Multilayer network modularity[1] is defined as

$$Q_m = \frac{1}{2\mu} \sum_{ijsr} \left[\left(a_{ijs} - \frac{k_{is}k_{js}}{2m_s} \right) \delta(s, r) + c_{jsr}\delta(i, j) \right] \delta(\gamma_{i,s}, \gamma_{j,r}) \quad (6.2)$$

This extended quality function involves not just all pairs of actors (i, j) but also all pairs of layers (s, r). Variables μ and $\delta(\gamma_{i,s}, \gamma_{j,r})$ correspond respectively to m and $\delta(\gamma_i, \gamma_j)$ in the modularity formula (6.2), where μ also considers the links between different networks (i.e., two nodes in layers r and s are connected when they refer to the same actor j, increasing 2μ by c_{jsr}) and $\delta(\gamma_{i,s}, \gamma_{j,r})$ allows for assigning the same actor to different groups inside different layers. The sum is now made of two components. One is only computed when two actors in the same layer are considered (because of $\delta(s, r)$), corresponding to modularity. In fact, here $a_{ijs} = 1$ when i and j are connected in layer s and k_{is} is the degree of node i in the same layer. The second component, c_{jsr}, is only computed when we are considering the same actor j inside two different layers r and s. This term increases the quality function by c_{jsr} (typically, a constant value ranging from 0 to 1) whenever we assign the same individual to the same cluster on different layers.

---

[1] We have omitted the resolution parameter from this definition. For more details, please consider the aforementioned discussion by Fortunato and Barthélemy (2007) and Lancichinetti et al. (2011).

One practical problem in using this measure is how to set the c_{jsr} parameter. Because it defines the penalty to be paid if the same actor is assigned to different clusters in different layers, setting it to 0 for all actors and layers will ignore cross-layer links, and groups will be independently identified on every single layer. If c_{jsr} is set to a very high value, for example, 1, it becomes problematic to assign the same individuals to different groups on different layers, losing one of the major abilities of multilayer network modularity.

Another practical aspect to consider is what happens when we add more layers into our multilayer network. The contribution of interlayer relationships grows quadratically on the number of layers while the modularity part only grows linearly, meaning that for multilayer networks with a large number of layers, the impact of interlayer connectivity would be increasingly more relevant than direct intralayer connectivity.

Figure 6.10 shows the values of modularity for four different multilayer networks and three different settings for the interlayer parameter c_{jsr}, which is kept constant for all nodes and layers. As discussed earlier, $c_{jsr} = 0$ only considers intralayer connectivity in the computation of modularity, $c_{jsr} = .5$ provides a compromise between interlayer and intralayer connectivity, and $c_{jsr} = 1$ gives a larger weight to interlayer connectivity. The figure emphasizes the different components of this measure: on the top we can see two examples where the groups accurately correspond to both the edges inside each layer and the multilayer structure. In particular, well-connected groups of nodes belong to the same community, and the same nodes on different layers tend to belong to the same community. Even if the upper-right example shows that we can assign a node to different groups in different layers, we can still see a general alignment between interlayer and intralayer grouping.

It should be noted that modularities computed using different values of c_{jsr} cannot be compared because increasing c_{jsr} also increases the absolute value of modularity. For example, in the upper-right example, .48 does not indicate a less modular network than .61. However, we can see how the increase regarding the same example is proportionally lower than the one on the upper-left corner (from .48 to .68 and from .54 to .62, respectively). In other words, the more we consider interlayer links in the computation, the more modularity increases when actors are assigned to the same community through all the layers.

The two lower figures show an example of lower modularity values because the white and gray communities do not follow the structure of the ties. The bottom-left example has a low overall intralayer modularity, which can be seen when $c_{jsr} = 0$, and thus interlayer connections are not considered. When we consider them ($c_{jsr} = .5$ and $c_{jsr} = 1$), we can see that modularity is increasing

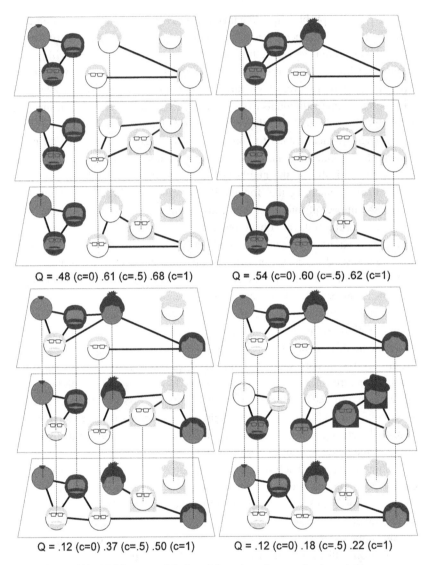

Q = .48 (c=0) .61 (c=.5) .68 (c=1)   Q = .54 (c=0) .60 (c=.5) .62 (c=1)

Q = .12 (c=0) .37 (c=.5) .50 (c=1)   Q = .12 (c=0) .18 (c=.5) .22 (c=1)

Figure 6.10. Multilayer modularity of four clusterings: nodes in each layer are assigned to two clusters (black and gray); the modularity of each assignment is reported under the multilayer network using three settings: $c_{jsr} = 1$, $c_{jsr} = .5$, and $c_{jsr} = 0$.

in the lower-left graph much more than in the lower-right one, where every node belongs to different clusters on different layers.

Once we have a definition of modularity, that is, how much a given assignment of the nodes to different communities complies with the network structure, we can use some heuristics to compute an assignment of high modularity, as done for single-layer networks. One famous approach, not usable for large networks because of its computational complexity but still very popular, consists in removing edges of high betweenness and considering each connected component as a community. The process of edge removal is repeated, recomputing at each step both the betweenness of the edges and the modularity of the assignment, until the maximum value of modularity is obtained (Newman, 2004). A similar approach, where removal is based on a multilayer version of clustering coefficient, was proposed by Bródka et al. (2013). For an extensive review of modularity optimization methods, we refer the reader to the aforementioned survey papers on single-layer clustering.

6.4 Multiple Actor Types

Most of the approaches defined in the previous sections assume that the same types of actors are present in different layers. Some exceptions are the methods based on network simplification, where two-mode and affiliation networks can be projected into a single-layer network with only one type of actor and then clustered using traditional methods, and multilayer modularity, which is general enough to allow the presence of different actors on different layers but has not been tested on these kinds of data to the best of our knowledge.

Although the reduction to single-layer networks seems to be a popular approach, some methods have also been developed to work directly on bipartite networks, for example, extending the concept of modularity to the case of two node types (Barber, 2007; Guimera et al., 2007). One popular method that explicitly takes advantage of the information provided by the different layers is RankClus (Sun et al., 2009), which combines ranking and clustering in a single method. As an example, having a bibliographic multilayer network with researchers and conferences, we can cluster researchers based on the conferences where they publish their work. Researchers publishing with important conferences would be more important in the definition of the clusters, and important conferences are themselves defined as those where important researchers publish their work.

6.5 Community Interpretation, Evaluation, and Description

Not all cliques or subgroups detected by any of the preceding methods will turn out to be meaningful: a certain number of groupings are expected to arise merely from chance, and it is nearly impossible for an algorithm to detect which are significant. The result of any subgroup detection technique will typically be a list of potential subgroups that should be interpreted and evaluated by the researcher. Interpretation of the result can be done on three different levels, as summarized by Wasserman and Faust (1994):

- individual actor;
- subset of actors; and
- whole group.

At the individual level, the interpretation will deal with the distinction between the actors who have been assigned to one or more groups and those who do not belong to any. At the level of a subset of actors, the interpretation will deal with what the members of a specific subgroup have in common, for example, which individual attributes can explain their membership. On a network level, the interpretation will deal with the presence and the number of subgroups within the network. Subgroup interpretation requires a qualitative understanding of the network, and although it is undoubtedly a difficult and complex task, it is not inherently different when it is performed on a multilayer structure.

Besides interpretation of the identified subgroups, one might be interested in evaluating the quality of the obtained clusters. This can be done in two different situations, depending on whether any ground truth is available. We will call the evaluation based on an existing ground truth *external evaluation* because it is based on external data, whereas we will call the evaluation done in the absence of a ground truth *internal evaluation* because it is based solely on data already available within the network. Subgroup evaluation, being based on the analysis of which actors have been placed within the same groups, is not affected by the multilayer structure of the network; therefore this task does not present any additional complexity in a multilayer scenario.

6.5.1 External Evaluation Measures

When ground truth is available, the problem is reduced to computing similarity between two clusterings. These measures of similarity can be divided into two groups: those based on pair counting and those based on information theory.

Given two partitionings $\mathbf{C}_u = \{C_{u1}, C_{u2}, \ldots, C_{um}\}$ and $\mathbf{C}_v = \{C_{v1}, C_{v2}, \ldots, C_{vr}\}$ of the same set of nodes, pair-counting-based measures show the proportion of agreement between the two partitionings.

The agreements between partitions $\mathbf{C}_u$ and $\mathbf{C}_v$ can be summarized using a contingency matrix as presented in Figure 6.11. In this matrix, n_{ij} is the number

$$\mathbf{C}_v$$

Class	v_1	v_2	$\ldots$	v_r	$\sum_{i\cdot}$
u_1	n_{11}	n_{12}	$\ldots$	n_{1r}	$n_{1\cdot}$
u_2	n_{21}	n_{22}	$\ldots$	n_{2r}	$n_{2\cdot}$
$\vdots$	$\vdots$	$\vdots$	$\ddots$	$\vdots$	$\vdots$
u_m	n_{m1}	n_{m2}	$\ldots$	n_{mr}	$n_{m\cdot}$
$\sum_{\cdot j}$	$n_{\cdot 1}$	$n_{\cdot 2}$	$\ldots$	$n_{\cdot r}$	n

$\mathbf{C}_u$ labels the rows.

Figure 6.11. A contingency matrix representing the agreements n_{ij} between two

of agreements, while $n_{i\cdot}$ is the number of elements of the ith group from the $\mathbf{C}_u$ partition and $n_{\cdot j}$ is the number of elements in the jth group in the $\mathbf{C}_v$ partition.

The Rand Index (RI) (Rand, 1971) is an approach for comparing two partitions and expresses the number of pairs of nodes that were placed within the same group in both partitions divided by all node pairs. Using the contingency matrix in Figure 6.11, this index can be expressed as

$$c\left(\mathbf{C}_u, \mathbf{C}_v\right) = \frac{\binom{n}{2} - \left[1/2\left(\sum_i\left(\sum_j n_{ij}\right)^2 + \sum_j\left(\sum_i n_{ij}\right)^2\right) - \sum\sum n_{ij}^2\right]}{\binom{n}{2}}$$

(6.3)

Note that $c\left(\mathbf{C}_u, \mathbf{C}_v\right) \in [0, 1]$, that is, it is 0 when the partitionings are dissimilar and 1 when the partitions are identical. Some alternative measures have also been defined, for example, Hubert and Arabie (1985) introduced the Adjusted Rand Index (ARI), which is a version of the RI corrected for chance.

Another very common measure is the Jaccard Index (Jaccard, 1901), which gives the ratio of node pairs that were clustered together in both partitionings by the node pairs clustered together in at least one partitioning.

The second group of external evaluation measures uses the mutual information (MI) between partitions, that is, the information both partitions share. These kinds of measures are based on the entropy and the joint entropy of the partitionings. Using the same contingency matrix presented in Figure 6.11, the MI is given by

$$\mathrm{MI}\left(\mathbf{C}_u, \mathbf{C}_v\right) = \sum_{i=1}^{m}\sum_{j=1}^{r}\frac{n_{ij}}{n}\log\frac{n_{ij}/n}{n_{i\cdot}n_{\cdot j}/n^2}$$

(6.4)

This measure can be normalized using a normalizing factor such as the joint entropy of the partitions, making the MI lie within the interval $[-1, 1]$ or $[0, 1]$. Variations of this measure with different normalizing factors or adjustments

with correction for chance are presented in detail by Danon et al. (2005) and
Vinh et al. (2010).

6.5.2 Internal Evaluation Measures

When no ground truth is available, determining the quality of a clustering must
be based on its intrinsic characteristics. According to Ben-David and Ackerman (2008, p. 2), a "clustering quality measure is a function that maps pairs of
the form (*data set, clustering*) to some ordered set (say, the set of non-negative
real numbers), so that these values reflect how good or cogent that clustering
is." Some general properties for good-quality measures have been proposed,
such as scale invariance, monotonicity, and richness (Ben-David and Ackerman, 2008; van Laarhoven and Marchiori, 2014), however, which of these properties are (most) important for a given problem depends on the purpose of the
analysis and which questions are asked. Natural candidates for the quality measure are *coverage* (i.e., the ratio between the intracommunity edges and the total
number of edges), *density*, and *modularity* (Fortunato, 2010; Newman, 2004).
Many existing quality functions are *additive*, which means that the overall quality of the clustering is given by the sum of the qualities of individual clusters.

Berlingerio et al. (2011b) have also discussed internal measures considering
the multilayer nature of the data. Given a set of actors who have been included
in the same community, we can consider their *variety*, that is, the number of
layers on which these actors are connected; *exclusivity*, that is, how many pairs
of actors are connected only on one layer; *homogeneity*, that is, how uniformly
the edges are distributed across the different layers; and *redundancy*, that is, the
number of pairs of actors connected on multiple layers.

Different research studies have also focused on hierarchical clustering,
where the result is a hierarchy of clusters that can also be seen as a system
of nested subgraphs. Queyroi et al. (2013) address the question of what is the
best candidate among different hierarchical clusterings of the same graph.

6.5.3 A Multiobjective Descriptive Approach

Communities found in a multilayer network can be described according to
several dimensions, and as a trade-off between compositional and structural
dimensions. We can foresee two main questions that researchers should address
when evaluating multilayer communities:

- to what extent and on how many layers (or on which layers) intra-cluster
  edges should be valued more than inter-cluster edges; and

- what the relation between the intracluster homogeneity of the node attributes should be, and how that can be evaluated on multiple layers.

Although according to Boden et al. (2012), good clusters should show a consistent behavior in all their dimensions, we have already discussed examples where this assumption might prevent discovering or understanding potentially useful clusters. This opens to the possibility that cluster evaluation within a multilayer context should be done in different ways depending on the social nature of the communities we are looking for. We might easily imagine communities that define themselves through their existence over multiple relations (e.g., friends who are also schoolmates and who practice social activities together) as well as groups that exist only within a single relation, and this constitutes an added or important value for that specific cluster. For example, research on online communities has shown that communities existing only online and thus with no overlapping with any other social layer can play an important role in terms of emotional support (Turner et al., 2001).

Addressing these points means to define a way to describe the multidimensional nature of multilayer cohesive subgroups instead of checking if a clustering is good or not as a whole. A specific subgroup in a multilayer network could be described taking into consideration four basic dimensions: structural quality, size, dimensionality, and level of novelty:

- *Structural quality.* A cohesive subgroup should still respect the basic structural requirements that we have described for single-layer cohesive subgroups. For structural quality, any measure from this section can be selected, like modularity, density, or redundancy, and multiple measures of structural quality can be used at the same time to emphasize different ways of forming a good community.
- *Size.* The size of the cohesive subgroup should be taken into account, and researchers should decide if and where to define a threshold of relevance.
- *Dimensionality.* How many layers should be taken into consideration? What role do they play in identifying the subgroups? Obviously, some specific domain knowledge would be best; otherwise, ideas introduced in Chapter 4 could be useful.
- *Novelty.* To assess novelty, we suggest using one of the proposed measures of overlap, such as the Jaccard Index, so that communities that are clearly distinct from the others are favored.

Once we have described the potential cohesive subgroups according to these four elements, we can then see these variables as different dimensions of a search space where each multidimensional point is a cluster. Good clusters can be selected based on custom settings of weights of the dimensions, or unweighted approaches like the Pareto front can be used to find all clusters that are potentially better than others according to any combination of these basic evaluation functions (Giotis et al., 2000).

7

Edge Patterns

There was a darkness; then a dizzy, sickening sensation of sight that
was not like seeing; I saw a Line that was no Line.

– The Square

In the previous chapter, we focused on actors: how to group them into communities. In this chapter, we focus on edges.

One of the most popular data mining tasks for social networks is *link* (or edge[1]) *prediction*: given the current status of a social network, which edges are likely to appear at a later time? This problem was originally defined for single-layer networks and is related to the topic of network evolution that we present in Chapter 8. In both cases, there is an underlying assumption about the social dynamics that lead to the appearance of new edges, for example, the fact that actors with many edges have a higher probability of receiving even more edges, or the fact that actors with many common neighbors have a higher probability of becoming neighbors themselves. However, with social network evolution models, the objective is typically the generation of synthetic social networks having some desired global properties, for example, a given clustering coefficient or degree distribution. In the case of edge prediction, the objective is to infer local edges, that is, to predict if an edge is going to appear between two given nodes, or to rank currently disconnected pairs of nodes according to the likelihood that they will become connected. We discuss the edge prediction problem in Section 7.1.

Although edge prediction for multilayer social networks can be seen as a direct extension of existing methods for single-layer networks, a specific kind of knowledge that only makes sense when we have multiple layers is the existence of layer correlations. In Chapter 2 we described different measures to

---

[1] *Link* is a synonym of *edge* used in the field of computer science.

Figure 7.1. The work layer of our running example depicted at two times t_0 and t_1.

detail the relationship between some predefined layers. However, when many layers exist, we may need automated methods to identify the specific combinations of layers showing significant correlations. We cover this problem in Section 7.2.

7.1 Edge Prediction

Edge prediction, as defined by Liben-Nowell and Kleinberg (2003), addresses the following question: which edges are going to be present at time t_1 given the edges existing at a previous time t_0? Figure 7.1 shows the work layer of our running example at two different points in time: in the figure, three new edges appear and one disappears at time t_1. The objective is to look at time t_0 and produce a ranked list of edges that are believed to appear or disappear soon.

The problem of edge prediction can be stated as a classification problem. We first choose a set of features to describe each pair of nodes in the network, for example, using some of the measures described in Chapter 3 applied to pairs of actors instead of single ones. For the prediction to be successful, these features must be associated to the actors' tendency to become connected or disconnected. Then, we also add one class attribute for each pair of nodes, indicating their connectivity status at time t_1. Table 7.1 shows how part of the work layer in our running example can be formatted as an edge prediction problem using two simple features: the product of the two nodes' degrees and the number of common neighbors. At this point, we can apply any classification algorithm to automatically learn the relationship between the feature attributes and the class attribute. In practice, we can learn a function that for each pair of nodes

Table 7.1. *Our work layer formatted to learn an edge prediction model*

Pair	Degree product	Comm. neigh.	Edge (t_0)	**Edge (t_1)**
Mark, Mat	6	1	no	**yes**
Mark, Bin	6	1	no	**no**
Mark, Sere	4	0	no	**no**
...	...	...	...	

Note: Each pair of actors is described using two features: the product of the numbers of neighbors of the two nodes and the number of common neighbors.

takes all their features as input and produces either a yes/no answer, stating if it is believed that those actors will get connected/disconnected, or – more typically – a score indicating the likelihood that this happens, which can be used to rank all pairs of nodes according to our belief that a new edge will appear or disappear among them.

This table can look slightly different depending on the specific formulation of the edge prediction problem. For example, we might have a trace of different times in the past when some edges had appeared and disappeared, therefore the column edge (t_0) could be replaced by a set of times when the edge was present. This has been shown to improve the accuracy of the predictions, exploiting the fact that edges that are often present or have recently been present have a higher chance of being present also in the near future. Most existing works have focused on the prediction of new edges and not on the prediction of edge disappearance. In this case, the column edge (t_0) would not be used, as we would only keep in the table pairs of actors who are not currently connected; that is, edge (t_0) = no.

A crucial task to achieve accurate predictions is the choice of good features.[2] Therefore we first provide some examples of features commonly used for single-layer networks, then we discuss how things change when multiple layers are considered.

---

[2] A specific classification algorithm to learn the relationship between feature attributes and connectivity status should also be chosen, but this is less specific to the case of social networks and does not need to be discussed here: all classification software libraries, e.g., the ones available in *R*, include several algorithms, e.g., decision trees, *k*-nearest neighbor, Bayesian approaches, artificial neural networks, and support vector machines, only to mention the most popular. Although some can slightly outperform the others, and some knowledge of how they work can lead to a more effective usage, ultimately they all perform the same task.

7.1.1 Structural Features for Single-Layer Networks

The following is a set of typical measures used as features in edge prediction tasks (Liben-Nowell and Kleinberg, 2003). Each measure takes two actors as input and, based on the network structure, produces a score to be used directly in our feature table. Let us indicate with $N(a)$ the neighbors of an actor a.

- A basic application of SNA measures consists in considering that actors who already have several edges have a higher probability of receiving new ones. Therefore, if we consider a pair of actors, we can use the product of their degrees as a feature: $\text{score}(a, b) = |N(a)| \times |N(b)|$.
- The number of common neighbors is also a basic and intuitive feature, this time involving the relationship between actors and not just actors one by one. This can be expressed as $\text{score}(a, b) = |N(a) \cap N(b)|$.
- The Jaccard coefficient applied to a neighborhood computes the proportion of common neighbors over the number of all neighbors, so that two actors with a lot of neighbors but many of them uncommon are not privileged too much: $\text{score}(a, b) = |\frac{N(a) \cap N(b)}{N(a) \cup N(b)}|$.
- The Adamic/Adar-based score puts more emphasis on having common neighbors who do not themselves have many neighbors, following the idea that actors with only a few edges are more selective and that their impact should be emphasized. This is defined as $\text{score}(a, b) = \sum_{c \in N(a) \cap N(b)} \frac{1}{\log |N(c)|}$.
- The previous features, except the product of the degrees, are only meaningful if the two actors have at least one common neighbor. This can be relaxed by using the inverse length of the shortest path between the two actors as a feature, or more sophisticated measures taking multiple paths into account, such as hitting time or PageRank (Lovasz, 1993; Newman, 2010).

7.1.2 The Multilayer Case

When multiple layers exist, the problem of edge prediction can be extended in two aspects. The first change consists in reformulating the problem so that we do not just predict the occurrence of a new edge but a more complex event including information about the layers, for example, the specific layer where the edge is going to appear. The second change consists in using information about the relationships between the layers to define new features.

As we have seen in Chapter 2, multilayer models can be used to represent different scenarios. In the context of edge prediction, we can distinguish two main cases: when nodes on the different layers represent a common set of actors and when they represent entities of different types.

Common Actors on Different Layers

When a multilayer network represents a set of actors connected on different social networks, or by different types of relational ties, the problem of edge prediction can be reformulated so that we try to predict not only the pair of authors between whom an edge is going to appear, but also the layer where this is happening (Rossetti et al., 2011).

This is the most conservative extension of the original edge prediction problem, and all the features used for single-layer networks can be reused, computing them on the layer that we want to predict. In this case, if we have two layers A and B, we would compute the number of common neighbors on layer A and the number of common neighbors on layer B, and given a pair of actors (a_i, a_j), we would use the first feature to compute the likelihood that an edge will appear (or disappear) on the first layer, and the second feature for the second layer. A specific case of this problem has been studied by Leskovec et al. (2010), trying to predict two kinds of edges: positive and negative.

Beyond the basic approach, we can exploit relationships between different layers to build new features. The main idea is that if a connection on layer A is often associated with a connection on layer B, then we can have a feature to predict the appearance of an edge on B whose value is proportional to the likelihood of the association. Some research has been done on this problem (Ahmad et al., 2010; Rossetti et al., 2011), suggesting that the correlations between layers can actually improve the accuracy of the predictions. However, we are not aware of systematic studies addressing a large number of different data sets and alternative metrics of edge correlation among layers. We get back to the automated computation of layer correlations in the second part of this chapter.

Different Types of Nodes

When the different layers contain nodes of different types, rather than referring to a common set of actors, then the edge prediction task changes more significantly. While the general setting of the solution is the same (defining a target, choosing some features, and learning the relationship between the features and the target to compute a scoring function and rank events based on their likelihood), the features defined may not be directly applied, or they may not use all the available information. For example, if we think of a classic two-mode network, where individuals are associated with a set of organizations where they work, there are no edges between individuals, so there is no concept of common neighbors on this layer, and edges can only occur between nodes on different layers. Though this may seem a complication, which we can simplify by projecting these two layers into a single layer only containing individuals, it is also an opportunity. In fact, instead of predicting simple edges between an

Table 7.2. *Metapaths in a Twitter example: Notation and meaning*

	Notation	Meaning
mp_1	$U \leftarrow U$	user a_i follows user a_j
mp_2	$U \rightarrow U$	user a_i is followed by user a_j
mp_3	$U \leftarrow T \rightarrow U$	a_i and a_j are mentioned in the same tweet
mp_4	$U \rightarrow T \rightarrow U$	a_i posts a tweet which mentions a_j
mp_5	$U \leftarrow T \leftarrow U$	a_i is mentioned by a tweet posted by a_j
mp_6	$U \leftarrow T \leftarrow U \rightarrow T \rightarrow U$	a_i and a_j are mentioned on tweets by the same user
mp_7	$U \leftarrow T \leftarrow U \rightarrow U$	a_i is mentioned by a tweet posted by a follower of a_j

actor a_i and an actor a_j, we can try to predict the appearance of more complex structures (paths) involving more nodes of different types, using an approach developed for HINs.

As a concrete example, consider a Twitter network where we have two layers containing respectively users (generically notated as U) and tweets (T) and three kinds of directed edges: from users to users (follows), from users to tweets (posts), and from tweets to users (mentions). Then, instead of having intralayer targets like "a_i starts following a_j," we can define as a target an event like "users a_i and a_j are mentioned in the same tweet." Instead of predicting a single edge, we try to predict two edges from the twitter layer to the user layer. This can be represented as a so-called *meta-path* (Sun and Han, 2012) $U \leftarrow T \rightarrow U$.

Then, we can use meta-paths also to compute features. In Table 7.2 we show some meta-paths for the Twitter example, with their meanings. Each of these (except the one we choose as a target, in this case mp_3) can be used as a basis for defining features. For example, we may make the hypothesis that if a_i follows a_j (mp_1), it is more probable that a_i and a_j will be at some point mentioned in the same tweet. Or, if the same user mentions both a_i and a_j in different tweets (mp_6), this increases the chances that someone (maybe the same user) will mention them in the same tweet.

The last step needed to build a table like Table 7.1 for the multilayer case with multiple types of nodes is to associate a numerical value (or more values) to each of the meta-paths we choose to build our features. One possibility is to count the number of paths in the multilayer network matching the corresponding meta-path for the two actors under consideration. This type of feature has been called *path count* (Sun and Han, 2012):

Definition 7.1 (Path count) Path count measures the number of path instances between two objects following a given meta-path.

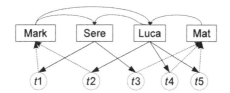

Figure 7.2. A two-layer network with users and tweets.

Figure 7.2 shows an example of a multilayer network with four users and five tweets. The path count for meta-path mp_6 (Table 7.2) and this network for the pair of actors (Mark, Matteo) is 3:

(i) Mark $\leftarrow t1 \leftarrow$ Sere $\rightarrow t3 \rightarrow$ Matteo
(ii) Mark $\leftarrow t2 \leftarrow$ Luca $\rightarrow t4 \rightarrow$ Matteo
(iii) Mark $\leftarrow t2 \leftarrow$ Luca $\rightarrow t5 \rightarrow$ Matteo

7.2 Layer Associativity

In the previous section, we saw how the main addition of multilayer edge prediction with respect to the single-layer case is the hypothesis that the presence (or absence) of an edge between two actors on a specific layer may change the probability that those actors will be connected on another layer.

We can actually be more precise and compute *association rules* between sets of layers to learn more about their mutual relationships. However, we do not want to compute all possible correlations, but only those that are frequent and statistically significant.

7.2.1 Basic Configurations: Pairs of Actors

We start by considering pairs of actors. For each pair with at least one edge connecting them, we list all the layers where they are connected. An example of this representation for a portion of the AUCS data set is shown in Table 7.3. From this, we look for patterns in the following form: "when two actors are connected on layers $l_{i_1}, \ldots, l_{i_n}$, then it is likely that they are also connected on layers $l_{j_1}, \ldots, l_{j_m}$." This is a basic data mining task, and it can be solved in two steps: first finding sets of layers that appear together frequently enough, then extracting the aforementioned patterns.

Step 1: Finding Frequent Sets of Layers
Before extracting association rules between layers, we want to filter out unfrequent cases: to believe that an association is not happening by chance, we need

Table 7.3. *Part of the AUCS multilayer network,*
where, for each connected pair of actors, all the
layers on which they are connected are grouped

Pair	Layers
U102,U139	lunch
U106,U118	coauthor, leisure, lunch, work
U106,U123	Facebook, work
U106,U041	leisure, lunch, work
U110,U072	lunch, work

to observe it several times. The number of occurrences needed to consider a set of layers as frequent is typically a parameter set by the analyst, because threshold considerations are different for different problems.

Definition 7.2 (Support) The *support* of a set of layers X, notated $s(X)$, is the proportion of connected pairs of actors who are directly connected on all those layers.

If we look at the example in Table 7.3, the support of the layer work is $\frac{4}{5}$, because it connects four out of five pairs of actors. The support of the set {lunch, work} is instead $\frac{3}{5}$, because these two layers appear together only in three cases. As said, the analyst can set a minimum support to discard sets of layers not appearing together frequently enough.

If we look at the whole AUCS network, we find the top 6 most frequent sets of layers indicated in Table 7.4.

Table 7.4. *Most frequent layers,*
ranked by the percentage of
connected pairs of nodes with an
edge in each of the indicated layers

Frequency	Layer
0.548	work
0.545	lunch
0.351	Facebook
0.276	work, lunch
0.248	leisure
0.171	lunch, leisure

Table 7.5. *Top 4 association rules ranked by confidence*

Rank	Rule	Support	Lift	Confidence
c1	leisure, coauthor → work	0.025	1.64	0.9
c2	coauthor → work	0.051	1.56	0.857
c3	lunch, coauthor → work	0.03	1.544	0.846
c4	work, leisure → lunch	0.112	1.525	0.832

Step 2: Extracting and Evaluating Layer Association Rules

Once we have selected frequent sets of layers, we can try to extract rules from them. For example, we can take the two layers {lunch, work}, which appear among more than 27 percent of the connected pairs of actors, as we have shown in Table 7.4. From this, we can say that the rules lunch → work (read as, when two actors are connected on the lunch layer then they are also connected on the work layer) and work → lunch appear frequently. However, they are not always true: for example, in some cases, the lunch layer is present alone without the work one. Therefore frequency is not enough.

Two well-known measures to rank the found rules are *confidence* and *lift*. Confidence measures the proportion of times when a rule is true:

Definition 7.3 (Confidence) Given an association rule X → Y, its *confidence* is defined as $\frac{s(X \cup Y)}{s(X)}$.

A potential misuse of confidence comes from the fact that a high confidence may happen because the set Y is very frequent. As an example, if all connected actors are also connected on layers Y, the rule X → Y will have confidence 1 independently of X. Therefore, lift measures an increase of expectations also considering the frequency of Y: if two sets of layers with support, respectively, $s(X)$ and $s(Y)$, are independently distributed in the multilayer network, we would expect to find both X and Y on a fraction $s(X) \cdot s(Y)$ of the connected actors. If the observed number of pairs of actors connected on all layers in Y is significantly higher or lower than this, then the rule indicates a potentially interesting dependency between X and Y.

Definition 7.4 (Lift) Given an association rule $X \to Y$, lift is defined as $\frac{s(X \cup Y)}{s(X)s(Y)}$

We can now go back to the AUCS network and check the top rules according to these two alternative measures, indicated respectively in Table 7.5 and Table 7.6.

Table 7.6. *Top 4 association rules ranked by lift*

Rank	Rule	Support	Lift	Confidence
11	work, leisure → coauthor	0.025	3.185	0.189
12	coauthor → work, leisure	0.025	3.185	0.429
13	leisure → work, coauthor	0.025	2.017	0.103
14	work, coauthor → leisure	0.025	2.017	0.5

From Table 7.5 we can see, for example, that approximately 86 percent of the cases being connected on the coauthor layer also results in having a work connection (rule c2). It is worth noticing that

(i) this only indicates co-occurrence and not causation; and
(ii) the inverted rule may not have the same confidence, for example, in the AUCS network, work determines coauthor only in approximately 10 percent of the cases.

Then, looking at rule c1, we can see that being connected on both the leisure and the coauthor layers raises the confidence of finding a work edge to 90 percent.

Though the previous results are certainly interesting, the high confidences are also determined by the high frequency of working relationships – this being the layer connecting the most actors. If we look at rule 11 in Table 7.6, we can see how having a connection on the work and leisure layers only indicates a connection on the coauthor layer in a small percentage of cases, because the coauthor layer is very sparse. However, a coauthorship edge is 3.185 times more likely to be present when work and leisure also exist than for a randomly chosen pair of actors. It is worth noticing the combined effect of these two layers. Being connected on the leisure layer lifts the chances of being connected also on the coauthor layer by 1.921. Being connected on the work layer lifts the chances of being connected also on the coauthor layer by 1.564. As said, being connected on both leisure and work increases this to 3.185.

7.2.2 Generalized Associations

We conclude this chapter by mentioning that the previous approach can be theoretically extended to more complex configurations. For example, we might consider triads instead of pairs of actors and represent different combinations of relationships. Given three actors a_i, a_j, a_k, they might form a closed triangle on a single layer or a closed triangle using two different types of edges, as we discussed in Section 3.2.4 regarding the multilayer clustering coefficient.

The main problem in studying these more complex patterns is computational: the number of items in our table would quickly become very large. However, for small and sparse networks, configurations other than pairs of actors connected on different layers can be studied. ERGMs are defined exactly with this aim, and as an example, they have been used for the case of multiple types of edges by Lazega and Pattison (1999). Additional details regarding other configurations of interest that can be used to define ERGMs can be found in the book edited by Lusher et al. (2012).

PART III

Dynamical Processes

8

Formation of Multilayer Social Networks

> Well, now I will gradually return to Flatland and you shall see my section become larger and larger.
>
> *– The Sphere*

Understanding network formation and evolution is crucial for a wide variety of network tasks. Whether used to support theories or for the practical tasks of planning for future size and structure, understanding the possible implications of interventions or extrapolating from a smaller data set to a larger one, they all require the ability to create and evolve networks according to a specified model. Any network model is typically evaluated on its ability to reproduce factors of interest for the network in question. This means that a first necessary step to be done to select the specific model we need is to answer the following rather difficult questions: What kinds of characteristics are really important for us? What factors should be incorporated into the model we decide to use? Obviously, these relevant factors change according to both the domain we are in and our final goals.

After a long tradition of social network research, we now have a general understanding of what elements should be taken into account when we think of a model able to create a network showing some level of similarity with the networks we observe in the real world. At minimum these factors include degree(s), the degree-degree correlations (assortativity and disassortativity), and the clustering coefficient. The present chapter first provides a quick overview of how these elements have been implemented in the currently available models for network formation, and then it presents the state of the research about the extension to multilayer networks.

8.1 General Properties for Social Network Formation

8.1.1 Degree Distribution

The first consideration for the formation of social networks is the degree distribution, or how likely or common it is for people to have a given number of connections. As we may expect, it is far more likely for someone to have a small number of connections than it is to have a large number of connections. Besides this commonsense expectation, many years of analysis of social networks have revealed that unlike, for example, height, there is no "typical" number of connections: the degree distribution of social networks is almost invariably fat-tailed (Amaral et al., 2000; Adamic et al., 2001; Clauset et al., 2009). Another way of putting it is that outliers are "common." Upon reflection, this should be obvious: very few people know of anyone twice as tall as them, and no one knows anyone 10 times as tall as she is, but all of us are very likely to know of someone who has 2, 10, 100, or even 1,000 times as many social connections as ourselves. As such, when considering models of social network formation, it is very important that the model be able to incorporate and reproduce this feature. One common way to incorporate this feature into modeling, as we will see in detail later, is *preferential attachment*, where connections are not assigned randomly but rather in accordance with a fitness value partly or entirely based on the current degree of the node.

8.1.2 Correlations

As mentioned several times throughout the volume, we might expect different social relations to show some level of correlation (this is discussed in Chapters 2 and 3). For example, in the AUCS network, we might expect to find some level of correlation between the coauthor layer and the work layer. These relations between multiple types of connections have been long explored in the context of single multiplex networks (Tolsdorf, 1976), and as we see later, they are also central in multilayer models. In addition to these layer-level correlations, we might also focus on similar dynamics that take place at the actor level: it is typical for individuals in social networks to be connected to individuals with whom they have something in common. Within this perspective, this is one of the major driving forces for understanding social networks (McPherson et al., 2001). Though often understood on a categorical level, that is, based on common or similar attributes like age or gender, it is also possible to observe how actors tend to be connected with actors of similar degree far more often than we would expect by chance alone. The origin of this property has often been described as a desire to "stay in one's league," as it were, and it has often been connected with the broader concept of social capital (Rivera et al., 2010). When incorporating this property into a model, these correlations are sometimes built in, but they are often also imposed after the fact by modifying an already created network.

8.1.3 Clustering

A third important property of social networks is the high degree of clustering: friends of your friends are much more likely to be your friend than random individuals, and not only that, but they are likely to become your friends if they are not. Explanations of this property are varied, from the fact that we generally like people who are similar in at least some ways to ourselves, to the simple fact that you are more likely to encounter them at all. This phenomenon is related to, but distinct from, the *small world* phenomenon famously published by Watts and Strogatz (1998), which refers to the length of the average path between any two nodes on the network. Any nonregular network will have a small average path length, but many nonsocial networks (such as infrastructure networks) are not highly clustered. This feature, like the preceding, is sometimes incorporated directly into models and sometimes provisioned for separately.

With these considerations in mind, we can now move to explicitly discussing some models that satisfy these conditions, first in single-layer networks and later in the multilayer context. A summary of the models discussed can be found in Table 8.1.

8.2 Single-Layer Network Formation

For the purposes of this book, we recognize two standard categories of network generation models: edge assignment (EA) models and network growth (NG) models.[1] In EA models, the size of the network is fixed at creation, and edges are added or removed according to particular dynamics, until either steady state or a desired end state is reached. With NG models, the network gains or loses nodes as well as edges. In general, social network membership in offline social networks (e.g., work networks) is best modeled by EA models, as the dynamics of the nodes are typically much slower than those of the edges, and neglecting the former is likely to be of negligible concern (Newman et al., 2001). In contrast, online social networks generally have comparable node and edge dynamic time scales, and so an NG model may be more appropriate.

---

[1] These are, of course, not the only ways to classify network generation models.

Table 8.1. *Summary of various network generation models and some of their important properties in the context of social networks*

Model	Type	Degree distr.	Correlations	High clust.
ER (Erdös and Rényi, 1959)	Single EA	Poisson	No	No
Configuration (Molloy and Reed, 1995)	Single EA	Arbitrary	No	No
BA (Barabási and Albert, 1999)	Single NG	Power law	No	No
(Toivonen et al., 2006)	Single NG	Power law	Assortative	Yes
Forest Fire (Leskovec et al., 2007)	Single NG	Power law	Assortative	Yes
Butterfly (McGlohon et al., 2008)	Single NG	Power law	No	Yes
Copying (Krapivsky and Redner, 2005)	Single NG	Poisson out, power law in	No	Yes
Citation (Šubelj and Bajec, 2013)	Single NG	Power law	Disassortative	Yes
Zhou et al. (2008)	Single NG	Power law	Assortative	Yes or No
Medus and Dorso (2014)	Single NG	Power law	No	Yes
xSocial (Nan Du et al., 2010)	Multi	Power law	No	Yes
Klimek and Thurner (2013a)	Multi-EA	Poisson	No	Yes
Lee et al. (2012)	Multi-EA	Poisson	Either cross-layer	No
Podobnik et al. (2012)	Multi-NG	Power law	Assortative cross-layer	No
Nicosia et al. (2013); Kim and Goh (2013)	Multi-NG	Power law	Either cross-layer	No
Magnani and Rossi (2013a)	Multi-NG	Power law	Assortative cross-layer, link overlap	Yes

8.2.1 EA Models

Two standard EA models are the Erdˊos-Rènyi (ER) model (Erdös and Rényi, 1959) and the configuration model (Molloy and Reed, 1995). The ER model is one of the earliest network models, and it is still useful for being very analytically tractable and a good null model to analyze the importance of network structure. For example, we can compare statistics from an empirical network to those from an ER model with the same number of nodes and edges, to highlight their differences, or we can test new network metrics on both empirical and ER networks, to check if they can distinguish between the two. Beyond these uses, the ER model can be a good fit for social networks where considerable effort is required to have a link established or where other constraints exist, such as limited total population size or limited group size (Amaral et al., 2000; Newman et al., 2001).

The ER model is a two-parameter model: N, the number of nodes, and p, the probably for a link to exist between each pair of nodes. For $p = 0$, the ER model gives an empty graph, and for $p = 1$, it gives the complete graph. In the range $0 < p < 1$ lies the simplest family of nontrivial graphs. Each node has $N - 1$ potential neighbors, and thus the average degree of each node for large N is $\langle k \rangle = p(N - 1) \approx pN$. When dealing with large networks, the average degree is often specified instead of the connection probability, due to p being very small in most large real-world networks, whereas $\langle k \rangle$ is a more tractable number. The degree distribution generated by the ER model follows a Poisson distribution in the limit $N \rightarrow \infty$:

$$P(k) = \frac{\langle k \rangle^k e^{-\langle k \rangle}}{k!} \tag{8.1}$$

with $\langle k \rangle = Np$.

The configuration model is also a two-parameter model. The first parameter, as in all EA models, is still N, the number of nodes, but for the configuration model, the second parameter is the degree of each node in the network. Often, rather than the individual degrees, a configuration model will be specified by a degree distribution, with each node being assigned a random degree from the distribution, with the condition that the sum of the degrees must be an even number. The steps to constructing a network using a specified degree distribution are as follows:

1. Assign each node n a degree drawn at random from the degree distribution; if the total degree of all nodes is odd, replace a node's degree with a new random degree until the total degree is even.
2. Create a list where each node appears a number of times equal to its degree.

3. While this list still has elements remaining, pick and remove two elements randomly from the list and place a link between them. (Optional: Check to see if this would create a self- or repeated link, and if so, replace the two chosen elements and repeat.)

The configuration model can accurately represent the fat-tailed degree distribution of most real-world social networks, although the networks it creates are neither assortative nor with a high clustering coefficient. To reproduce these properties while maintaining the overall degree distribution, it is typical to perform pairwise edge swaps to progressively move the network towards the desired configuration. In particular, for assortativity, Xulvi-Brunet and Sokolov (2004) introduced a method by which two sets of connected nodes are pairwise selected and then rewired either with probability p, such that the two higher-degree nodes are connected and the two lower-degree nodes are connected, or else rewired randomly with probability $p - 1$. This process is repeated until the assortativity reaches the desired steady state value. By varying p, a network of desired assortativity can be generated. A similar method can be used to increase the clustering coefficient: pairwise selecting edges, and then swapping their end points with probability 1 if the operation closes a triangle, or with some probability $p < 1$ if it does not.

It may also be desirable to start from the specific configuration of a known network and randomize it appropriately. An edge swapping method described later can be used (with restrictions on permissible edge swaps as desired to preserve assortativity, clustering, etc.) to generate a random realization of a given network rather than reconstructing it via, for example, a configuration model. For example, to randomize the network while preserving assortativity, after selecting an edge at random, we can select the second edge only from the set of edges where the ends possess the same respective degrees. As a rule of thumb, the network will be sufficiently randomized after ≈ 100 swaps per edge (Milo et al., 2004).

8.2.2 NG Models

One of the most popular and basic NG models is the Barabasi-Albert (BA) preferential attachment model made famous by Barabási and Albert (1999) and first investigated as a network growing model by Price (1976). In this model, the network is initialized with a seed of m_0 fully connected nodes. Then, at each time step, a new node of degree $m < m_0$ is added, with its neighbors selected preferentially according to their proportional degrees, that is, the probability p_i that a node i with degree k_i is chosen as a neighbor is $\frac{k_i}{\sum_j k_j}$. In the long time/large size limit, this produces a network with a power-law degree distribution $P(k) = \frac{2m^2}{k^3}$, no assortativity, and a low clustering coefficient.

Although the BA model can be made assortative or highly clustered through random rewiring, as mentioned – and indeed Xulvi-Brunet and Sokolov (2004) used a BA model in demonstrating their algorithm – there are also a number of algorithms for inherently generating assortative, clustered networks that are therefore well suited to creating social networks. One such model is that introduced by Toivonen et al. (2006).

In the Toivonen model, the explicit preferential attachment is replaced by implicit preferential attachment. The network begins (as in most growth models) with a seed of m_0 fully connected nodes. Then, at each time step, links are formed to, on average, $\langle m_r \rangle \geq 1$ randomly selected nodes. Next, an average of $\langle m_s \rangle \geq 0$ neighbors of the randomly selected nodes are also linked to. Depending on m_r and m_s, this generates networks with power-law degree distribution $P(k) \sim k^{-\gamma}$, where $3 < \gamma < \infty$. There are a number of other similar models, including the Forest Fire model (Leskovec et al., 2007), the Butterfly model (McGlohon et al., 2008), the Copying model (Krapivsky and Redner, 2005), and the Citation model (Šubelj and Bajec, 2013). One limitation of the Toivonen model is that it cannot generate power-law degree distributions with an exponent smaller than 3, which many real-world networks have.

A model that lifts this limitation (in exchange for adding the limitation of fixing the network size at model initialization) is a preferential attachment version of the configuration model introduced by Zhou et al. (2008). In this model, the network is again initialized by a fully connected network of size m_0. Then, at each time step, a new node is introduced into the network with random degree $1 \leq k \leq \min(m_0 + t - 1, k_{\max})$, where $k_{\max}$ is the maximum degree satisfying $NP(k) \geq 1$, where $P(k)$ is the degree distribution specified. If the degree chosen does not satisfy $N_k \leq NP(k)$, where N_k is the number of nodes with degree k, the procedure is repeated until it does. After a valid degree is chosen, we select the k nodes closer in degree (i.e., maximally assortative) that satisfy the condition $N_{k+1} \leq NP(k + 1)$. In the case of ties, selecting the newest possible nodes to add will generate a network with a high clustering coefficient (selecting at random generates an assortative small-world network, but one with a low clustering coefficient). The process is repeated until the network reaches the specified size N.

Lastly, recognizing that triadic closure is an important feature in social networks, a recent triadic closure model was proposed by Medus and Dorso (2014). Starting from a network with m_0 nodes and l_0 edges, at each time step, we connect a node to one of its second nearest neighbors with probability q and to a random node with probability $q - 1$, disallowing multiple and self-edges. Additionally, with probability λ, we add a new node to the network and connect it to a single randomly chosen node. This is repeated until the network reaches a chosen average network degree $\langle k \rangle$, where $\langle k(t) \rangle = 2(m_0 + (1 + \lambda)t/(m_0 + \lambda t))$. With appropriate parameter choice, this generates networks with power-law degree distribution $P(k) \sim k^{-\gamma}$, where $3 < \gamma < \infty$.

8.3 Multilayer Properties

The most straightforward method of generating a multilayer network would be simply to repeatedly use single-layer network models and then connect them. Most of the standard methods of single-layer network formation can easily be extended to multilayer networks, and many have been. However, when doing this, there are some additional properties that must be considered if the resultant networks are to be sufficiently realistic. One of the major problems that we have to face in this regard is that the actual knowledge of real-world multilayer networks is still rather limited. Although we have a large amount of empirical data for single-layer networks, data that have been used to create and to test the network formation models we have presented, we still do not have many data sets that can be used to test multilayer models. Therefore, although we might have expectations based on our general understanding of social phenomena and social networks, we still do not have a precise definition of what characteristics a model for multilayer social networks should achieve.

In this chapter we focus on properties and models for the structural co-evolution of multiple layers. This is of course only one aspect of the more general problem of network formation and evolution: while evolving in time, a layer will be influenced not only by the structure of other layers but also by the status of the actors. For example, if actors have different opinions about a topic, this can be due to their current connections, but it can also influence the creation of new connections – see, for example, the survey on this topic for single-layer networks by Gross and Blasius (2008). We expect these types of studies to be extended to the multilayer context in the future.

8.3.1 Interlayer Correlation

As we have briefly introduced previously, there are cases when some degree of coordination between the edges on different layers of a network should be expected. A hypothetical layer containing a collection of LinkedIn connections might be expected to show a high level of correlation with an offline work layer: links in one network are likely to be represented in another. Although this correlation seems to be reasonable, we still do not know how strong it should be, and in many cases, we might even be surprised by the absence of or the low values observed in empirical data. For example, when observing this on the AUCS multilayer network, we might be surprised by how the lunch layer shows a strong correlation with the work layer, until we realize the context of the data collection (a university department). When designing multiple social networks, it is important to account for the presence or absence of these connections, either directly in the model or imposed on top.

8.3.2 Degree-Degree Correlations

Much as, within a single-layer network, nodes are more likely to be connected to other nodes of similar degree, in a multilayer network scenario, actors might be expected to have similar degrees in every layer that they are a part of. While certainly some individuals do show a radically different level of social involvement across different spheres, we do not have enough examples of real-world multilayer data to say in which case this can be expected or how this value should be interpreted. This property is often handled either by explicit copying of nodes or links from one layer to another or by having a cross-layer fitness function in the case of preferential attachment.

Evidence of this phenomenon can be found in real data. Figure 8.1 shows the correlation between the degrees of the same set of users on three OSNs: Twitter, FriendFeed, and YouTube (Magnani and Rossi, 2013a). Each circle in the plot represents a user, and users with a high x or y coordinate are among the top users on the corresponding OSN according to their degree centrality (more precisely, x and y coordinates correspond to the ranking of the user, 0 for the user with lowest degree centrality up to 7628 for the user with the highest degree centrality in that OSN).

These data show not only that we can observe degree-degree correlations across layers (FriendFeed and Twitter) but also that correlation can vary significantly depending on the layers. Therefore models generating more than two layers should be able to express different layer dependencies. While not visible in the plot, these three layers have significantly different sizes: respectively, 37,997, 67,123, and 1185 edges on FriendFeed, Twitter, and YouTube.

8.3.3 Randomization Methods

As mentioned earlier, when they are not directly incorporated into the model, the various properties necessary to make what we believe can be considered realistic multilayer social networks are often arrived at by randomization

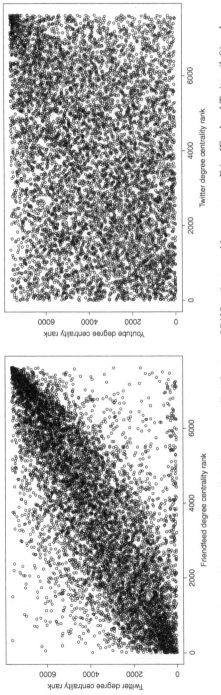

Figure 8.1. User ranking (according to their degree centrality) for a set of 7628 real users with accounts on FriendFeed and Twitter (left) and Twitter and YouTube (right). Pearson correlation indexes are, respectively, .75 and .21.

methods, in particular, by performing Monte Carlo node identity swaps to increase the values in question, that is, pick two actors i and j, and two layers d_1 and d_2, and swap them with probability 1 if they increase the quantity of interest, and with probability $p < 1$ if they do not.

One problem that may arise is when trying to simultaneously optimize for more than one of these conditions, for example, link overlap and assortativity. Node degree is often correlated across layers, but such correlations are not absolute. Consider a pair of actors i and j in two layers L_1 and L_2. If actor i is a hub in both layers, but actor j is a hub in only L_1, then copying an ij link from L_1 to L_2 will increase link overlap but decrease assortativity. Restricting oneself to only accepting swaps that move all desired parameters toward the desired value is, of course, one method of dealing with this; however, it can easily lead to rejecting almost all potential swaps, potentially trapping the networks in configurations very similar or identical to the starting point. One method of averting this local trapping is to consider k-fold edge selection rather than pairwise edge selection. Though originally proposed for single-layer networks (Tabourier et al., 2011), the multiple edge swapping can be very useful for multilayer networks, as the swap permutations grow factorially with k. As an alternative to the increased complexity of multiple edge swapping, it may be easier simply to alternate which parameter one is optimizing for in a given step, until the system as a whole reaches equilibrium.

Rather than using Monte Carlo methods as described to introduce structural features into multilayer networks, it is of course also possible to build models with features that directly introduce those correlations as part of the growth or assignment properties, and in what follows, we discuss a number of these methods, along with other notable features they may have.

8.4 Multilayer Formation Models

Even without fully formalized multilayer models, there are a couple of approaches that have obtained remarkable results modeling multiplex networks and confronting the results with empirical data. One of the first such models, which does not fit directly into the two preceding classes, was an agent-based model for a two-layer online social network. The model, called xSocial by its authors (Nan Du et al., 2010), is designed to replicate user behavior on a discussion board–like site (one layer) that also allows users to choose friends (second layer). At each time, every agent can perform three independent actions (write a message, add a friend, and comment on a message) guided by a one-dimensional random walk mechanism. Writing a message corresponds to adding a new node in the message layer, and the time this node is created is recorded and used in establishing the likelihood of users to comment (link) to this message. When adding a friend, an agent chooses the new friend either by preferential attachment according to the users, activity (degree in the comment network) or by the number of messages on which they have commented together (i.e., the weight of edges obtained by the projection of the discussion network onto the users). The likelihood of choosing these actions varies by agent according to a preference value f_i. When adding a comment, the user prefers newer, more popular messages and thus chooses a message j with a probability $P(j) \sim \frac{\text{\#of comments}+1}{\text{\#of time steps since creation}+1}$. Thus the two networks co-evolve. Despite being relatively simple and having no free parameters (the unique user preferences were set uniformly randomly between 0 and 1), the model generates a network that is remarkably similar to both the FriendView and Flickr networks, including similar power degree distribution, edge weights, and triangle-weight properties (Du et al., 2009).

Echoing the work of Medus and Dorso (2014), Klimek and Thurner (2013b) focused on the importance of triadic closure as a unifying mechanism to explain three scaling exponents of social networks, including the linking probability for new nodes joining the network as a function of degree of the existing (linked-to) node ($\Pi(k) \sim k^\lambda$), the degree distribution ($P(k) \sim k^{-\gamma}$), and the clustering coefficient of nodes as a function of their degree ($c(k) \sim k^{-\beta}$). Their model initially begins with an ER network with N nodes and $l = N/2$ edges. The network is then evolved dynamically according to the following steps:

1. Choose a node i at random. If $k_i < 2$, add a link between i and a randomly chosen node. If $k_i \geq 2$, with probability r (triadic closure parameter), choose two random neighbors of i and create a link between them; otherwise, with probability $1 - r$, choose one neighbor of i and one node from the entire network at random and create a link between them.
2. With probability p (node-replacement parameter), choose a node at random and first remove all of its links, and then add m new random links to any nodes in the network (replacing it). Repeat these steps until the three measures $\Pi(k)$, $P(k)$, and $c(k)$ reach steady state levels.

The results of the model were then compared to a multiplex network data set collected from the German online game Pardus. This data set included six distinct layers, of which the three positive (communication, trade, and friendship) layers were all able to be well fit by the model. As the model has fewer free parameters (only p and r affect the exponents λ, γ, and β) than parameters to be fit, this is indicative that triadic closure is likely to be fundamental across multiple types of positive relationships. The data set also included three negative (enmity, attacks, and revenge) networks, but as long-established research shows that triads are not common in negative relationships (Heider, 1946), the inability of the model to fit those networks is expected.

8.4.1 Multilayer Edge Assignment Models

There have been few truely multiplex EA models. This is perhaps due to the fact that, as node insertion is unnecessary for EA models, they are simply less conceptually difficult to expand. One exception is that of Lee et al. (2012), who introduced a family of two-layer ER models and looked at the impact of correlations in the joint degree distributions of the two layers. They found that positive cross-layer degree correlations led to quicker onset but lower growth of a giant connected component, which has important implications for spreading and diffusion processes, as seen in Chapter 9.

8.4.2 Multilayer Network Growth Models

NG models require more adaptation for the multilayer network framework than EA models. In particular, it is typically undesirable to treat node creation as random. Multilayer NG models thus often incorporate duplication of actors from other layers in addition to completely new creation. This is an important feature, as it is rare for someone to exist only on a single social layer, so provisions for having representation in multiple layers is important.

An NG model that incorporates cross-layer preferential attachment was introduced by Podobnik et al. (2012). In this model, each of two interdependent networks BA_1 and BA_2 (corresponding to two layers in a multilayer network) begins with a small number (m_0) of nodes. At each time step t, a new BA_1 node j is added with (i) $m_1 (\leq m_0)$ edges that link the new node j to m_1 already existing nodes in BA_1, and with (ii) m_{12} edges that link j to m_{12} already existing nodes in BA_2. The nodes in BA_1 and BA_2 linked to j are chosen based on a version of preferential attachment: the probability Π that a new node j in BA_1 is connected to node i in BA_1 depends on the total degree of node i including both BA_1 and BA_2 nodes (total connectivity). Similarly, the same probability Π controls whether a new node j in BA_1 is connected to node i' in BA_2. We define the growth of the BA_2 layer similarly. At each time step t, we add to the BA_2 layer a new node j' with $m_2 (\leq m_0)$ edges that link j' preferentially to m_2 different nodes already present in BA_2 and with m_{21} edges that link j' preferentially to m_{21} already existing nodes in BA_1. After t time steps, the four parameters of the model (m_1, m_2, m_{12}, and m_{21}) lead to a network of two layers with $t + m_0$ nodes in both BA_1 and BA_2, an average degree $\langle k_i \rangle = 2m_1 + m_{12} + m_{21}$ for BA_1 and $\langle k_i \rangle = 2m_2 + m_{12} + m_{21}$ for BA_2. This generates power-law degree distributed layers of the form $P_1(k) \sim (k)^{-[(1/\beta_1)+1]}$ with $\beta_1 = \frac{m_1+m_{21}}{2m_1+m_{12}+m_{21}}$ for BA_1 and $P_2(k) \sim (k)^{-[(1/\beta_2)+1]}$ with $\beta_2 = \frac{m_2+m_{12}}{2m_2+m_{21}+m_{12}}$ for BA_2. Owing to the preferential attachment process considering the total degree, the degree distributions for both inter- and intra-layer degrees for each network are identical.

A later work by Nicosia et al. (2013) presents yet another extension of preferential attachment models to multilayer networks. This model is extended to non-linear preferential attachment where the nonlinearity of the attachment is allowed to differ for different layers (i.e., for a two-layer network $\Pi \sim k_1^\alpha k_2^\beta$, with $\alpha, \beta \in R$). By varying the values of α and β, assortative or disassortative networks can be generated that are variously heterogeneous or homogeneous in degree distribution, although a mean-field attempt to analytically derive their parameters was found to be ineffective. To generate assortative layers with a power-law degree distribution, the two constraints are $\alpha + \beta \leq 1$ with $\alpha, \beta \geq 0$; that is, attachment in both networks must be positive, but not more than linear. Kim and Goh (2013) independently arrived at a similar model where a linear preferential attachment incorporates the degree in different layers, either bi- or unidirectionally.

Though the models above have cross-layer degree-degree correlations, the link overlap across networks is merely random, which is not expected of real-life social networks. One NG model that does incorporate explicit link overlap in its network construction was developed by Magnani and Rossi (2013a). We reproduce this simple multilayer network formation example on two layers N_1 and N_2 here. The model is an NG model with two key features. First, to model the differing growth speeds of the two layers, we include a possibility of inaction rather than uniformly introducing a new node or edge into each layer at each time step t_i. The second fundamental change necessary for this network model is allowing an action on one layer to be influenced by a previous action on another one. In our example, an edge is created in N_1 due to the presence of that same edge in N_2. Practically speaking, if you already know someone, for example, you are friends on Facebook, this may increase the probability that you will also connect on another online social network such as Twitter. Although both example social networks are online, the model functions equivalently with offline social networks. In summary, according to this model, at every time t_i, there are three possible events on each layer (see Figure 8.2):

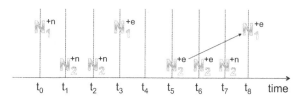

Figure 8.2. Abstract view of the joint evolution of two layers. Time step t_4 shows an example of event 1: nothing happens. Time step t_8 shows an example of event 3: external dynamics. All other time stamps show event 2: internal dynamics.

1. With probability p: nothing happens, that is, the layer remains unchanged.
2. With probability $q < 1 - p$: the layer grows according to internal dynamics, that is, something happens independently of the other layer. For example, a Twitter user may find a tweet interesting and thus start following its author (internal edge creation), or someone with no prior social network usage may join Facebook for the first time (internal node creation). The ratio between edge and node addition is chosen to control the average degree of the network. Although this model accounts for various levels of positive correlation between two layers – from no correlation to absolute mirroring – it is not able to reproduce negative effects, such as edges that are removed from one layer because a connection between the same two actors has been established on another layer. In the original presentation of this model, the attachment process was modeled as a BA preferential attachment process, though any growth process (Copying model, Toivonen model, etc.) can also be used.
3. With probability $1 - q - p$, the layer grows according to external dynamics, that is, something happens because of the configuration of an external layer. For example, a Twitter user joins Facebook and follows one of his prior Facebook friends (external node creation), or an existing Facebook user may friend someone on Facebook he had already been following on Twitter (external edge creation).

As earlier, the ratio between node and edge addition controls the average degree of every layer. In the case of external node creation, there is an additional consideration on the choice of which node to be imported and the corresponding creation of a link. Two possible actions are allowed:

1. The new node is imported from the other layer entirely at random, meaning that the choice is not influenced by other nodes already in the target layer. Here, though the node creation is externally influenced, the resultant link is created through internal dynamics.

2. The new node is chosen only from the set of nodes connected to individuals already in the target layer.

In practice, these actions can be exemplified as follows. A user, say, Cici, has an account on Twitter and an account on Facebook. At some point, another Facebook user creates an account on Twitter. Under option (1), this is just a random user who decided to join Twitter. Under option (2), this is a friend of Cici on Facebook who decided to join Twitter and start following Cici.

9

Information and Behavior Diffusion

I exhorted all my hearers to divest themselves of prejudice and to
become believers in the Third Dimension.

– The Square

9.1 Diffusion in Networks

What information will spread through a social network? This is one of the most
important questions about social networks, and the relationship between network structure and information has been at the center of research activity for
many years. The simple idea that information and concepts propagate over the
observable network connecting the actors of a specific community is too fascinating not to lead generations of researchers to try to answer this fundamental
question. The existence of a strong relation between social network structure
and information propagation processes has been observed many times over the
years, at least since Katz and Lazarsfeld (1955) published their pivotal work
on the flow of mass communication, which essentially looked, albeit within a
different frame, at the role that opinion leaders played in networks. Despite this
long-existing tradition of research, the full dynamic that connects networks and
diffusion processes is still an open problem. In this chapter we set up a framework with which to examine the conditions under which it is possible to study
how information spreads throughout a multilayer network. First, as we have
done so far, the necessary concepts are introduced for single-layer networks,
and then multilayer extensions are examined.

9.1.1 A Complex Circular Problem

Despite the wide body of research and the growing number of empirical data
sets – often made of massive data gathered from online social networks such as

those used by Yang and Leskovec (2010) and Bakshy et al. (2012) – a clear identification and measurement of the role played by network structure within propagation processes remains an open problem. There are few areas of research
where such a number of network properties converge, in a sometimes contra-
dictory way, to create a phenomenon that is extremely difficult to observe. As
Nahon and Hemsley (2013) put it in their work about virality:

> When everything lines up – the right content, with the right source at the right time
> of the day – then a viral event can emerge as a result of many people deciding
> something is remarkable, and then doing just that: remarking on, and sharing, some
> bit of content. (p. 80)

The main problem when observing propagation processes in multilayer networks through empirical data is to determine if what we see is an actual internal
propagation process or if it could be created by an external process (Bakshy
et al., 2012). Without specific data, it is often impossible to determine whether
a specific sequence of actions performed by two connected actors (e.g., Mat
and Cici sharing the same link on Facebook) is due to an internal propagation
process (e.g., Cici saw the link shared by Mat and decided to reshare it) or to an
external element (e.g., they both received the same mailing list that morning,
containing an interesting piece of information).

A central problem is to understand the role played by homophily in this process. Researchers have observed how social networks, both online and offline,
show a large degree of homophily, but what role does this play in diffusion
processes? Do actors that are closely connected behave similarly because they
communicate a piece of information (thus we can observe a diffusion process),
or are they connected because they occupy a similar social position and have
access to the same (external) sources of information? In this second situation,
their sharing processes would be independent of the existence of a network
connection (Shalizi and Thomas, 2011).

Often information propagation and behavior diffusion are observed and
described as very similar phenomena. In the same way in which an actor propagates new pieces of information through her social network, she can easily
propagate a new behavior or the adoption of specific technology. Nevertheless,
besides some similarities, these two phenomena present very different characteristics.

When we discuss how information propagates through the network, we
should take into account the role played by strong and weak ties within information flows: from Granovetter (1973) we know how weak ties play a necessary
role in information flow, facilitating the access to information that is not available within the group defined by strong ties (that are expected to have access

to the same or related information sources). We also have empirical evidence suggesting that weak ties drive the diffusion process within large networks with a low cost of dissemination, such as OSNs (Bakshy et al., 2012).

In contrast to information diffusion, behavior diffusion shows different dynamics where influence and propagation result from having multiple densely connected contacts who have adopted a specific behavior (Aral and Walker, 2011; Centola and Macy, 2007). This is often modeled by *threshold models* – which we discuss later in this chapter – that take into consideration not only the existence of a connection between two actors in the network but also the other connections that represent the social dimension that is often present behind our decision of whether to adopt a specific behavior.

The chapter is then structured following this distinction between information propagation and behavior diffusion. In both cases we first introduce briefly the concepts as they have been developed in single-layer networks, and then we present the major challenges that occur when we try to extend these concepts within a multilayer scenario.

9.2 Modeling Information Spreading

Information spreading, whether online or offline, has usually been modeled essentially as a contact process. Individuals are considered to be in one of two states: either they know something, or they do not. Any individual knowing a fact can spread it to anyone he is connected to. Much as the term "going viral" implies, this can be thought of as a kind of disease epidemic, where the disease corresponds to the knowledge in question. While some researchers have expressed concerns about the metaphor of information as a virus (Jenkins et al., 2009; Huberman and Adamic, 2004; Wu et al., 2004), it has a great deal of success across many research areas and is now a widespread way of representing the incredibly fast information diffusion processes that are mainly realized with mass media technologies.[1]

While various factors can influence the individual decision to share or not to share information – many more than what can influence if and how an individual will share a real virus, for the sake of simplicity these have generally been compressed down into a single variable, which is allowed to take on

---

[1] Although a lot of the initial fortune of the viral metaphor is due to the idea of a grassroots unstoppable process that could be started by anyone, more recent research has shown the role of mass media as super hubs and as gatekeepers in contemporary viral propagation through digital communication networks (Nahon and Hemsley, 2013).

different values for different pieces of information and for different actors. This information spreading parameter (β) ranges between 0 and 1 and indicates, at a high level of simplification, how much a single piece of information is worth spreading and how much a single actor is susceptible to this influence. If we go back to the very first lines of this book, when we mentioned how Keith Urbahn tweeted about the death of Osama Bin Laden, we might safely assume that this specific piece of information had a large perceived importance, remembering of course that different actors may have found it more or less worth retweeting or otherwise sharing.

Despite the differences that exist within any network, one of the beneficial consequences of modeling the spreading of information in this way is that the average value of β across the network, combined with information about the structure of the network itself, can be used to define a critical level to predict whether a given piece of information is over or under the threshold of propagation. The initial assumption is thus that by knowing the structure of a specific network and its susceptibility to propagating a specific piece of information, we can know in advance if a given propagation will actually take place.

One way of showing this concept is expressed through *phase diagrams* (see Figure 9.1): by plotting information about the connectivity of the network (κ, where higher values indicate more connections) on one axis and information spreading information (β) on another, we can visually see the existence of a critical line that separates those combinations that are likely to spread from those that are not. From this diagram, we can notice a few things, first among which is that as networks become more connected (κ increases), less attractive information (smaller β) can spread. We can also see that, equivalently, as β increases, information will spread on less connected networks (smaller κ), but that past a certain point, it does not matter how attractive information is to spread: even when all actors immediately share the information ($\beta = 1$), the information does not spread throughout the network. This is due to those networks lacking a *giant component*, that is, a connected component containing most of the nodes, meaning that most users cannot find a path to each other. Under the simplistic assumption that the network represents all the information we need to study the diffusion process, information cannot be shared along connections that do not exist.

One consequence of the existence of the critical line is that near it, small changes in either the network or information spreading properties can drastically impact the outcome. Far away from the critical line, cutting half the connections in the network may only lower the number of people hearing the information by a few percent. On the other hand, near the critical line, adding

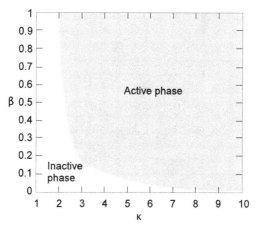

Figure 9.1. A simple phase diagram showing what combinations of network parameters (κ) and information parameters (β) will result in the information spreading or not. In the active phase (gray), information spreads throughout the network. In the inactive phase (white), information remains local. Near the critical line, small changes in either parameter can mean two nearly identical events can have wildly different results.

as few as 10 percent additional connections will often mean the difference between information heard by dozens and information heard by thousands. Alterations to the likelihood of spreading information likewise have similar dramatic effects near the critical line; however, in the context of social interactions, it is of course much harder to control a user's actions than it is to control his connections.

9.2.1 Simple Epidemic Models

The modeling of information spreading in a population has adopted concepts and models originally developed to study how diseases were transmitted within a given population. In these models the population in question is divided into disjoint classes. The most simple approach divides the population into just two classes: the susceptible class S, which consists of individuals who are vulnerable to a disease but are not currently infected, and the class I, which consists of those individuals currently infected with the disease and capable of infecting other individuals. While those two classes make up the minimum necessary to model an epidemic or information spreading, it is useful also to consider a third class: the recovered or removed class (R), which comprises those individuals who have previously been infected but can no longer infect others or be

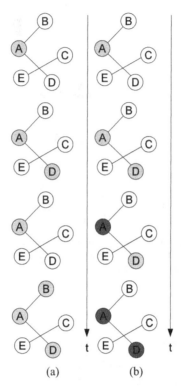

(a)   (b)

Figure 9.2. Network examples for (a) the SIS model, where an individual who stops spreading information can begin spreading it again if triggered, and (b) the SIR model, where an individual who ceases spreading information will never spread again. White nodes represent susceptible actors, light gray nodes represent infected actors, and dark gray nodes represent recovered actors.

reinfected, either because of some sort of lasting immunity or owing to death from the disease.

Mapping this approach within the realm of information means that those actors who have not heard the information will correspond to the susceptible (S) class, those who have heard the information and are currently willing to share the information will constitute the infected (I) class, and those actors who have decided that they will no longer spread the information will be in the recovered (R) class.

Various models can be constructed depending on allowable transitions between these three (or other) states, but two of the most common are the so-called susceptible/infected/susceptible (SIS) model (Figure 9.2a), and the so-called susceptible/infected/recovered (SIR) model (Figure 9.2b). For those

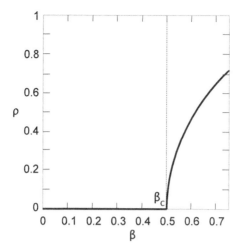

Figure 9.3. A simple phase diagram, equivalent to a vertical slice from Figure 9.1, showing the average fraction of the network reached (ρ) for different values of the likelihood of the information being spread (β). Below the critical point (β_c), a zero fraction of the network is reached. Above the critical point, the information spreads to an appreciable fraction of the network.

interested, a detailed description of these models can be found in Anderson and May (1992). In the context of information spreading, the SIS model has been used to represent long-term societal trends that, although they may fall out of an individual's current notice, are likely to reoccur in the future, such as political issues. The SIR model, conversely, has been used to represent *fads* or *gossip*. Fad refers to a strong but short-lived enthusiasm for something, like using a specific language expression, typically motivated by its novelty and popularity more than its intrinsic quality. Similarly, gossip is typically targeting new information about personal affairs. Therefore an individual is unlikely to resume spreading once the peak of diffusion has passed, even if he comes into contact with the same information later.

Although the long-term behavior of the two models is different (with SIS reaching a steady state or cycle and SIR having a single peak followed by die-off), they share a common set of initial trajectories starting from a purely susceptible population, namely, that the initial infection/information will either stay confined to its local environment or spread throughout a globally significant portion of the population. The separation between these two scenarios is fully represented by a line, as shown earlier in Figure 9.1, but it is customary to calculate a single value for the information spreading parameter at which the system moves between these two states, known as a *critical point* (see Figure 9.3), and methods for calculating it are presented in the following, first for single-layer and then for multilayer networks. This figure should be interpreted as a vertical slice across the phase diagram for a given network, such that the size of the population reached can be visualized conveniently.

9.2.2 Additional Properties for Information Diffusion

It is easy to derive the critical points and phase diagrams for random regular networks; however, as we discussed in Chapter 8, real social networks deviate from this model in a number of ways. We should thus examine what are the peculiar characteristics of social networks that have an impact on information diffusion processes.

Degree Distribution

The effects of the fat-tailed degree distribution on the critical point can be dramatic. Scale-free networks with an exponent greater than 2 have actually been shown to have a critical point asymptotically close to zero (Pastor-Satorras and Vespignani, 2001). In other words, every piece of information will eventually be spread throughout the community. Barthélemy et al. (2004) showed that not only does the threshold vanish but the time required for the information to spread also vanishes. This result is supported by real-world data that show typical saturation times of less than a day for extremely large networks such as those of Twitter and Digg (Lerman and Ghosh, 2010).

Assortativity

As mentioned before, some real-world social networks show a high level of assortative behavior (Newman, 2003), including the AUCS running example used throughout this text. Several authors have shown assortativity to enhance epidemic spreading in networks (Van Mieghem, 2011; Goltsev et al., 2008, 2012), even going so far as to push the threshold to zero in networks with an otherwise finite threshold (Vázquez and Moreno, 2003). Although not extremely common in social networks, dissortative behavior has the opposite effect of raising the critical threshold and lowering outbreak size.

Clustering

In contrast to the preceding factors, which are similar for SIS and SIR epidemic models, the impact of clustering on information differs. For SIS networks, the epidemic threshold decreases with increasing clustering (Van Mieghem, 2011), as highly clustered portions of the community serve as hotbeds of discussion that are able to repeatedly involve the rest of the network. In contrast, for SIR networks, the epidemic threshold increases with increasing clustering

(Keeling, 1999; Newman, 2003): the information will spread throughout local clusters but then can die out before it is able to spread throughout the network.

9.2.3 Derivations

Giant Components

A necessary, but not sufficient condition for information spreading is the existence of a giant connected component, that is, the network needs to have a nonzero fraction of its members connected to one another. If the network is fragmented into disparate parts, then obviously no information will spread outside its local cluster. Because almost all realistic examples of social networks have shown the presence of giant components (Newman et al., 2002), we provide only the final result in what follows; for a derivation, see, for example, the work by Newman et al. (2001).

The condition for the existence of a giant component is

$$\frac{\sum_k p_k k^2}{\sum_k p_k k} = \kappa = 2 \tag{9.1}$$

where p_k is the probability distribution for a node to have degree k. In other words, the ratio of the second to first moment of the degree distribution must be higher than 2 for a giant component to emerge. In an ER network, this occurs when the average number of connections is two, meaning that it is possible for information to spread as long as each individual has, on average, one additional person to spread information to, besides the person she heard it from.

Critical Condition

Suppose that we have a network with a giant component as defined in the previous section; that network will be above the threshold that allows for long-range connectivity within the network. Given this condition, an interesting question could concern how many connections we can remove at random before the giant component is destroyed. Starting from an initial degree distribution P_k and removing links with probability q, we arrive at a new distribution P_k^* for the altered network with

$$P_k^* = \sum_{k_0=k}^{\infty} P_{k_0} \binom{k_0}{k} q^{(k_0-k)}(1-q)^k \tag{9.2}$$

We can derive the critical failure probability, q_c, by substituting the first and second moments of this degree distribution into Eq. (9.1) These first and second moments are

$$\langle k^* \rangle = \langle k \rangle (1 - q) \tag{9.3}$$

and

$$\langle (k^*)^2 \rangle = \langle k \rangle q (1 - q) + \langle k^2 \rangle (1 - q)^2 \tag{9.4}$$

Setting $\kappa^* = 2$ and solving, we find

$$q_c = 1 - \frac{1}{\kappa - 1} \tag{9.5}$$

Realistically, information spreading can occur at any time; however, there is seldom any issue with assuming that information occurs in discrete time steps, perhaps on the order of a minute. The spread of disease or information is thus governed by two parameters: infected individuals I come into contact and infect all susceptible individuals S with probability β per time step, and individuals cease to be infected after an average time t_R. The *transmissibility* T, or the total chance that an infected individual will transmit the infection to a susceptible neighbor, is then

$$T = 1 - (1 - \beta)^{t_R} \tag{9.6}$$

Now, we vary the number of connections that each person has by assuming they are nodes on a network with a particular degree distribution $P(k)$. Imagine that we start with a single infected individual of degree k_0. The probability of this node infecting exactly k of its k_0 edges is given by a binomial probability distribution $\binom{k_0}{k} T^k (1 - T)^{(k_0 - k)}$. The probability distribution of all possible infected nodes is

$$P_{k_0} \binom{k_0}{k} T^k (1 - T)^{(k_0 - k)} \tag{9.7}$$

which is simply Eq. (9.2) with $T = (1 - q)$. Thus we can immediately conclude from Eq. (9.5) that

$$T_c = \frac{1}{\kappa - 1} \tag{9.8}$$

Although β and t_R are likely to vary across a network, as different individuals have different reactions to different diseases/information, it has been shown (Newman, 2001a) that if β or t_R is an independently identically distributed random variable drawn from some distribution $P(\beta)$ or $P(t_R)$, the epidemic threshold depends simply on the first moment of T,

$$\langle T \rangle = \int_0^\infty P(t_R) dt_R \sum_{\beta=0}^\infty P(\beta) P(t_R) (1 - \beta)^{t_R} \tag{9.9}$$

and the critical condition is $\langle T \rangle_c = (\kappa - 1)^{-1}$.

Eigenvalue Approach

An alternate approach to calculating the critical threshold for SIS epidemic spreading using the largest eigenvalue of the adjacency matrix was developed by Wang et al. (2003). This condition is

$$\beta_c = \frac{\delta}{\lambda_{1,A}} \tag{9.10}$$

where $\lambda_{1,A}$ is the largest eigenvalue of the adjacency matrix and where $\delta \sim t_R^{-1}$. Equivalently, $T_c = 1 - (1 - \delta/\lambda_{1,A})^{1/\delta}$. This critical condition agrees exactly with the preceding model for ER networks, where $\lambda_{1,A} = (\kappa - 1) = \langle k \rangle$, but differs for scale-free networks, where the authors claim it offers increased accuracy.

9.2.4 Extensions to Multilayer Networks

With simple information spreading, the move to multilayer networks carries one important rule: information will always spread at least as fast and as far as it would on a single network, and often faster. This is trivially true in the single network case: adding more connections to a single network always provides more avenues for spreading the information. Mathematically, adding links always increases κ, and, as we saw, the critical threshold varies inversely with κ.

The real effects of multilayer network structure on information spreading go beyond this: Cozzo et al. (2013) showed not only that the epidemic threshold in a multilayer network lower than the flattened projection of the same network but also that in a two-layer network, when both layers are active, the multilayer representation could reach more than twice as many individuals on average.

Derivations

To simplify the derivation on multilayer networks, in the following, we consider only the case of two layers, but the matrix approaches used are completely general for N layer networks. In all cases we assume that a giant component exists. We present two cases that have been studied: first we examine a complete overlap model with variable spreading parameters, and next we examine a partial overlap model.

A multilayer network equivalent of the single network generating function approach was developed by Leicht and D'Souza (2009). As with the single-layer network, we present only the result; for the derivation, we direct the reader to Leicht and D'Souza's paper.

For a two-layer network with layers designated α and β, a giant component first appears when

$$\left(1 - \bar{k}_\alpha^\alpha\right)\left(1 - \bar{k}_\beta^\beta\right) = k_\alpha^{\bar{\beta}} k_\beta^\alpha \qquad (9.11)$$

and of course continues to exist for any set of strictly higher ks.

Given that a giant component exists, we can find the epidemic threshold by following, for example, the work by Min and Goh (2013). Their model assumes that all nodes are present in all layers but does incorporate not only a difference in spreading rates across the two layers but also the possibility of a penalty to the spreading rate in layers other than the one through which the individual was informed. In other words, if you heard a piece of information through Twitter, you are less likely to share that information on, for example, Facebook than you are to reshare it through Twitter, because of the additional overhead in switching services and transferring the information. This is a rather interesting aspect because it can be used to model on one side the technical effort required to move a piece of information to a different layer but also the perceived relational difference between two layers, for example, if I received some piece of gossip through my friendship layer, it might take a while before I decide – if ever – to share it through my work layer.

The critical condition, as always, is that the largest eigenvalue of a matrix be equal to unity; however, in this case, the matrix in question is for a two-layer network:

$$\begin{pmatrix} T_{11}(\kappa_1 - 1) & T_{21}K_1 \\ T_{12}K_2 & T_{22}(\kappa_2 - 1) \end{pmatrix} \qquad (9.12)$$

where T_{ij} is the transmissibility for an i node infecting a j node, κ_i is the second moment of the degree distribution on layer i in isolation, and $K_i = \langle k_i k_j \rangle / \langle k_i \rangle$. In general, we restrict $T_{ij} \leq T_{ii}, T_{jj}$. The largest eigenvalue of the preceding matrix can be calculated explicitly:

$$\Lambda = \frac{1}{2}\left[T_{11}(\kappa_1 - 1) + T_{22}(\kappa_2 - 1) \right.$$
$$\left. + \sqrt{(T_{11}(\kappa_1 - 1) - T_{22}(\kappa_2 - 1))^2 + 4T_{12}T_{21}K_1K_2}\right] \qquad (9.13)$$

As noted earlier, this is always greater than or equal to the eigenvalues of the individual layers, $\Lambda \geq \max(\lambda_1 = T_{11}\kappa_1, \lambda_2 = T_{22}\kappa_2)$, validating the assertion that the epidemic threshold in a multilayer network cannot be larger than that on the individual layers.

This model is similar to a model proposed by Buono et al. (2014), which allows for only partial overlap in the network by adding in an overlap parameter q that indicates the fraction of nodes present in both layers. As individuals are rarely present in all layers (as it happens when we consider several OSNs), we can combine the two models. This reduces the off-diagonal terms of the matrix and gives

$$\begin{pmatrix} T_{11}(\kappa_1 - 1) & T_{21}qK_1 \\ T_{12}qK_2 & T_{22}(\kappa_2 - 1) \end{pmatrix} \tag{9.14}$$

with eigenvalue condition

$$\Lambda = \frac{1}{2}\left[T_{11}(\kappa_1 - 1) + T_{22}(\kappa_2 - 1) \right.$$
$$\left. + \sqrt{(T_{11}(\kappa_1 - 1) - T_{22}(\kappa_2 - 1))^2 + 4T_{12}T_{21}q^2K_1K_2} \right] \tag{9.15}$$

9.3 Opinion Formation and Behavior Adaptation

In the previous sections, we focused on spreading of information modeled according to simple contagion dynamics. Formation of opinion and adoption of behavior follow somewhat different dynamics. Though we can easily acquire and share new information, opinions and consequent behaviors seem to be more stable – and their diffusion often requires that the actor have more than a single contact with the new behavior.

In particular, experimental evidence suggests that a behavior requires some level of social reinforcement that is triggered by collective action from our network (Centola and Macy, 2007). If you are, for example, initially disinterested to see a movie, it may not matter that a single friend of yours attempts to change your mind, even if he repeatedly and convincingly attempts to do so. Alternatively, if many of your friends attempt to entice you to see it, you may be willing to do so, even if each of them only mentions it once. Similarly, if only one of your connections moves to a new social network, you may not find it worth the effort until several of your friends are on. As such, the simple contagion model presented for information does not hold for opinions and behaviors, and we must instead turn to complex contagion models as defined by McAdam and Paulsen (1993).

Centola and Macy (2007) underline four major reasons why diffusion of behaviors should follow complex contagion models:

1. *Strategic complementarity.* Knowing about something new is rarely enough to induce someone to change her behavior (Gladwell, 2006). Many innovations are costly, especially for early adopters, but less so for those who wait.

2. *Credibility.* New practices often lack credibility until relevant people in your network have adopted them. Markus (1987) found this adoption pattern for media technology.
3. *Legitimacy.* When a specific behavior is adopted by several people within the network, it acquires legitimacy, at least internally to that part of the network (Grindereng, 1967).
4. *Emotional contagion.* Most theoretical models of collective behavior share the basic assumption that there are expressive and symbolic impulses in human behavior that can be communicated and amplified in spatially and socially concentrated gatherings (Aminzade and McAdam, 2002; Collins, 2009).

The best-known complex contagion model for networks is the Watts threshold model (Watts, 2002). This is an evolution of a deterministic SI model. In this model, in addition to a degree, each node i has a randomly chosen threshold value $0 < \phi_i < 1$. At the beginning of the simulation, a random set of nodes is chosen to begin in state I. At each time step, nodes in state S change to state I if at least a fraction ϕ_i of their neighbors are in state I, remaining there forever. In this model, ϕ replaces β as the information spreading parameter.

Relative versus Absolute Threshold Models

In social networks, it is important to differentiate between relative and absolute threshold models. Watts's model, whose transition diagram is represented in Figure 9.4, is a relative threshold model. In relative threshold models, what matters is the fraction of connections: if you only have 3 connections, you may be willing to form an opinion or adopt a behavior if two of them differ from you, whereas in the scenario where you have 300, it may take 200 of them to change your state. Collective actions, such as participation in a given social network, generally fall into this category, as non-adopters are generally assumed to belong to a competing service. In contrast, for an absolute threshold model (Granovetter, 1978), what matters is the simple number of contacts: a threshold might be, for example, 3 contacts, regardless of whether you have 3 connections or 300. Belief in urban legends, rumors, or conspiracy theories may best be modeled by an absolute threshold model. A single connection is likely insufficient, but the presence of nonbelieving connections does not hinder the adoption of the belief.

Absolute threshold models are generally less studied than relative threshold models, as they lack the qualitatively different phenomena that relative threshold models show. Instead, absolute threshold models show similar behavior to

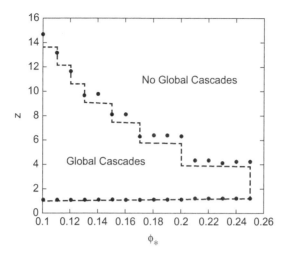

Figure 9.4. Phase diagram reproduced from Watts (2002) showing the emergence and disappearance of global cascades as the threshold parameter ϕ and average network degree z for a uniform random graph. Watts, Duncan J. 2002. A Simple Model of Global Cascades on Random Networks. *Proceedings of the National Academy of Sciences (PNAS)*, 99(9). Copyright (2002) National Academy of Sciences, USA.

simple information spreading, only with a higher critical threshold and lower cascade sizes.

The aforementioned models have qualitatively different features from the simple contagion model. In particular, while adding connections in a simple contagion model can only enhance spreading, in a relative threshold model, adding connections tends to suppress spreading, because every new link increases the number of infected neighbors you must have on average to become infected yourself. In fact, for a given average threshold ϕ, spreading can only occur on networks with $1 < \langle k \rangle < 1/\phi$.

Before moving on to multilayer networks, a brief note on clustering for both relative and absolute threshold models: although clustering does not have a large impact on the critical threshold, Centola et al. (2007) show that for small average degrees, a highly clustered structure decreases the expected size of global cascades, whereas after a certain value of average degree, clustering increases the expected cascade size.

9.3.1 Extension to Multilayer Networks

There are several different approaches when considering threshold models on multilayer networks. The naive approach of flattening the network almost invariably produces a network with an average degree that is far too high for any cascade to exist. Brummitt et al. (2012) instead developed a model where an actor becomes infected if any layer it is present in exceeds its threshold criteria: $\phi < \max(I_i/k_i)$, where I_i are the number of infected neighbors in layer i. As more layers are added, the area where global cascades occur increases. An interesting feature of this model is that cascades can occur even when one layer is above the threshold at which cascades would normally disappear, as long as another layer is below this threshold, and vice versa. Thus, by adding isolated (or highly connected) communities, information can be spread in communities that are otherwise too highly connected (or isolated) for this to occur.

Yagan and Gligor (2012) have introduced an alternate extension of the Watts threshold model. Here the threshold value is calculated by summing the parameters across all the layers, and each layer has an associated influence strength c_i, which may take on any positive value. This represents that, for example, in determining which programming language to learn, your work colleagues may be more influential than your friends. The threshold condition for an m-layer is thus

$$\phi_i < \frac{\sum_{i=1}^{m} c_i I_i}{\sum_{i=1}^{m} c_i k_i} \tag{9.16}$$

This model shows some similar features to the preceding one, namely, that by varying c_i, the epidemic threshold can be made to appear and vanish depending on the nature of layers. In particular, for $c_i > 1$, cascades can occur even when all layers have $\langle k_i \rangle < 1$.

9.3.2 Other Diffusion Processes

Although this chapter focuses on contagion-based information and behavior diffusion, we would be remiss if we did not at least briefly mention the many other important types of diffusion research that, while not necessarily directly relevant to social networks, may have indirect applications or provide insight into the history of the field of multilayer networks in general. Although many diffusion processes have been investigated on multilayer networks, including synchronization (Gambuzza et al., 2015), competing information (Sahneh et al., 2014), and even the spread of bankruptcies (Brummitt and Kobayashi, 2015), we would like in particular to highlight three. For a more thorough survey, please consult Salehi et al. (2015).

One of the first and most important diffusion problems studied in the model known as network of networks was that of cascading failures (Buldyrev et al., 2010). Inspired by the 2003 blackout that affected all of Italy, Buldyrev et al.

(2010) showed that, far from being a freak accident, the vulnerability of interdependent networks to catastrophic failure was an intrinsic property of the system. Still an active and important area of research, to the best of our knowledge, this kind of cascade has not been studied in the context of social networks, and there is no obvious scenario where nodes represent human beings.

More saliently, the voter model has also been recently extended to the multilayer network case. The voter model (Clifford and Sudbury, 1973) is a standard framework for studying how social imitation leads to opinion formation and can be thought of as a kind of I_1I_2 model, where initially each individual is in one of two states and may change the state of his neighbors to match. Previously much studied on single-layer networks, Diakonova et al. (2014) found a novel phase transition between consensus and "shattered" phases depending on the network parameters in the multilayer model. This topic is an object of current research – for example, in their still unpublished work, Chmiel and Sznajd-Weron (2015) extend the simple case to a (unanimous) threshold model and claim that for socially realistic models, multilayer networks produce significant changes in observed behavior. Diakonova et al. (2015) also claim that attempts to reduce a multilayer network to a single layer may produce large deviations in behavior, once again highlighting the necessity to properly treat layer multiplicity. We expect research in this area to expand in the coming years.

Lastly, game theoretic approaches on networks (Galeotti, 2010) constitute a fascinating topic worthy of a book in its own right that is being extended in new and novel ways to multilayer networks. Much as contagion models were first solved in the uniform mixing case and later extended to networks, so has been the concept of strategic equilibrium: given that not every game player is connected to every other, which strategies will survive or dominate? A sample of research in this area includes the work by Gómez-Gardeñes et al. (2012), who showed that the survival of cooperation in multilayer networks is intrinsically linked to the network structure, and by Ramezanian et al. (2015), who derived an initial framework for how network structure impacts strategy adoption.

PART IV

Conclusion

10

Future Directions

In order to complete the range of thy experience, I conduct thee
downward to the lowest depth of existence, even to the realm of
Pointland, the Abyss of No dimensions.

– The Sphere

Multilayer networks constitute an extremely active field of research. While we
were writing this manuscript, we had to change, update, and amend the text
many times because of all the relevant research and ideas that were being published. Despite all our efforts, we are certain that much new research, and possibly some major advances, will be published before this book becomes available.

This should probably be considered a good sign and will not undermine the
main goal of the volume: besides providing an introduction to multilayer social
networks and a set of initial concepts and metrics to introduce the reader to this
exciting area, our main objective was to suggest an initial organization of the
material in this area, which is still spread across multiple research fields that
have only recently begun talking regularly to each other.

Getting to the topic of this chapter, as it often happens when research areas
are extremely heterogeneous and are being developed autonomously by scholars as different as physicists, computer scientists, and sociologists, it is not easy
to identify a single clear direction for future research, and even trying to provide a frame to what exists poses serious challenges. We often had to make
hard choices to propose a structure that was as homogeneous as possible and
still cover the major areas of research – and we are aware that we have not
completely reached this objective.

Although we are fully aware of all these limitations, and although we do not
think that this work could be as comprehensive as some of the existing volumes
on traditional social network analysis or network theory, we think that this kind
of work can help a diverse and dispersed community to be more aware of what

is going on and to settle some key concepts before moving forward. Following this ambition, we have decided to conclude this book by outlining some of what we think might constitute future research trends of broad interest in this field.

10.1 New Models and Measures

Recent studies in multilayer SNA have adopted complex models, allowing the representation of generic sets of features on both edges and nodes. However, many of these studies have been either theoretical or applied to well-known, controlled, and specific data, for example, bibliographic publication networks. For what concerns this book, that is, the specific case of social networks, the most obvious future research direction is the application of existing models and measures to a larger number of real-world scenarios.

Particular for social networks, and especially for online social networks, there is an exciting opportunity to combine network analysis with natural language processing to analyze how content drives network structure. Homophily has been shown for almost every attribute humans possess, and it would be useful and interesting to confirm or deny that this is true, for example, for the language, sentiment, or topics of their social media content.

Partially owing to the heterogeneous nature of the research areas that inspired them, the various models that we have described have generated different frameworks and software tools that can be used to perform the required analyses. Both the young MuxViz[1] package and the more established Statnet[2] are moving toward a more user-friendly graphical user interface. However, a general understanding of the R software environment (or other programming languages) is still required, as is also the case for the multinet[3] library that we used to compute most of the analyses in the book. Preferences for a specific framework might also play a role in the choice of a model. We must consider this coevolution of tool and model development and, it is hoped, try to minimize the fragmentation based on this diversity, while not being unnecessarily constrained.

Although it has been shown for most of the new measures that they can find something not measurable using traditional approaches, we do not have a clear understanding of the interpretability of these findings in the context of a social network, and it is also unclear whether those motivating examples for these

[1] http://www.muxviz.net/.
[2] http://statnet.csde.washington.edu/.
[3] https://github.com/magnanim/multiplenetwork.

measures – for example, the presence of actors with an important bridging role between layers but unimportant inside each single layer – occur in real data.

For what concerns the practical usage of multilayer networks, a topic that has not been investigated in detail is the management of missing data. In particular, we still need to understand the effect of specific types of missing data on the results of analysis measures and data mining methods and to develop solutions for those cases where a significant effect is expected. Various imputation techniques have been proposed in the past to recover or estimate missing data (Sadikov et al., 2011). Although no general approach can guarantee a general solution to the missing data problem, imputation methods as well as approaches based on data removal are often used in research practices concerning single-layer networks.

At the same time, not all the measures developed for traditional SNA have been extended for multilayer models, and some, like betweenness, have been extended in multiple ways, leading to very correlated measures where it is still unclear whether their small differences are significant. So far most of the research on multilayer networks has focused on combinations of simple and homogenous types of layers, for example, with undirected edges among the same set of actors. The most immediate future development that we expect is the study of multilayer models including combinations of directed networks, bipartite networks, attributed graphs, and even more features unified in the same model. The greater flexibility offered by multilayer networks will allow researchers to represent and study social phenomena that, until now, required an excessive level of simplification. As an example, an interesting aspect would be to evaluate new metrics specific to time-varying phenomena on multilayer social networks.

Some of the measures that over the years have been developed for single-layer networks have already been extended to multilayer networks: we have presented many of these in Chapter 3, and it is easy to predict that more will come. Nevertheless, we hope also to see a growing number of new metrics that move beyond what already exists. The extension of traditional concepts is undoubtedly necessary, and in some cases, it might constitute a challenging goal. It might be perceived as the continuation, within a different set of network models, of the work on multiple relations that has been an ongoing process in areas such as relational algebra applied to multiplex networks. At the same time, we believe that the new conceptual structure introduced by multilayer networks offers the opportunity to define new measures and concepts that were simply impossible with single-layer models. What these might be and how this will happen is hard to say: some examples are the measures of layer relevance, which make no sense without multiple layers. Looking at the history of how the most common metrics have been introduced, we can say that often these have emerged as attempts to address practical problems (from centrality in groups to strength of communities); therefore we might expect that the same will happen as soon as multilayer models step outside the domain of synthetic networks and real cases are investigated.

While multilayer data collection is undoubtedly more complex than single-layer data collection, the growing availability of OSN data as well as the digital traces left by a growing number of everyday social interactions (from phone calls to physical proximity) will probably produce an increasing number of multilayer network data sets. Among the various metrics that could be introduced, we hope, at least for applications within the field of the social sciences, that researchers will focus on those metrics that can explain how actors manage their identities and their relational resources through multiple layers of social connections. What pushes the various layers that define our everyday experience toward a higher or lower level of similarity? What kinds of strategies do actors implement to maintain separate social contexts by limiting the similarities between various layers? Among others that might have more theoretical foundations, these questions seem to be extremely timely owing to the increasing social concern about what has been defined as the collapse of context.

Another important research direction would be to explore how these metrics affect the propagation of information. As an example, it would be interesting to measure the correlation between metrics indicating the presence of multilayer communities (Bothorel et al., 2015) and the metrics to characterize spreading processes summarized in this paper.

Quite obviously, metrics enable the measurement of multilayer social networks and are thus necessary elements to expand the study of multilayer networks in a large variety of areas, as we see later.

10.2 Multilayer Network Visualization

An old motto says that "seeing is believing." Indeed, many phenomena are first observed, and then suitable models are built to explain the observations, and there is no doubt that the sociograms and their accessibility have helped greatly the diffusion of SNA and a general familiarity with network concepts. To be able to see the most central actor or to have a visual understanding of the community structure of a network is a great advantage both for seasoned researchers and for the larger public of potential readers. Although visual exploration and manipulation of single-layer networks has been a major area of development during recent years (think, e.g., of the huge popularity reached by software like Gephi (Bastian et al., 2009), offering a visual approach to network analysis), only a few works have addressed the problem of multilayer network visualization.

As we have pointed out in Chapter 5, even though using 3-dimensional models (or, more precisely, 2.5-dimensional representations) to visualize multilayer networks might appear as the most obvious thing to do, showing great continuity with traditional visualization approaches, there might be limits – as they exist for single-layer networks – to how many layers or nodes can be effectively visualized. The aforementioned early works on multilayer network visualization have not been corroborated by third-party studies, being very recent. Within this perspective, we see two possible directions: one is to continue the already existing work on algorithms for network visualization in the multilayer domain, for example, extending force-based layouts to consider both intra- and interlayer edges, which has not been done yet, to the best of our knowledge; the second one is to develop new approaches to network visualization that move beyond the initial idea of the sociogram. An intriguing aspect of this second direction is that rethinking a deeply intuitive concept like the sociogram is a challenge that can hardly be accomplished within a single discipline but will require a truly interdisciplinary approach ranging from visual arts and design to computer science.

Whatever the future of multilayer network visualization may be, in our opinion, it will have an impact on two main areas of research: information diffusion and community analysis. In both cases, the approaches based on sociograms have been extremely successful in giving us a good grasp of network phenomena, but how these could be visualized within multilayer structures and if it will be possible to use these visualizations to explore multilayer network data remain open problems.

10.3 Communities and Other Groups

Community detection in multilayer networks is an active research area, and as such, it presents a number of open problems. As we have seen in Chapter 6, many existing methods come from the combination of two well-established areas: graph clustering and multidimensional relational clustering. Therefore we can see two main classes of open problems: challenges particular to the graph clustering task that are also present when single-layer data are considered, which are the easiest to list, as they have also been discussed in the literature, and those specifically related to the combination of multiple layers.

An example of the first category are algorithms to discover overlapping clusters. While the majority of graph clustering methods partition the nodes of the graph into disjoint sets, many authors have pointed out that in real contexts, individuals often belong to multiple communities. For simple graphs, this has motivated the development of specific methods: as an example, Wang et al. (2011) developed an extended version of modularity applicable to overlapping clusters. However, there are still open questions, such as how to measure the significance of overlapping nodes and how to interpret the resulting communities (Xie et al., 2013). Some work in this direction exists, for example, Yang et al. (2013) have used multilayer networks for detecting overlapping communities, stating that the resulting communities can be interpreted more easily by analyzing the attributes of the nodes belonging to each community. However, quality and interpretation issues are, again, still open questions.

The second category of open problems includes the exponential explosion in the number of layer combinations to be considered during the clustering process. Although this is a well-known problem in relational data mining, it does not apply to traditional community detection, and thus it has not been addressed in this context before. Despite some promising attempts to address this problem developed in the area of subspace clustering, in our opinion, this aspect demands a lot more research to be able to apply clustering algorithms to real multilayer social networks, for example, to evaluate the effects of specific heuristics. Given the intrinsic computational complexity of the problem, a possible direction involves the consideration of domain knowledge to focus the community detection process on promising combinations of dimensions.

As a last relevant problem, early works on community detection on multilayer networks have focused on finding static communities, which is a preliminary and necessary step to study their evolution. Here researchers can partially reuse the same approaches used to find evolving communities on simple graphs, in particular the comparison of nodes clustered at different time stamps to identify evolutionary steps (*create*, *merge*, *split*, etc.). However, the existence of communities spanning multiple layers may also require a revision of the concept of the evolutionary step developed for single-layer communities.

While community detection represents one of the main tasks in network analysis, actors can be grouped in other ways. In particular, there is a long tradition in SNA about the identification of actors having the same position in a network and actors playing the same role – two types of groups that have been typically addressed using block modeling methods. We refer the reader to a recent paper by Vega et al. (2015) that extends a block modeling approach so that multilayer measures can be included in the method – for example, to find all actors with a bridging role between layers.

10.4 Formation, Diffusion, and Temporal Processes

The last area of future development we want to discuss is related to all the dynamical processes that can be studied on multilayer networks. These processes are still actively studied in the context of single-layer networks, and a multilayer approach seems to be able to offer new promising research directions. In addition, dynamical processes are strictly related to other nondynamical aspects: as an example, in Chapter 8, we have presented some models describing the forces leading to a specific structure of a multilayer social network. How is this related to community detection? Which models generate multilayer social networks exposing a modular structure? Among dynamical processes, spreading processes, in particular, offer many unsolved problems to address, and here we identify some that we consider very relevant.

As we have discussed in different parts of the book, collecting real multilayer data is not easy (Stopczynski et al., 2014), but it is even harder when one tries to gather data on both the spreading process and the structure of the underlying multilayer network. So far almost every existing work on multilayer network diffusion has been based on synthetic data, but despite the undeniable challenges, this kind of research is necessary if we want to be able to test models and theories against real-world phenomena. One of the major challenges to be faced in collecting these kinds of data is that there are few companies, organizations, or institutions owning many layers about the same actors. While to some extent, this is reassuring in terms of surveillance on our activities, it constitutes a problem from a research perspective. Network sampling strategies can be used to address this issue by reducing the complexity and the cost of collecting large, real multilayer networks (Mehdiabadi et al., 2012b; Salehi and Rabiee, 2013). Thus it is worth exploring how different sampling approaches can impact the measurement of spreading processes (Mehdiabadi et al., 2012a).

The study of behavior propagation is extremely interesting within a multilayer structure because it requires the development of suitable diffusion models that take into consideration the existence and interactions of different layers with different properties and qualitative values. Whether we are focusing on information propagation or on behavior diffusion, an obvious research direction would be to combine this with temporal information. Networks exhibit a mutable structure, meaning that nodes and links change over time (Holme and Saramäki, 2012). Spreading processes on dynamic single-layer networks have received a lot of attention (Vazquez et al., 2007; Volz and Meyers, 2009; Taylor et al., 2012; Gauvin et al., 2013). However, studying this problem in time-varying multilayer networks is more difficult (Snijders et al., 2013). Given the large interest in the topic of propagation and the interesting perspective opened by the multilayer approach, we expect to see many more studies in this area in the future.

While simple information is well studied, the more complicated versions of information spreading are only now starting to receive attention and will likely become more and more popular in future years. In particular, voter models on networks provide valuable insights into political and belief structures that even complex contagions cannot model.

The interactions between network evolution and spreading processes have also received attention with respect to single-layer networks: the underlying assumption is that how the network is used to propagate the information can explain how the network is going to evolve (Gross et al., 2006; Gross and Blasius, 2008; Marceau et al., 2011; Rossi and Magnani, 2012). This problem becomes more complex when multilayer social networks are considered, raising interesting questions such as if the communication that is happening on a layer can determine a change in a different layer.

As a final point, outbreak detection is a task that aims at identifying the large propagation of items in a network as early as possible (Leskovec et al., 2007). In our opinion, the problem of outbreak detection is also worth exploring in the area of multilayer social networks, with potential applications in the early identification of online social media misinformation that might have dangerous effects – as an example, people diffusing unverified information about policemen killing demonstrators that could finally lead to violent behavior.

10.5 Big Open Data

A common problem that emerged in the previous sections of this chapter, certainly a problem not unique to SNA, is the challenge of obtaining real data. Synthetic models are useful for generalizations, analytical tractability, and experimentation, but the ability to connect our results and prove our predictions in real-world situations is useful within academia and mandatory everywhere else. There are numerous technical, legal, economic, political, and even moral challenges around collecting social data in particular. The technical challenges around efficient algorithms and efficient storage are likely to increase as we become more and more interconnected in more and more ways, but similarly we can expect these widely useful technologies to improve, demanding only that we stay abreast of ongoing technical developments. More challenging will be the legal and economic issues of acquiring and sharing data: the value of social network data is increasing, and persuading the companies that own those data to share them for collaborative advancement is a serious challenge. Lastly are the political and moral challenges regarding privacy. Anonymization methods previously thought to be sufficient are being shown to be inadequate, and in highly interconnected multilayer networks, information about one layer can be leveraged to reveal information in many others. Of course, even should these challenges be overcome, these large open data sets will certainly raise new research challenges and reveal unexplained phenomena.

Thank you for reading, and we leave you with this final thought:

> Yet I exist in the hope that these memoirs, in some manner, I know not how, may find their way to the minds of humanity in Some Dimension, and may stir up a race of rebels who shall refuse to be confined to limited Dimensionality. (Abbott, 1884, p. 100)

Glossary

2-star Three nodes, with one node in the center with two adjacent edges connecting it to the two other nodes. A triangle contains three 2-stars, depending on which node we consider in the center.

Actor One of the real-world entities whose connections are studied in SNA, for example, an individual in a social network.

Adjacency matrix A matrix where the element (i, j) indicates whether nodes i and j are connected (1) or not (0), or the weight of the connection.

Assortativity Indicates a preference for actors to connect with similar actors.

Betweenness A widely used indicator of nodes' centrality in networks. It measures the proportion of shortest paths in a network passing through a specific node or edge.

Clique A set of nodes in an undirected graph where for each pair of nodes there is an edge between them.

Closeness centrality A popular indicator of actor centrality in networks. It measures how close an actor is to all the other actors of a network on average.

Clustering coefficient A measure of how much actors tend to form groups in a network. For an actor, it is defined as the ratio between the number of edges between its neighbors and the number of potential edges between them. On a global level, it can be computed as the average clustering coefficient among all nodes with at least two neighbors.

Connected component A set of nodes in a network where for every pair of nodes there is a path connecting them.

Degree A widely used indicator of actor centrality in networks. It measures the number of edges adjacent to an actor.

Diameter The maximum distance between two nodes in a network.

Directed network A network characterized by directional relations, for example, $A \rightarrow B$.

Distance Length of one of the shortest paths between two nodes. It is the smallest number of edges that has to be traversed to move from node A to node B.

Dyad A subgroup of two nodes.

Edge A relationship between two nodes, for example, a *following* relationship between two nodes representing two Twitter accounts. Synonyms used in the literature include *link, arc, (relational) tie, bond, connection.*

179

Exclusive relevance A measure of the impact of removing a set of layers on the connectivity of an actor.

Facebook Launched in 2004, it is the most used OSN in the world. Users signed in to the system can create profiles, add other users to their friends, write private messages and public messages (posts), share pictures and videos, and participate in discussions organized in groups or fan pages.

Fad A strong but short-lived enthusiasm for something.

Giant component On an empirical social network, this term is used to indicate the largest connected component when this contains a large portion of the nodes. On random graphs, a giant component is said to be present when, independently of the size of the network, there is a high probability to find a connected component containing a large fraction of the nodes; that is, the bigger the network we generate, the larger the component becomes.

Gossip Talking about personal affairs of individuals. This term also refers to a class of algorithms based on nodes in a network exchanging information with neighbors to solve a global problem.

Graph A mathematical representation of entities (nodes) connected by some relationships (edges).

Hashtag On Twitter, a keyword starting with the symbol #.

Interdependence The proportion of shortest paths traversing multiple layers over the number of all shortest paths.

k-Core (of a graph) A (connected) subgraph where all nodes have degree at least k.

Layer Part of a multilayer network used to organize nodes and edges into different groups, for example, different OSNs.

LinkedIn Launched in 2003, it is a business-oriented OSN. Users signed in to the system can create profiles, add other users to their contacts, write private messages, share content, and upload a professional CV.

Multigraph A graph where multiple edges can be present between the same pair of nodes.

Multiplex relationship A relationship existing over a number of cultural domains. Multiplex relationships are usually broad and general rather than specific and concrete.

Node An element of a graph. Formally, an element $v \in V$ in a graph $G = (V, E)$. A node typically represents an actor (e.g., an individual in a social network) or some projection of an actor (e.g., an account on an OSN). Synonyms used in the literature include *vertex* and *site*.

Path A sequence of edges sharing common end points, for example, an edge between n_i and n_j followed by an edge between n_j and n_k.

Relevance A measure of the impact of a set of layers on the connectivity of an actor.

Simple graph A graph with at most one edge between any pair of nodes (as opposed to multigraphs, where multiple edges are allowed), with only one type of edge and with no edges between a node and itself. Formally, a simple graph is a pair $G = (V, E)$, where V is a set of nodes and $E \subseteq V \times V$, with $(v, v) \notin V$.

Snowball sampling It is a sampling strategy that relies on existing connections between the actors under investigation. Subjects already involved in the data collection recruit future subjects among their acquaintances. It is widely used when the population to study is hidden or difficult to reach.

Social aggregator Social network aggregation platforms are meta social networks that allow users to to share, through a unified profile, contents and activities originally produced within other OSNs.

Transitivity A measure of the tendency to close triangles in a network. If T is the number of triangles and S is the number of 2-stars, transitivity is defined as $\frac{3T}{S}$ (where 3 is due to the fact that for every triangle there are three corresponding 2-stars).

Triad A subgroup of three nodes.

Triangle A subgroup of three nodes with an edge between any two of them.

Twitter It is an OSN. Users signed in to the system can create profiles and share private or public messages of maximum 140 characters called *tweets*. Users can follow each others' tweets, but the system does not force a reciprocal relation. Although tweets are usually visible only to the followers of a user, they can be aggregated using hashtags.

Bibliography

Abbott, Edwin A. 1884. *Flatland: A romance of many dimensions*. Seely.

Adamic, Lada A., Lukose, Rajan M., Puniyani, Amit R., and Huberman, Bernardo A. 2001. Search in power-law networks. *Physical Review E*, **64**(4), 046135.

Ahmad, Muhammad Aurangzeb, Borbora, Zoheb, Srivastava, Jaideep, and Contractor, Noshir. 2010. Link prediction across multiple social networks. Pages 911–918 of *International Conference on Data Mining Workshops*. IEEE.

Alamsyah, Andry, and Rahardjo, Budi. 2014. Community detection methods in social network analysis. *Advanced Science Letters*, **20**(1), 250–253.

Allard, Antoine, Noël, Pierre-André, Dubé, Louis J., and Pourbohloul, Babak. 2009. Heterogeneous bond percolation on multitype networks with an application to epidemic dynamics. *Physical Review E*, **79**(3), 036113.

Amaral, Luis A. Nunes, Scala, Antonio, Barthelemy, Marc, and Stanley, H. Eugene. 2000. Classes of small-world networks. *Proceedings of the National Academy of Sciences*, **97**(21), 11149–11152.

Aminzade, Ron, and McAdam, Doug. 2002. Emotions and contentious politics. *Mobilization: An International Quarterly*, **7**(2), 107–109.

Anderson, Roy M., and May, Robert M. 1992. *Infectious Diseases of Humans: Dynamics and Control*. Oxford University Press.

Aral, Sinan, and Walker, Dylan. 2011. Creating social contagion through viral product design: A randomized trial of peer influence in networks. *Management Science*, **57**(9), 1623–1639.

Atig, Mohamed Faouzi, Cassel, Sofia, Kaati, Lisa, and Shrestha, Amendra. 2014. Activity profiles in online social media. Pages 850–855 of *Advances in Social Networks Analysis and Mining (ASONAM)*. IEEE.

Avrachenkov, Konstantin, Ribeiro, Bruno, and Towsley, Don. 2010. Improving random walk estimation accuracy with uniform restarts. Pages 98–109 of *Algorithms and Models for the Web-Graph*. Springer.

Bakshy, Eytan, Rosenn, Itamar, Marlow, Cameron, and Adamic, Lada A. 2012. The role of social networks in information diffusion. Pages 519–528 of *International Conference on World Wide Web (WWW)*. ACM.

Barabási, Albert-László. 2002. *Linked: How Everything Is Connected to Everything Else and What It Means for Business, Science, and Everyday Life*. Basic Books.

Barabási, Albert-László, and Albert, Réka. 1999. Emergence of scaling in random networks. *Science*, **286**(5439), 509–512.

Barber, Michael J. 2007. Modularity and community detection in bipartite networks. *Physical Review E*, **76**, 066102.

Barigozzi, Matteo, Fagiolo, Giorgio, and Garlaschelli, Diego. 2010. Multinetwork of international trade: A commodity-specific analysis. *Physical Review E*, **81**(4), 046104.

Barrett, Louise, Henzi, Peter, and Lusseau, David. 2012. Taking sociality seriously: The structure of multi-dimensional social networks as a source of information for individuals. *Philosophical Transactions of the Royal Society of London, Series B*, **367**(1599), 2108–2118.

Barthélemy, Marc, Barrat, Alain, Pastor-Satorras, Romualdo, and Vespignani, Alessandro. 2004. Velocity and hierarchical spread of epidemic outbreaks in scale-free networks. *Physical Review Letters*, **92**(17), 178701.

Bastian, Mathieu, Heymann, Sebastien, and Jacomy, Mathieu. 2009. Gephi: An open source software for exploring and manipulating networks. Pages 361–362 of *International Conference on Weblogs and Social Media*, vol. 8. AAAI.

Battiston, Federico, Nicosia, Vincenzo, and Latora, Vito. 2014. Structural measures for multiplex networks. *Physical Review E*, **89**(3), 032804.

Bearman, Peter S., Moody, James, and Stovel, Katherine. 2004. Chains of affection: The structure of adolescent romantic and sexual networks. *American Journal of Sociology*, **110**(1), 44–91.

Ben-David, Shai, and Ackerman, Margareta. 2008. Measures of clustering quality: A working set of axioms for clustering. Pages 121–128 of *Advances in Neural Information Processing Systems*. NIPS Foundation.

Bennacer, Nacéra, Nana Jipmo, Coriane, Penta, Antonio, and Quercini, Gianluca. 2014. Matching user profiles across social networks. Pages 424–438 of *Advanced Information Systems Engineering*. Lecture Notes in Computer Science, vol. 8484. Springer International.

Berlingerio, Michele, Coscia, Michele, and Giannotti, Fosca. 2011a. Finding and characterizing communities in multidimensional networks. Pages 490–494 of *International Conference on Advances in Social Networks Analysis and Mining (ASONAM)*. IEEE.

Berlingerio, Michele, Coscia, Michele, and Giannotti, Fosca. 2011b. Finding redundant and complementary communities in multidimensional networks. Pages 2181–2184 of *International Conference on Information and Knowledge Management (CIKM)*. ACM.

Berlingerio, Michele, Coscia, Michele, Giannotti, Fosca, Monreale, Anna, and Pedreschi, Dino. 2011c. Foundations of multidimensional network analysis. Pages 485–489 of *International conference on Social Network Analysis and Mining (ASONAM)*. IEEE.

Berlingerio, Michele, Pinelli, Fabio, and Calabrese, Francesco. 2013. ABACUS: Frequent pAttern mining-BAsed Community discovery in mUltidimensional networkS. *Data Mining and Knowledge Discovery*, **27**(3), 294–320.

Bernard, H. Russel, Killworth, Peter, Kronenfeld, David, and Sailer, Lee. 1984. The problem of informant accuracy: The validity of retrospective data. *Annual Review of Anthropology*, **13**(1), 495–517.

Bernard, Jessie. 2012. *Sociology of Community: A Collection of Readings*. Routledge.

Bertini, Flavio, Sharma, Rajesh, Iannì, Andrea, and Montesi, Danilo. 2015. Profile resolution across multilayer networks through smartphone camera fingerprint. Pages 23–32 of *International Database Engineering and Applications Symposium (IDEAS)*. ACM.

Bhargava, Mudit, Mehndiratta, Pulkit, and Asawa, Krishna. 2013. Stylometric analysis for authorship attribution on Twitter. Pages 37–47 of *Big Data Analytics*. Lecture Notes in Computer Science, vol. 8302. Springer International.

Boccaletti, Stefano, Bianconi, Ginestra, Criado, Regino, Del Genio, Charo I., Gómez-Gardeñes, Jesús, Romance, Miguel, Sendiña Nadal, Irene, Wang, Zhen, and Zanin, Massimiliano. 2014. The structure and dynamics of multilayer networks. *Physics Reports*, **544**(1), 1–122.

Boden, Brigitte, Günnemann, Stephan, Hoffmann, Holger, and Seidl, Thomas. 2012. Mining coherent subgraphs in multi-layer graphs with edge labels. Pages 1258–1266 of *International Conference on Knowledge Discovery and Data Mining (KDD)*. ACM.

Bonchi, Francesco, Gionis, Aristides, Gullo, Francesco, and Ukkonen, Antti. 2012. Chromatic correlation clustering. Pages 1321–1329 of *International Conference on Knowledge Discovery and Data Mining (KDD)*. ACM.

Borgatti, Stephen P, and Everett, Martin G. 2006. A graph-theoretic perspective on centrality. *Social Networks*, **28**(4), 466–484.

Borgatti, Stephen P., Mehra, Ajay, Brass, Daniel J., and Labianca, Giuseppe. 2009. Network analysis in the social sciences. *Science*, **323**(5916), 892–895.

Bothorel, Cecile, Cruz, Juan David, Magnani, Matteo, and Micenkova, Barbora. 2015. Clustering attributed graphs: models, measures and methods. *Network Science*, **3**(3), 408–444.

Bott, Helen. 1928. Observation of play activities in a nursery school. *Genetic Psychology Monographs*, **4**, 44–88.

boyd, danah. 2008. *Taken Out of Context: American Teen Sociality in Networked Publics*. PhD thesis, University of California, Berkeley.

Bright, David A., Greenhill, Catherine, Ritter, Alison, and Morselli, Carlo. 2015. Networks within networks: Using multiple link types to examine network structure and identify key actors in a drug trafficking operation. *Global Crime*, **16**(3), 219–237.

Bródka, Piotr, Skibicki, Krzysztof, Kazienko, Przemyslaw, and Musial, Katarzyna. 2011a. A degree centrality in multi-layered social network. Pages 237–242 of *International Conference on Computational Aspects of Social Networks (CASoN)*. IEEE.

Bródka, Piotr, Stawiak, Pawel, and Kazienko, Przemyslaw. 2011b. Shortest path discovery in the multi-layered social network. Pages 497–501 of *International Conference on Social Network Analysis and Mining (ASONAM)*. IEEE.

Bródka, Piotr, Kazienko, Przemyslaw, Musial, Katarzyna, and Skibicki, Krzysztof. 2012. Analysis of neighbourhoods in multi-layered dynamic social networks. *International Journal of Computational Intelligence Systems*, **5**(3), 582–596.

Bródka, Piotr, Filipowski, Tomasz, and Kazienko, Przemyslaw. 2013. An introduction to community detection in multi-layered social networks. Pages 185–190 of *Information Systems, E-learning, and Knowledge Management Research*. Springer.

Brummitt, Charles D., and Kobayashi, Teruyoshi. 2015. Cascades in multiplex financial networks with debts of different seniority. *Physical Review E*, **91**(6), 62813.

Brummitt, Charles D., D'Souza, Raissa M., and Leicht, Elizabeth A. 2012. Suppressing cascades of load in interdependent networks. *Proceedings of the National Academy of Sciences of the United States of America*, **109**(12), E680–689.

Buldyrev, Sergey V., Parshani, Roni, Paul, Gerald, Stanley, H. Eugene, and Havlin, Shlomo. 2010. Catastrophic cascade of failures in interdependent networks. *Nature*, **464**(7291), 1025–1028.

Buono, Camila, Alvarez-Zuzek, Lucila G., Macri, Pablo A., and Braunstein, Lidia A. 2014. Epidemics in partially overlapped multiplex networks. *PloS One*, **9**(3), e104373.

Burt, Ronald S. 1987. A note on missing network data in the general social survey. *Social Networks*, **9**(1), 63–73.

Burt, Ronald S., and Schott, Thomas. 1989. Relational contents in multiple network systems. Pages 185–213 of *Research Methods in Social Network Analysis*. University of California, Irvine.

Cai, Deng, Shao, Zheng, He, Xiaofei, Yan, Xifeng, and Han, Jiawei. 2005a. Community mining from multi-relational networks. *European Conference on Principles and Practice of Knowledge Discovery in Databases*, **3721**, 445–452.

Cai, Deng, Shao, Zheng, He, Xiaofei, Yan, Xifeng, and Han, Jiawei. 2005b. Mining hidden community in heterogeneous social networks. Pages 58–65 of *International Workshop on Link Discovery (LinkKDD)*. ACM.

Celli, Fabio, Di Lascio, F. Marta L., Magnani, Matteo, Pacelli, Barbara, and Rossi, Luca. 2010. Social network data and practices: The case of Friendfeed. In: *International Conference on Social Computing, Behavioral Modeling and Prediction (SBP)*, vol. 6007. Lecture Notes in Computer Science. Springer.

Centola, Damon, and Macy, Michael. 2007. Complex contagions and the weakness of long ties. *American Journal of Sociology*, **113**(3), 702–734.

Centola, Damon, Eguíluz, Víctor M., and Macy, Michael W. 2007. Cascade dynamics of complex propagation. *Physica A: Statistical Mechanics and Its Applications*, **374**(1), 449–456.

Chmiel, Anna, and Sznajd-Weron, Katarzyna. 2015. Phase transitions in the q-voter model with noise on a duplex clique. *Physical Review E*, **92**(5),052812.

Clauset, Aaron, Shalizi, Cosma Rohilla, and Newman, Mark. E. J. 2009. Power-law distributions in empirical data. *SIAM Review*, **51**(4), 661–703.

Cleveland, William S., and McGill, Robert. 1984. Graphical perception: Theory, experimentation, and application to the development of graphical methods. *Journal of the American Statistical Association*, **79**(387), 531–554.

Clifford, Peter, and Sudbury, Aidan W. 1973. A model for spatial conflict. *Biometrika*, **60**, 581–588.

Collins, Randall. 1988. *Theoretical Sociology*. Harcourt College.

Collins, Randall. 2009. *The Sociology of Philosophies*. Harvard University Press.

Contractor, Noshir. 2009. The emergence of multidimensional networks. *Journal of Computer-Mediated Communication*, **14**(3), 743–747.

Coscia, Michele, Giannotti, Fosca, and Pedreschi, Dino. 2011. A classification for community discovery methods in complex networks. *Statistical Analysis and Data Mining*, **4**(5), 512–546.

Cozzo, Emanuele, Ba, Raquel A, Meloni, Sandro, and Moreno, Yamir. 2013. Contact-based social contagion in multiplex networks. *Physical Review E*, **88**(5), 050801.

Cozzo, Emanuele, Kivelä, Mikko, De Domenico, Manlio, Solé, Albert, Arenas, Alex, Gómez, Sergio, Porter, Mason A., and Moreno, Yamir. 2015. Structure of triadic relations in multiplex networks. *New Journal of Physics*, **17**, 073029.

D'Agostino, Gregorio, and Scala, Antonio (eds.). 2014. *Networks of Networks: The Last Frontier of Complexity*. Springer.

Danon, Leon, Díaz-Guilera, Albert, Duch, Jordi, and Arenas, Alex. 2005. Comparing community structrue identification. *Journal of Statistical Mechanics: Theory and Experiment*, **2005**(09), P09008.

Davis, Allison, Gardner, Burleigh B., and Gardner, Mary R. 1941. *Deep South: A Social Anthropological Study of Caste and Class*. University of Chicago Press.

De Domenico, Manlio, Porter, Mason A., and Arenas, Alex. 2014. MuxViz: A tool for multilayer analysis and visualization of networks. *Journal of Complex Networks*, **3**(2), 159–176.

De Domenico, Manlio, Solé-Ribalta, Albert, Omodei, Elisa, Gómez, Sergio, and Arenas, Alex. 2015a. Centrality in interconnected multilayer networks. *Nature Communications*, **6**, 6868.

De Domenico, Manlio, Nicosia, Vincenzo, Arenas, Alexandre, and Latora, Vito. 2015b. Structural reducibility of multilayer networks. *Nature Communications*, **6**.

Diakonova, Marina, San Miguel, Maxi, and Eguíluz, Víctor M. 2014. Absorbing and shattered fragmentation transitions in multilayer coevolution. *Physical Review E*, **89**(6), 62818.

Diakonova, Marina, Nicosia, Vincenzo, Latora, Vito, and Miguel, Maxi San. 2015. Irreducibility of multilayer network dynamics: The case of the voter model. *arXiv:1507.08940*.

Dickison, Mark, Havlin, S., and Stanley, H. E. 2012. Epidemics on interconnected networks. *Physical Review E*, **85**, 066109.

Du, Nan, Faloutsos, Christos, and Akoglu, Bai Wang Leman. 2009. Large human communication networks: Patterns and a utility-driven generator. Pages 1–9 of *International Conference on Knowledge Discovery and Data Mining (KDD)*. ACM.

Erdös, Paul, and Rényi, Alfréd. 1959. On random graphs. *Publicationes Mathematicae*, **6**, 290–297.

Fisher, Claude S. 1982. *To Dwell among Friends: Personal Networks in Town and City*. University of Chicago Press.

Fortunato, Santo. 2010. Community detection in graphs. *Physics Reports*, **486**(3–5), 75–174.

Fortunato, Santo, and Barthélemy, Marc. 2007. Resolution limit in community detection. *Proceedings of the National Academy of Sciences of the United States of America*, **104**(1), 36–41.

Frank, Ove. 1979. Sampling and estimation in large social networks. *Social Networks*, **1**(1), 91–101.

Frank, Ove. 2005. Network sampling and model fitting. Pp. 31–56 of *Models and Methods in Social Network Analysis*, Cambridge University Press.

Frank, Ove. 2011. Survey sampling in networks. Pp. 389–403 in *The SAGE Handbook of Social Network Analysis*. Sage.

Freeman, Linton C. 1979. Centrality in social networks conceptual clarification. *Social Networks*, **1**(1), 215–239.

Freeman, Linton C. 1992. The sociological concept of "group": An empirical test of two models. *American Journal of Sociology*, **98**(1), 152–166.

Freeman, Linton C. 1996. Some antecedents of social network analysis. *Connections*, **19**(1), 39–42.

Gaito, Sabrina, Rossi, Gian Paolo, and Zignani, Matteo. 2012. Facencounter: Bridging the gap between offline and online social networks. Pages 768–775 of *International Conference on Signal Image Technology and Internet Based Systems (SITIS)*. IEEE.

Galeotti, Andrea. 2010. Network games. *Review of Economic Studies*, **77**(1), 218–244.

Gambuzza, Lucia Valentina, Frasca, Mattia, and Gomez-Gardeñes, Jesus. 2015. Intra-layer synchronization in multiplex networks. *EPL (Europhysics Letters)*, **110**(2), 20010.

Garton, Laura, Haythornthwaite, Caroline, and Wellman, Barry. 2006. Studying online social networks. *Journal of Computer-Mediated Communication*, **3**(1).

Gauvin, Laetitia, Panisson, André, Cattuto, Ciro, and Barrat, Alain. 2013. Activity clocks: Spreading dynamics on temporal networks of human contact. *Scientific Reports*, **3**, 3099.

Giotis, Aristides, Giannakoglou, Kyriakos C., and Périaux, Jacques. 2000. A reduced-cost multi-objective optimization method based on the pareto front technique, neural networks and PVM. In *European Congress on Computational Methods in Applied Sciences and Engineering (ECCOMAS)*.

Girvan, Michelle, and Newman, Mark E. J. 2002. Community structure in social and biological networks. *Proceedings of the National Academy of Sciences*, **99**(12), 7821–7826.

Gjoka, Minas, Butts, Carter T, Kurant, Maciej, Markopoulou, Athina, and Member, Ieee. 2011. Multigraph sampling of online social networks. *IEEE Journal on Selected Areas in Communications*, **29**(9), 1893–1905.

Gladwell, Malcolm. 2006. *The Tipping Point: How Little Things Can Make a Big Difference*. Little, Brown.

Gluckman, Max. 1955. *The Judicial Process among the Barotse of Northern Rhodesia*. Manchester University Press.

Goga, Oana, Loiseau, Patrick, Sommer, Robin, Teixeira, Renata, and Gummadi, Krishna P. 2015. On the reliability of profile matching across large online social networks. Pages 1799–1808 of *International Conference on Knowledge Discovery and Data Mining (KDD)*. ACM.

Goltsev, A. V., Dorogovtsev, S. N., and Mendes, J. F. F. 2008. Percolation on correlated networks. *Physical Review E*, **78**(5), 51105.

Goltsev, Alexander V., Dorogovtsev, Sergey N., Oliveira, Joao G., and Mendes, Jose F. F. 2012. Localization and spreading of diseases in complex networks. *Physical Review Letters*, **109**(12), 128702.

Gómez-Gardeñes, Jesús, Reinares, Irene, Arenas, Alex, and Floría, Luis Mario. 2012. Evolution of cooperation in multiplex networks. *Scientific Reports*, **2**, 620.

Goodreau, Steven M. 2007. Advances in exponential random graph (p*) models applied to a large social network. *Social Networks*, **29**(2), 231–248.

Granovetter, M. 1978. Threshold models of collective behavior. *American Journal of Sociology*, **83**(6), 1420–1443.

Granovetter, Mark. 1976. Network sampling: Some first steps. *American Journal of Sociology*, **81**(6), 1287–1303.

Granovetter, Mark S. 1973. The strength of weak ties. *American Journal of Sociology*, **78**(6), 1360–1380.

Grindereng, Margaret P. 1967. Fashion diffusion. *Journal of Home Economics*, **59**(3), 171–174.

Gross, Thilo, and Blasius, Bernd. 2008. Adaptive coevolutionary networks: A review. *Journal of the Royal Society*, **5**(20), 259–271.

Gross, Thilo, D'Lima, Carlos, and Blasius, Bernd. 2006. Epidemic dynamics on an adaptive network. *Physical Review Letters*, **96**(20), 208701.

Guimera, Roger, Sales-Pardo, Marta, and Amaral, Luis A. Nunes. 2007. Module identification in bipartite and directed networks. *Physical Review E*, **76**, 036102.

Hakimi, Seifollah Louis. 1965. Optimum distribution of switching centers in a communication network and some related graph theoretic problems. *Operations Research*, **13**(3), 462–475.

Halu, Arda, Mondragón, Raul J., Panzarasa, Pietro, and Bianconi, Ginestra. 2013. Multiplex PageRank. *PloS One*, **8**(10), e78293.

Heider, Fritz. 1946. Attitudes and cognitive organization. *The Journal of Psychology*, **21**(1), 107–112.

Hoffman, Dean G., and Rodger, Christopher A. 1992. The chromatic index of complete multipartite graphs. *Journal of Graph Theory*, **16**(2), 159–163.

Hogan, Bernie. 2010. The presentation of self in the age of social media: Distinguishing performances and exhibitions online. *Bulletin of Science, Technology, and Society*, **30**(6), 377–386.

Holland, Paul W., and Leinhard, Samuel. 1973. Structural implications of measurement error in sociometry. *Journal of Mathematical Sociology*, **3**(1), 85–111.

Holme, Petter, and Saramäki, Jari. 2012. Temporal networks. *Physics Reports*, **519**(3), 97–125.

Hristova, Desislava, Musolesi, Mirco, and Mascolo, Cecilia. 2014. Keep your friends close and your Facebook friends closer: A multiplex network approach to the analysis of offline and online social ties. Article 8102 in *International Conference on Weblogs and Social Media (ICWSM)*. AAAI.

Huang, Lailei, and Liu, Jiming. 2010. Characterizing multiplex social dynamics with autonomy oriented computing. Pages 277–287 of *Life System Modeling and Intelligent Computing*. Springer.

Huberman, Bernardo A., and Adamic, Lada A. 2004. Information dynamics in the networked world. Pages 371–398 of *Complex Networks*. Springer.

Hubert, Lawrence, and Arabie, Phipps. 1985. Comparing partitions. *Journal of Classification*, **2**(1), 193–218.

Iacobucci, Dawn, and Wasserman, Stanley. 1990. Social networks with two sets of actors. *Psychometrika*, **55**(4), 707–720.

Iofciu, Tereza, Fankhauser, Peter, Abel, Fabian, and Bischoff, Kerstin. 2011. Identifying users across social tagging systems. Article 2779 in *International Conference on Weblogs and Social Media (ICWSM)*. AAAI.

Jaccard, Paul. 1901. Étude comparative de la distribution florale dans une portion des Alpes et des Jura. *Bulletin del la Société Vaudoise des Sciences Naturelles*, **37**, 547–579.

Jain, Paridhi, Kumaraguru, Ponnurangam, and Joshi, Anupam. 2013. @I Seek 'Fb.Me': Identifying users across multiple online social networks. Pages 1259–1268 of *International Conference on World Wide Web (WWW)*. ACM.

Jenkins, Henry, Li, Xiaochang, Krauskopf, Ana Domb, and Grean, J. B. 2009. *If It Doesn't Spread, It's Dead (Part One): Media Viruses and Memes*.

Jin, Emily, Girvan, Michelle, and Newman, Mark E. J. 2001. Structure of growing social networks. *Physical Review E*, **64**(4), 046132.

Johansson, Fredrik, Kaati, Lisa, and Shrestha, Amendra. 2013. Detecting multiple aliases in social media. Pages 1004–1011 of *Advances in Social Networks Analysis and Mining (ASONAM)*. ACM.

Johansson, Fredrik, Kaati, Lisa, and Shrestha, Amendra. 2015. Timeprints for identifying social media users with multiple aliases. *Security Informatics*, **4**(1).

Kadushin, Charles. 2012. *Understanding Social Networks: Theories, Concepts, and Findings*. Oxford University Press.

Kane, Gerald C., Alavi, Maryam, Labianca, Giuseppe Joe, and Borgatti, Steve. 2012. What's different about social media networks? A framework and research agenda. *MIS Quarterly*, **38**(1), 275–304.

Kapferer, Bruce. 1972. *Strategy and Transaction in an African Factory: African Workers and Indian Management in a Zambian Town*. Vol. 43. Manchester University Press.

Katz, Elihu, and Lazarsfeld, Paul Felix. 1955. *Personal Influence: The Part Played by People in the Flow of Mass Communications*. Free Press.

Kazienko, Przemysaw, Bródka, Piotr, Musial, Katarzyna, and Gaworecki, Jarosaw. 2010. Multi-layered social network creation based on bibliographic data. Pages 407–412 of *2010 IEEE Second International Conference on Social Computing*. IEEE.

Keeling, Matthew J. 1999. The effects of local spatial structure on epidemiological invasions. *Proceedings of the Royal Society of London, Series B*, **266**(1421), 859–867.

Kenett, Dror Y., Gao, Jianxi, Huang, Xuqing, Shao, Shuai, Vodenska, Irena, Buldyrev, Sergey V., Paul, Gerald, Stanley, H. Eugene, and Havlin, Shlomo. 2014. Network of interdependent networks: Overview of theory and applications. Pages 3–36 of D'Agostino, Gregorio, and Scala, Antonio (eds.), *Networks of Networks: The Last Frontier of Complexity*. Understanding Complex Systems. Springer International.

Kim, Jung Yeol, and Goh, K.-I. 2013. Coevolution and correlated multiplexity in multiplex networks. *Physical Review Letters*, **111**(5), 058702.

Kivelä, Mikko, Arenas, Alexandre, Barthelemy, Marc, Gleeson, James P., Moreno, Yamir, and Porter, Mason A. 2014. Multilayer networks. *Journal of Complex Networks*, **2**(3), 203–271.

Klimek, Peter, and Thurner, Stefan. 2013a. Triadic closure dynamics drives scaling laws in social multiplex networks. *New Journal of Physics*, **15**(6), 063008.

Klimek, Peter, and Thurner, Stefan. 2013b. Triadic closure dynamics drives scaling laws in social multiplex networks. *New Journal of Physics*, **15**(6), 63008.

Kossinets, Gueorgi. 2006. Effects of missing data in social networks. *Social Networks*, **28**(3), 247–268.

Krackhardt, David. 1988. Predicting with networks: Nonparametric multiple regression analysis of dyadic data. *Social Networks*, **10**(4), 359–381.

Krackhardt, David. 1999. The ties that torture: Simmelian tie analysis in organizations. *Research in the Sociology of Organizations*, **16**(1), 183–210.

Krapivsky, P. L., and Redner, S. 2005. Network growth by copying. *Physical Review E*, **71**(3), 36118.

Labitzke, S., Taranu, I., and Hartenstein, H. 2011. What your friends tell others about you: Low cost linkability of social network profiles. In *International ACM Workshop on Social Network Mining and Analysis*. ACM.

Lancichinetti, Andrea, Radicchi, Filippo, Ramasco, José J., and Fortunato, Santo. 2011. Finding statistically significant communities in networks. *PloS One*, **6**(4), e18961.

Laumann, Edward O., Marsden, Peter V., and Prensky, David. 1989. The boundary specification problem in network analysis. Pages 61–87 of *Research Methods in Social Network Analysis*. George Mason University Press.

Lazega, Emmanuel, and Pattison, Philippa E. 1999. Multiplexity, generalized exchange and cooperation in organizations: A case study. *Social Networks*, **21**(1), 67–90.

Lazega, Emmanuel, Jourda, Marie-Thérèse, Mounier, Lise, and Stofer, Rafaël. 2008. Catching up with big fish in the big pond? Multi-level network analysis through linked design. *Social Networks*, **30**(2), 159–176.

Lee, Kyu-Min, Kim, Jung Yeol, Cho, Won-kuk, Goh, K.-I., and Kim, I.-M. 2012. Correlated multiplexity and connectivity of multiplex random networks. *New Journal of Physics*, **14**, 033027.

Leicht, E. A., and D'Souza, Raissa M. 2009. Percolation on interacting networks. In *International Workshop and Conference on Network Science (NetSci)*.

Lerman, Kristina, and Ghosh, Rumi. 2010. Information contagion: An empirical study of the spread of news on Digg and Twitter social networks. Pp. 90–97 in *International Conference on Weblogs and Social Media (ICWSM)*. AIII.

Leskovec, Jure, Krause, Andreas, Guestrin, Carlos, Faloutsos, Christos, VanBriesen, Jeanne, and Glance, Natalie. 2007. Cost-effective outbreak detection in networks. *International Conference on Knowledge Discovery and Data Mining (KDD)*, 420.

Leskovec, Jure, Lang, Kevin J., Mahoney, Michael W., and Dasgupta, Anirban. 2008. Statistical properties of community structure in large social and information networks. P. 695 in *Proceeding of the 17th International Conference on World Wide Web (WWW)*. ACM.

Leskovec, Jure, Lang, Kevin J., Dasgupta, Anirban, and Mahoney, Michael W. 2009. Community structure in large networks: Natural cluster sizes and the absence of large well-defined clusters. *Internet Mathematics*, **6**(1), 29–123.

Leskovec, Jure, Huttenlocher, Daniel, and Kleinberg, Jon. 2010. Predicting positive and negative links in online social networks. Page 641 of *International Conference on World Wide Web (WWW)*. ACM.

Liben-Nowell, David, and Kleinberg, Jon. 2003. The link prediction problem for social networks. Pp. 556–559 in *ACM Conference on Information and Knowledge Management (CIKM)*. ACM.

Longabaugh, William. 2012. Combing the hairball with BioFabric: A new approach for visualization of large networks. *BMC Bioinformatics*, **13**(1), 1–16.

Lovasz, Laszlo. 1993. Random walks on graphs: A survey. In *Combinatorics, Paul Erdös is Eighty*. Springer.

Lusher, Dean, Koskinen, Johan, and Robins, Garry (eds.). 2012. *Exponential Random Graph Models for Social Networks: Theory, Methods, and Applications*. Cambridge University Press.

Magnani, Matteo, and Montesi, Danilo. 2010. A survey on uncertainty management in data integration. *ACM Journal of Data and Information Quality*, **2**(1), 5–33.

Magnani, Matteo, and Rossi, Luca. 2011. The ML-model for multi-layer social networks. Pages 5–12 of *International Conference on Social Network Analysis and Mining (ASONAM)*. IEEE.

Magnani, Matteo, and Rossi, Luca. 2013a. Formation of multiple networks. Pages 257–264 of *Social Computing, Behavioral-Cultural Modeling and Prediction (SBP)*. Lecture Notes in Computer Science, vol. 7812. Springer.

Magnani, Matteo, and Rossi, Luca. 2013b. Pareto distance for multi-layer network analysis. Pages 249–256 of *Social Computing, Behavioral-Cultural Modeling and Prediction (SBP)*. Lecture Notes in Computer Science, vol. 7812. Springer.

Magnani, Matteo, Montesi, Danilo, and Rossi, Luca. 2013. Factors enabling information propagation in a social network site. Pages 411–426 of *The Influence of Technology on Social Network Analysis and Mining*. Springer.

Malhotra, Anshu, Totti, Luam, Meira, Wagner, Jr., Kumaraguru, Ponnurangam, and Almeida, Virgilio. 2012. Studying user footprints in different online social networks. Pages 1065–1070 of *International Conference on Advances in Social Networks Analysis and Mining (ASONAM)*. IEEE.

Marceau, Vincent, Noël, P. A., Pierre-André, Hébert-Dufresne, Laurent, Allard, Antoine, and Dubé, Louis J. 2011. Modeling the dynamical interaction between epidemics on overlay networks. *Physical Review E*, **84**(2), 026105.

Markus, M. Lynne. 1987. Toward a "critical mass" theory of interactive media universal access, interdependence and diffusion. *Communication Research*, **14**(5), 491–511.

Marsden, Peter V. 1990. Network diversity, substructures, and opportunities for contact. Pp. 397–410 in *Structures of Power and Constraint: Papers in Honor of Peter Blau*. Cambridge University Press.

Marwick, Alice E., and boyd, danah. 2011. I tweet honestly, I tweet passionately: Twitter users, context collapse, and the imagined audience. *New Media and Society*, **13**(1), 114–133.

Mastrandrea, Rossana, Fournet, Julie, and Barrat, Alain. 2015. Contact patterns in a high school: A comparison between data collected using wearable sensors, contact diaries and friendship surveys. *PloS One*, **10**(9), 1–26.

McAdam, Doug, and Paulsen, Ronnelle. 1993. Specifying the relationship between social ties and activism. *American Journal of Sociology*, **99**(3), 640–667.

McGlohon, Mary, Akoglu, Leman, and Faloutsos, Christos. 2008. Weighted graphs and disconnected components. Pages 524–532 of *International Conference on Knowledge Discovery and Data Mining (KDD)*, vol. 360. ACM.

McPherson, Miller, Smith-Lovin, Lynn, and Cook, James M. 2001. Birds of a feather: Homophily in social networks. *Annual Review of Sociology*, **27**, 415–444.

Medus, Andrés D., and Dorso, Claudio O. 2014. Memory effects induce structure in social networks with activity-driven agents. *Journal of Statistical Mechanics: Theory and Experiment*, **9**(9), P09009.

Mehdiabadi, Motahareh Eslami, Rabiee, Hamid R., and Salehi, Mostafa. 2012a. Diffusion-aware sampling and estimation in information diffusion networks. Pages

176–183 of *International Conference on Privacy, Security, Risk and Trust and 2012 International Conference on Social Computing*. IEEE.

Mehdiabadi, Motahareh Eslami, Rabiee, Hamid R., and Salehi, Mostafa. 2012b. Sampling from diffusion networks. Pages 106–112 of *International Conference on Social Informatics*. IEEE.

Milo, Ron, Itzkovitz, Shalev, Kashtan, Nadav, Levitt, Reuven, Shen-Orr, Shai, Ayzenshtat, Inbal, Sheffer, Michal, and Alon, Uri. 2004. Superfamilies of evolved and designed networks. *Science*, **303**(5663), 1538–1542.

Min, Byungjoon, and Goh, K. I. 2013. Layer-crossing overhead and information spreading in multiplex social networks. *arXiv:1307.2967*.

Minor, Michael J. 1983. New directions in multiplexity analysis. Pp. 223–244 in *Applied Network Analysis*, ed. Ronald S. Burt and Michael J. Minor. Sage.

Molloy, Michael, and Reed, Bruce. 1995. A critical point for random graphs with a given degree sequence. *Random Structures and Algorithms*, **6**(2–3), 161–180.

Monge, Peter R., and Contractor, Noshir S. 2003. *Theories of Communication Networks*. Vol. 91. Oxford University Press.

Moreno, J. L. 1934. *Who Shall Survive? A New Approach to the Problem of Human Interrelations*. Nervous and Mental Disease.

Morris, R. G., and Barthelemy, M. 2012. Transport on coupled spatial networks. *Physical Review Letters*, **109**(12), 128703.

Morstatter, Fred, Pfeffer, Jurgen, Liu, Huan, and Carley, Kathleen M. 2013. Is the sample good enough? Comparing data from Twitter's streaming API with Twitter's firehose. *International Conference on Weblogs and Social Media (ICWSM)*. AIII.

Moustafa, Rida E. 2011. Parallel coordinate and parallel coordinate density plots. *Computational Statistics*, **3**(2), 134–148.

Mucha, Peter J., Richardson, Thomas, Macon, Kevin, Porter, Mason A., and Onnela, Jukka-Pekka. 2010. Community structure in time-dependent, multiscale, and multiplex networks. *Science*, **328**(5980), 876–878.

Nahon, Karine, and Hemsley, Jeff. 2013. *Going Viral*. Polity.

Nan, Du, Wang, Hao, and Faloutsos, Christos. 2010. Analysis of large multi-modal social networks: Patterns and a generator. Pp. 393–408 in Balcázar, José Luis, Bonchi, Francesco, Gionis, Aristides, and Sebag, Michèle (eds.), *Machine Learning and Knowledge Discovery in Databases*. Lecture Notes in Computer Science, vol. 6321. Springer.

Newman, Mark E. J. 2001a. Scientific collaboration networks: I. Network construction and fundamental results. *Physical Review E*, **64**, 016131.

Newman, Mark E. J. 2001b. Scientific collaboration networks: II. Shortest paths, weighted networks, and centrality. *Physical Review E*, **64**, 16132.

Newman, Mark E. J. 2002. Spread of epidemic disease on networks. *Physical Review E*, **66**(1), 016128.

Newman, Mark E. J. 2003. Mixing patterns in networks. *Physical Review E*, **67**(2), 26126.

Newman, Mark E. J. 2004. Detecting community structure in networks. *The European Physical Journal B*, **38**(2), 321–330.

Newman, Mark E. J. 2005. A measure of betweenness centrality based on random walks. *Social Networks*, **27**(1), 39–54.

Newman, Mark E. J. 2010. *Networks: An Introduction*. Oxford University Press.

Newman, Mark E. J., Strogatz, Steven H., and Watts, Duncan J. 2001. Random graphs with arbitrary degree distributions and their applications. *Physical Review E*, **64**, 026118.

Newman, Mark E. J., Watts, Duncan J., and Strogatz, Steven H. 2002. Random graph models of social networks. *Proceedings of the National Academy of Sciences of the United States of America*, **99**(suppl 1), 2566–2572.

Ng, Michaek K.-P., Li, Xutao, and Ye, Yunming. 2011. MultiRank: Co-ranking for objects and relations in multi-relational data. Pages 1217–1225 of *International Conference on Knowledge Discovery and Data Mining (KDD)*. ACM.

Nicosia, Vincenzo, Bianconi, Ginestra, Latora, Vito, and Barthelemy, Marc. 2013. Growing multiplex networks. *Physical Review Letters*, **111**, 058701.

Opsahl, Tore. 2013. Triadic closure in two-mode networks: Redefining the global and local clustering coefficients. *Social Networks*, **35**(2), 159–167.

Padgett, John F., and McLean, Paul D. 2006. Organizational invention and elite transformation: The birth of partnership systems in Renaissance Florence. *American Journal of Sociology*, **111**(5), 1463–1568.

Padrón, Benigno, Nogales, Manuel, and Traveset, Anna. 2011. Alternative approaches of transforming bimodal into unimodal mutualistic networks: The usefulness of preserving weighted information. *Basic and Applied Ecology*, **12**(8), 713–721.

Pastor-Satorras, Romualdo, and Vespignani, Alessandro. 2001. Epidemic spreading in scale-free networks. *Physical Review Letters*, **86**(14), 3200–3203.

Pei, Jian, Jiang, Daxin, and Zhang, Aidong. 2005. On mining cross-graph quasi-cliques. Pages 228–238 of *International Conference on Knowledge Discovery and Data Mining (KDD)*. ACM.

Podobnik, Boris, Horvatic, Davor, Dickison, Mark, and Stanley, H. Eugene. 2012. Preferential attachment in the interaction between dynamically generated interdependent networks. *Europhysics Letters*, **100**(5), 50004.

Price, Derek J. de Solla. 1976. A general theory of bibliometric and other cumulative advantage processes. *Journal of the American Society for Information Science*, **27**(5), 292–306.

Provan, Keith G., and Sebastian, Juliann G. 1998. Networks within networks: Service link overlap, organizational cliques, and network effectiveness. *Academy of Management Journal*, **41**(4), 453–463.

Queyroi, François, Delest, Maylis, Fédou, Jean-Marc, and Melançon, Guy. 2013. Assessing the quality of multilevel graph clustering. *Data Mining and Knowledge Discovery*, **28**(4), 1107–1128.

Raacke, John, and Bonds-Raacke, Jennifer. 2008. MySpace and Facebook: Applying the uses and gratifications theory to exploring friend-networking sites. *Cyberpsychology and Behavior*, **11**(2), 169–174.

Raad, Elie, Chbeir, Richard, and Dipanda, Albert. 2010. User profile matching in social networks. Pages 297–304 of *International Conference on Network-Based Information Systems (NBiS)*. IEEE.

Rainie, Lee, and Wellman, Barry. 2012. *Networked: The New Social Operating System*. MIT Press.

Ramezanian, Rasoul, Salehi, Mostafa, Magnani, Matteo, and Montesi, Danilo. 2015. Diffusion of innovations over multiplex social networks. Pages 1–5 of *International Symposium on Artificial Intelligence and Signal Processing (AISP)*. IEEE.

Rand, William M. 1971. Objective criteria for the evaluation of clustering methods. *Journal of the American Statistical Association*, **66**(336), 846–850.

Redondo, Denis, Sallaberry, Arnaud, Ienco, Dino, Zaidi, Faraz, and Poncelet, Pascal. 2015. Layer-centered approach for multigraphs visualization. Pages 50–55 of *International Conference on Information Visualisation (iV)*. IEEE.

Reitz, Karl P. 1988. Social groups in a monastery. *Social Networks*, **10**(4), 343–357.

Renoust, Benjamin, Melançon, Guy, and Munzner, Tamara. 2015. Detangler: Visual analytics for multiplex networks. *Computer Graphics Forum*, **34**(3), 321–330.

Ribeiro, Bruno, and Towsley, Don. 2010. Estimating and sampling graphs with multidimensional random walks. Pp. 390–403 in *Annual Conference on Internet Measurement (IMC)*. ACM.

Rivera, Mark T., Soderstrom, Sara B., and Uzzi, Brian. 2010. Dynamics of dyads in social networks: Assortative, relational, and proximity mechanisms. *Annual Review of Sociology*, **36**, 91–115.

Roberts, Nancy, and Everton, Sean F. 2011. *Roberts and Everton Terrorist Data: Noordin Top Terrorist Network (Subset)*. http://www.thearda.com/Archive/Files/Descriptions/TERRNET.asp.

Robins, Garry. 2015. *Doing Social Network Research: Network-Based Research Design for Social Scientists*. Sage.

Rocklin, Matthew, and Pinar, Ali. 2013. On clustering on graphs with multiple edge types. *Internet Mathematics*, **9**(1), 82–112.

Roethlisberger, Fritz J., and Dickson, William J. 1939. *Management and the Worker*. Cambridge University Press.

Rossetti, Giulio, Berlingerio, Michele, and Giannotti, Fosca. 2011. Scalable link prediction on multidimensional networks. Pages 979–986 of *International Conference on Data Mining Workshops*. IEEE.

Rossetti, Giulio, Pappalardo, Luca, and Pedreschi, Dino. 2012. How well do we know each other? Detecting tie strength in multidimensional social networks. Pp. 485–489 in *ASONAM Workshop on Complex Social Network Analysis*. ACM.

Rossi, Luca, and Magnani, Matteo. 2012. Conversation practices and network structure in Twitter. In *Sixth International AAAI Conference on Weblogs and Social Media (ICWSM)*. AIII.

Rossi, Luca, and Magnani, Matteo. 2015. Towards effective visual analytics on multiplex and multilayer networks. *Chaos, Solitons, and Fractals*, **72**, 68–76.

Rumsey, Deborah J. 1993. *Nonresponse Models for Social Network Stochastic Processes (Markov Chains)*. PhD thesis, Ohio State University.

Sabidussi, Gert. 1966. The centrality index of a graph. *Psychometrika*, **31**(4), 581–603.

Sadikov, Eldar, Medina, Montserrat, Leskovec, Jure, and Garcia-Molina, Hector. 2011. Correcting for missing data in information cascades. Pages 55–64 of *International Conference on Web Search and Data Mining (WSDM)*. ACM.

Sahneh, F. D., Chowdhury, F. N., Brase, G., and Scoglio, C. M. 2014. Individual-based information dissemination in multilayer epidemic modeling. *Mathematical Modelling of Natural Phenomena*, **9**(2), 136–152.

Salehi, Mostafa, and Rabiee, Hamid R. 2013. A measurement framework for directed networks. *IEEE Journal on Selected Areas in Communications*, **31**(6), 1007–1016.

Salehi, Mostafa, Sharma, Rajesh, Marzolla, Moreno, Magnani, Matteo, Siyari, Payam, and Montesi, Danilo. 2015. Spreading processes in multilayer networks. *IEEE Transactions on Network Science and Engineering*, **2**(2), 65–83.

Schank, Thomas, and Wagner, Dorothea. 2005. Approximating clustering coefficient and transitivity. *Journal of Graph Algorithms and Applications*, **9**(2), 265–275.

Seierstad, Cathrine, and Opsahl, Tore. 2011. For the few not the many? The effects of affirmative action on presence, prominence, and social capital of women directors in Norway. *Scandinavian Journal of Management*, **27**(1), 44–54.

Shalizi, Cosma Rohilla, and Thomas, Andrew C. 2011. Homophily and contagion are generically confounded in observational social network studies. *Sociological Methods and Research*, **40**(2), 211–239.

Sharma, Rajesh, Magnani, Matteo, and Montesi, Danilo. 2014. Missing data in multiplex networks: A preliminary study. Pp. 401–407 in *Third International Workshop on Complex Networks and their Applications*.

Sharma, Rajesh, Magnani, Matteo, and Montesi, Danilo. 2015. Investigating the types and effects of missing data in multilayer networks. Pp. 392–399 in *International Conference on Advances in Social Networks Analysis and Mining (ASONAM)*. ACM.

Simmel, Georg. 1902a. The number of members as determining the sociological form of the group I. *American Journal of Sociology*, **8**(1), 1–40.

Simmel, Georg. 1902b. The number of members as determining the sociological form of the group II. *American Journal of Sociology*, **8**(2), 158–196.

Skvoretz, John, and Agneessens, Filip. 2007. Reciprocity, multiplexity, and exchange: Measures. *Quality and Quantity*, **41**(3), 341–357.

Snijders, Tom A. B., Lomi, Alessandro, and Torló, Vanina Jasmine. 2013. A model for the multiplex dynamics of two-mode and one-mode networks, with an application to employment preference, friendship, and advice. *Social Networks*, **35**(2), 265–276.

Söderberg, Bo. 2003. Random graph models with hidden color. *Acta Physica Polonica B*, **34**(July), 5085–5102.

Solé-Ribalta, Albert, De Domenico, Manlio, Gómez, Sergio, and Arenas, Alex. 2014. Centrality rankings in multiplex networks. Pages 149–155 of *ACM conference on Web Science (WebSci)*. ACM.

Stephenson, Karen, and Zelen, Marvin. 1989. Rethinking centrality: Methods and examples. *Social Networks*, **11**(1), 1–37.

Stopczynski, Arkadiusz, Sekara, Vedran, Sapiezynski, Piotr, Cuttone, Andrea, Madsen, Mette My, Larsen, Jakob Eg, and Lehmann, Sune. 2014. Measuring large-scale social networks with high resolution. *PloS One*, **9**(4), e95978.

Sun, Yizhou, and Han, Jiawei. 2012. *Mining Heterogeneous Information Networks: Principles and Methodologies*. Synthesis Lectures on Data Mining and Knowledge Discovery. Morgan and Claypool.

Sun, Yizhou, Han, Jiawei, Zhao, Peixiang, Yin, Zhijun, Cheng, Hong, and Wu, Tianyi. 2009. RankClus: Integrating clustering with ranking for heterogeneous information network analysis. Pages 565–576 of *International Conference on Extending Database Technology (EDBT)*. ACM.

Szell, Michael, Lambiotte, Renaud, and Thurner, Stefan. 2010. Multirelational organization of large-scale social networks in an online world. *Proceedings of the National Academy of Sciences of the United States of America*, **107**(31), 13636–41.

Tabourier, Lionel, Roth, Camille, and Cointet, Jean-Philippe. 2011. Generating constrained random graphs using multiple edge switches. *Journal of Experimental Algorithmics*, **16**, 1–7.

Taylor, Michael, Taylor, Timothy J., and Kiss, Istvan Z. 2012. Epidemic threshold and control in a dynamic network. *Physical Review E*, **85**(1), 016103.

Toivonen, Riitta, Onnela, Jukka-Pekka, Saramäki, Jari, Hyvönen, Jörkki, and Kaski, Kimmo. 2006. A model for social networks. *Physica A: Statistical Mechanics and Its Applications*, **371**(2), 851–860.

Tolsdorf, Christopher C. 1976. Social networks, support, and coping: An exploratory study. *Family Process*, **15**(4), 407–417.

Tonnies, Ferdinand. 1957. *Community and Society*. Courier.

Travers, Jeffrey, and Milgram, Stanley. 1967. An experimental study of the small world problem. *Psychology Today*, **2**, 60–67.

Tsatsaronis, George, Reimann, Matthias, Varlamis, Iraklis, Gkorgkas, Orestis, and Nø rvåg, Kjetil. 2011. Efficient community detection using power graph analysis. Pages 21–26 of *Proceedings of the 9th Workshop on Large-Scale and Distributed Informational Retrieval*. ACM.

Turner, Jeanine Warisse, Grube, Jean A., and Meyers, Jennifer. 2001. Developing an optimal match within online communities: An exploration of CMC support communities and traditional support. *Journal of Communication*, **51**(2), 231–251.

van Laarhoven, Twan, and Marchiori, Elena. 2014. An axiomatic study of objective functions for graph clustering. *Tech. rept. 1. CoRR, abs/1308.3383*.

Van Mieghem, Piet. 2011. The N-intertwined SIS epidemic network model. *Computing*, **93**(2–4), 147–169.

Vasquez, Alexei. 2006. Spreading dynamics on heterogeneous populations: Multitype network approach. *Physical Review E*, **74**(6), 066144.

Vázquez, Alexei, and Moreno, Yamir. 2003. Resilience to damage of graphs with degree correlations. *Physical Review E*, **67**(1), 15101.

Vazquez, Alexei, Rácz, Balázs, Lukács, András, and Barabási, Albert-László. 2007. Impact of non-poissonian activity patterns on spreading processes. *Physical Review Letters*, **98**(15), 158702.

Vega, Davide, Magnani, Matteo, Meseguer, Roc, and Freitag, Felix. 2015. Role and position detection in networks: Reloaded. Pp. 320–325 in *International Conference on Advances in Social Networks Analysis and Mining (ASONAM)*. IEEE.

Verbrugge, L. M. 1979. Multiplexity in adult friendships. *Social Forces*, **57**(4), 1286–1309.

Vinh, Nguyen Xuan, Epps, Julien, and Bailey, James. 2010. Information theoretic measures for clusterings comparison: Variants, properties, normalization and correction for chance. *Journal of Machine Learning Research*, **11**, 2837–2854.

Vitak, Jessica, Lampe, Cliff, Gray, Rebecca, and Ellison, Nicole B. 2012. Why won't you be my Facebook friend? Strategies for managing context collapse in the workplace. Pages 555–557 of *Proceedings of the 2012 iConference*. ACM.

Volz, Erik, and Meyers, Lauren Ancel. 2009. Epidemic thresholds in dynamic contact networks. *Journal of the Royal Society*, **6**(32), 233–241.

von Landesberger, Tatiana, Kuijper, Arjan, Schreck, Tobias, Kohlhammer, Jörn, van Wijk, Jarke J., Fekete, Jean-Daniel, and Fellner, Dieter W. 2011. Visual analysis of large graphs: State-of-the-art and future research challenges. *Computer Graphics Forum*, **30**(6), 1719–1749.

Vosecky, Jan, Hong, Dan, and Shen, Vincent Y. 2009. User identification across multiple social networks. Pages 360–365 of *International Conference on Networked Digital Technologies (NDT)*. IEEE.

Šubelj, Lovro, and Bajec, Marko. 2013. Model of complex networks based on citation dynamics. Pages 527–530 of *International Conference on World Wide Web
(WWW)*. ACM.

Wang, Bing, Cao, Lang, Suzuki, Hideyuki, and Aihara, Kazuyuki. 2011. Epidemic
spread in adaptive networks with multitype agents. *Journal of Physics A*, **44**(3),
035101.

Wang, Jianyong, Zhou, Zhiping, and Lizhu, Zeng. 2006. CLAN: An algorithm for mining closed cliques from large dense graph databases. Pages 73–73 of *International
Conference on Data Engineering (ICDE)*. IEEE.

Wang, Peng, Robins, Garry, Pattison, Philippa, and Lazega, Emmanuel. 2013. Exponential random graph models for multilevel networks. *Social Networks*, **35**(1), 96–115.

Wang, Yang, Chakrabarti, Deepayan, Wang, Chenxi, and Faloutsos, Christos. 2003. Epidemic spreading in real networks: An eigenvalue viewpoint. Pages 25–34 of *IEEE
Symposium on Reliable Distributed Systems*, vol. 0IEEE. Carnegie Mellon University.

Wasserman, Stanley, and Faust, Katherine. 1994. *Social Network Analysis: Methods
and Applications*. Structural Analysis in the Social Sciences, vol. 8. Cambridge
University Press.

Wasserman, Stanley, and Iacobucci, Dawn. 1991. Statistical modelling of onemode and
twomode networks: Simultaneous analysis of graphs and bipartite graphs. *British
Journal of Mathematical and Statistical Psychology*, **44**(1), 13–43.

Watts, Duncan J. 2002. A simple model of global cascades on random networks. *Proceedings of the National Academy of Sciences of the United States of America*,
99(9), 5766–5771.

Watts, Duncan J., and Strogatz, Steven H. 1998. Collective dynamics of small-world
networks. *Nature*, **393**(6684), 440–442.

Wellman, Barry Stephen, and Berkowitz, Stephen David (eds.). 1988. *Social structures:
A network approach*. Vol. 2. Cambridge University Press.

Wu, Fang, Huberman, Bernardo A., Adamic, Lada A., and Tyler, Joshua R. 2004. Information flow in social groups. *Physica A*, **337**(1–2), 327–335.

Xie, Jierui, Kelley, Stephen, and Szymanski, Boleslaw K. 2013. Overlapping community detection in networks: The state-of-the-art and comparative study. *ACM Computing Surveys*, **45**(4), 43.

Xulvi-Brunet, Ramon, and Sokolov, Igor M. 2004. Reshuffling scale-free networks:
From random to assortative. *Physical Review E*, **70**, 066102.

Yagan, Osman, and Gligor, Virgil. 2012. Analysis of complex contagions in random
multiplex networks. *Physical Review E*, **86**(3 Pt 2), 036103.

Yang, Jaewon, and Leskovec, Jure. 2010. Modeling information diffusion in implicit
networks. Pages 599–608 of *International Conference on Data Mining (ICDM)*.
IEEE.

Yang, Jaewon, McAuley, Julian, and Leskovec, Jure. 2013. Community detection in
networks with node attributes. Pages 1151–1156 of *International Conference on
Data Mining (ICDM)*. IEEE.

You, Gae-won, Hwang, Seung-won, Nie, Zaiqing, and Wen, Ji-Rong. 2011.
SocialSearch: Enhancing entity search with social network matching. Pages 515–
519 of *International Conference on Extending Database Technology (EDBT)*.
ACM.

You, Gae-won, Park, Jin-woo, Hwang, Seung-won, Nie, Zaiqing, and Wen, Ji-Rong. 2013. SocialSearch+: Enriching social network with web evidences. *World Wide Web*, **16**(5–6), 701–727.

Zachary, Wayne W. 1977. An information flow model for conflict and fission in small groups. *Journal of Anthropological Research*, **33**, 452–473.

Zafarani, Reza, and Liu, Huan. 2013. Connecting users across social media sites: A behavioral-modeling approach. Pages 41–49 of *International Conference on Knowledge Discovery and Data Mining (KDD)*. ACM.

Zappa, Paola, and Lomi, Alessandro. 2015. The analysis of multilevel networks in organizations: Models and empirical tests. *Organizational Research Methods*, **18**(3), 542–569.

Zappa, Paola, and Robins, Garry. 2016. Organizational learning across multi-level networks. *Social Networks*, **44**, 295–306.

Zeng, Zhiping, and Wang, Jianyong. 2006. Coherent closed quasi-clique discovery from large dense graph databases. Pp. 797–802 in *International conference on Knowledge Discovery and Data Mining (KDD)*. ACM.

Zhou, Jin, Xu, Xiaoke, Zhang, Jie, Sun, Junfeng, Small, Michael, and Lu, Jun-an. 2008. Generating an assortative network with a given degree distribution. *International Journal of Bifurcation and Chaos*, **18**(11), 3495–3502.

Index